SACRAL KINGSHIP IN ANCIENT ISRAEL

By

AUBREY R. JOHNSON

CARDIFF
UNIVERSITY OF WALES PRESS
1967

FIRST EDITION 1955
SECOND EDITION 1967

PRINTED IN GREAT BRITAIN

FOR
WINIFRED

PREFACE

THE following monograph is mainly concerned with two well-known groups of psalms, (i) the hymns which celebrate the Kingship of Yahweh, and (ii) the so-called royal psalms. Accordingly it may be regarded as one more illustration of the influence which Hermann Gunkel has exercised in the field of Old Testament study by his classification of the psalms according to their literary types and his stress upon the value of discovering, so far as possible, their original *Sitz im Leben*. By his wide application of the principles of *Formgeschichte* Gunkel has provided students of the Old Testament with an approach to their subject which, in my opinion, seems likely to lead in varying degrees beyond the simple correlation of obviously related types of literature to ideological syntheses which should enable us to recover more than one lost aspect of the religious thought and practice of ancient Israel. For this reason I have to add that the monograph also owes much to the emphasis which has been laid by Sigmund Mowinckel on the original cultic setting of so many of the psalms, although my conclusions are in many ways markedly different from his; and it is a pleasure to record here again in the preface, as I have already done in the body of the book,[1] my deep sense of indebtedness to this distinguished scholar, whose influence upon the course of Old Testament study during the last forty years has been so profound.

In this monograph I have returned to the theme with which I first ventured into print as a student of the Old Testament just twenty years ago,[2] and I have to thank Professor S. H. Hooke, as editor of the volume concerned, and the Reverend F. N. Davey of the Society for Promoting

---

[1] See below, p. 61, n. 1.

[2] 'The Rôle of the King in the Jerusalem Cultus', in *The Labyrinth. Further Studies in the Relation between Myth and Ritual in the Ancient World*, ed. S. H. Hooke (1935), pp. 71–111.

Christian Knowledge, its publishers, for readily granting me permission to employ again some of the language which I used on the former occasion. I indicated at the time that I hoped to return to the subject in due course,[1] but I little suspected that so long a period would elapse before I should feel justified in doing so. The fact is that I could see no hope of doing justice to this question of the cultic role of the king in ancient Israel until I knew more about Israelite ideas concerning God (or the gods) and mankind, and, in particular, the forms of communication which were thought possible between these two orders of being; and I planned a series of monographs for this purpose. Three of these have now appeared,[2] and I had hoped that by this time the number would be doubled. However, the widespread interest in the question of sacral kingship which has been aroused in recent years, particularly as a result of the views put forward by the so-called Uppsala School, has compelled me to return to the subject somewhat earlier than I intended, for I am disturbed to find that views are often attributed to me which I do not hold and, in fact, never have held. It is my earnest hope that this monograph, besides making my own position much clearer, may meet with acceptance as an attempt to deal constructively with this difficult problem, which has engrossed my attention ever since the time when, as a post-graduate student at Oxford nearly a quarter of a century ago, I first realized that its solution must be of the first importance for our understanding of both the Old and the New Testaments.

The text of the monograph reproduces what were substantially the Haskell Lectures, which I had the privilege of delivering before the Graduate School of Theology at Oberlin in the spring of 1951. I am happy to think that at last I am able to place on record in this way my deep appreciation of the honour which the Faculty did me in

[1] Op. cit., p. 110.

[2] *The One and the Many in the Israelite Conception of God* (1942), *The Cultic Prophet in Ancient Israel* (1944), *The Vitality of the Individual in the Thought of Ancient Israel* (1949).

issuing the invitation and the generous hospitality and kind consideration which my wife and I received from Dean Leonard Stidley and his colleagues throughout the very happy fortnight which we spent in their midst.

Sincere thanks are also due to a number of colleagues and friends, both at home and abroad, whose close interest in my monograph has meant much to me during the past five years. Where so many have been so kind it is difficult for me to make full acknowledgement, but there are several names which must be mentioned. Thus it is typical of the encouragement and the many acts of friendship which I have received from Professor G. R. Driver during more than twenty years that he read the whole of my typescript in its final draft with great care, and made a number of valuable suggestions for its improvement. The same is true of Professor H. H. Rowley, who, in addition to tracing several works which I needed, read through the monograph both in typescript and at the proof stage, and helped me on more than one occasion to choose the right expression for what I had in mind. I must also add a special word of thanks to Professor Otto Eissfeldt, Professor G. Levi Della Vida, and Father F. L. Moriarty, S.J., each of whom came to my aid by supplying me with copies of works which I had been unable to obtain through the normal channels. Finally in this connexion, I have to express my gratitude to the Reverend E. T. Ryder and, indeed, Mrs. Ryder, who kindly undertook the preparation of the indexes; I am greatly indebted to both these friends for the patience and care with which they have performed this most helpful service.

In conclusion, my warm thanks are due to the University of Wales Press for continuing to publish my monographs, and to the Oxford University Press for all the technical skill which has been placed so readily at our disposal once again.

AUBREY R. JOHNSON

Cardiff
August 1955

PREFACE TO THE SECOND EDITION

As with the earlier volumes in this series I have found reason to make only minor changes in the text for the purposes of a second edition; but once again the footnotes have been expanded, occasionally at some length, and in part this is indicative of the persistent and widespread interest in the subject of this monograph. Unfortunately I continue to find that, as I said in my earlier preface, views are often ascribed to me which I do not hold and, indeed, never have held; and occasional reference to such misrepresentation will now be found in the footnotes.[1]

In renewing my thanks to all those colleagues and friends who have aided me in the preparation of this work I must now add the names of Professor John Gray, Professor B. J. Roberts, Father James Swetnam, S.J., and the Reverend C. G. Williams who, in addition, has kindly undertaken the task of helping me with the checking of the indexes and the reading of the proofs.

Finally, I must also acknowledge with gratitude my deep sense of indebtedness to the Oxford University Press for all the technical skill so readily made available once more in the preparation of this edition.

AUBREY R. JOHNSON

Cardiff
October 1966

---

[1] The English reader has recently been offered a simple but glaring example of such misrepresentation in the case of H. J. Kraus, *Gottesdienst in Israel*, 2nd edit. rev. (1962), pp. 30 f., E.T. by G. Buswell, *Worship in Israel* (1966), p. 18, who cites this monograph, along with the original essay upon which it is based (as above, p. v, n. 2), to illustrate his claim that in the work of some of Mowinckel's followers 'the historical foundations of Israel's worship disappear more and more. Myth covers the whole field.' If anyone unfamiliar with my interpretation of the data will turn to the summary at the end of this volume (pp. 134–44, esp. 136 ff.), it will be a simple matter to determine what value is to be placed upon such a reference to my work. See also p. 90, n. 2.

PRINCIPAL ABBREVIATIONS

A.B.	Analecta Biblica.
A.D.	*The Assyrian Dictionary of the Oriental Institute of the University of Chicago* (1956–).
A.F.L.N.W.	Arbeitsgemeinschaft für Forschung des Landes Nordrhein-Westfalen.
A.f.O.	*Archiv für Orientforschung.*
A.H.	W. von Soden (ed.), *Akkadisches Handwörterbuch* (1959–).
A.J.S.L.	*American Journal of Semitic Languages and Literatures.*
A.L.B.O.	Analecta Lovaniensia Biblica et Orientalia.
A.N.V.A.O. II.	Avhandlinger utgitt av Det Norske Videnskaps-Akademi i Oslo, II. Hist.-Filos. Klasse.
A.O.	Der Alte Orient.
A.P.A.W.	Abhandlungen der Preussischen Akademie der Wissenschaften, Phil.-hist. Klasse.
A.R.M.	*Archives royales de Mari.*
A.R.W.	*Archiv für Religionswissenschaft.*
A.T.A.N.T.	Abhandlungen zur Theologie des Alten und Neuen Testaments.
A.T.D.	Das Alte Testament Deutsch.
B.A.	*The Biblical Archaeologist.*
B.A.S.O.R.	*Bulletin of the American Schools of Oriental Research.*
B.B.B.	Bonner Biblische Beiträge.
B.E.T.	Beiträge zur evangelischen Theologie.
B.H.T.	Beiträge zur historischen Theologie.
B.J.R.L.	*Bulletin of the John Rylands Library.*
B.K.A.T.	Biblischer Kommentar Altes Testament.
B.K.W.	Bible Key Words from Gerhard Kittel's *Theologisches Wörterbuch zum Neuen Testament.*
B.M.B.	*Bulletin du Musée de Beyrouth.*
B.O.T.	De Boeken van het Oude Testament.
B.P.(A.T.)	La Bible: *L'Ancien Testament* (Bibliothèque de la Pléiade).
B.V.S.A.W.L.	Berichte über die Verhandlungen der Sächsischen Akademie der Wissenschaften zu Leipzig, Phil.-hist. Klasse.
B.W.A.N.T.	Beiträge zur Wissenschaft vom Alten und Neuen Testament.
B.W.A.T.	Beiträge zur Wissenschaft vom Alten Testament.
B.Z.A.W.	Beihefte zur *Zeitschrift für die alttestamentliche Wissenschaft.*
C.A.H.	*The Cambridge Ancient History.*
C.B.	Cambridge Bible.
C.B.Q.	*The Catholic Biblical Quarterly.*
Cent.B.	The Century Bible.

C.I.S.	*Corpus Inscriptionum Semiticarum.*
C.R.B.	Cahiers de la *Revue Biblique.*
D	The Deuteronomic narrative (*or* code), or the Deuteronomic school.
D.B.S.	*Dictionnaire de la Bible: Supplément,* ed. L. Pirot, A. Robert, H. Cazelles, and A. Feuillet (1928–).
D.M.O.A.	Documenta et Monumenta Orientis Antiqui.
E	The Elohistic narrative (*or* code), or the Elohist.
E.B.	Études Bibliques.
E.B.	*Encyclopaedia Biblica,* ed. T. K. Cheyne and J. S. Black (1899–1903).
Echt.B.	Echter Bibel.
E.H.P.R.	Études d'histoire et de philosophie religieuses.
E.T.	*The Expository Times.*
F.R.L.A.N.T.	Forschungen zur Religion und Literatur des Alten und Neuen Testaments.
G.K.	Gesenius–Kautzsch, *Hebrew Grammar,* 2nd English edition, rev. by A. E. Cowley (1910).
G.T.M.M.M.	Det Gamle Testamente, oversatt av S. Michelet, S. Mowinckel og N. Messel.
G.U.O.S.T.	*Glasgow University Oriental Society: Transactions.*
H.A.T.	Handbuch zum Alten Testament.
H.K.	Handkommentar zum Alten Testament.
H.S.A.T.	Die Heilige Schrift des Alten Testamentes (Bonner Bibel).
H.S.A.T.	E. Kautzsch (ed.), *Die Heilige Schrift des Alten Testaments,* 4th edition, ed. A. Bertholet (1922–3).
H.T.R.	*Harvard Theological Review.*
H.U.C.A.	*Hebrew Union College Annual.*
I.B.	The Interpreter's Bible.
I.C.C.	The International Critical Commentary.
J	The Yahwistic narrative (*or* code), or the Yahwist.
J.A.O.S.	*Journal of the American Oriental Society.*
J.B.L.	*Journal of Biblical Literature.*
J.N.E.S.	*Journal of Near Eastern Studies.*
J.Q.R.	*Jewish Quarterly Review.*
J.S.S.	*Journal of Semitic Studies.*
J.T.S.	*The Journal of Theological Studies.*
K.A.I.	H. Donner and W. Röllig, *Kanaanäische and aramäische Inschriften,* i (1962), ii–iii (1964).
K.A.T.	Kommentar zum Alten Testament.
K.B.	L. Koehler and W. Baumgartner, *Lexicon in Veteris Testamenti Libros* (1953), including *Supplementum ad Lexicon in Veteris Testamenti Libros* (1958).
K.H.C.	Kurzer Hand-Commentar zum Alten Testament.

K.K.	Kurzgefasster Kommentar zu den heiligen Schriften Alten und Neuen Testamentes sowie zu den Apokryphen.
LXX	The Septuagint.
M.T.	The Massoretic Text.
M.U.N.	Mémoires de l'Université de Neuchâtel.
M.U.S.J.	*Mélanges de l'Université Saint-Joseph.*
M.V.A.G.	Mittheilungen der vorderasiatisch-ägyptischen Gesellschaft.
Nor.T.T.	*Norsk Teologisk Tidsskrift.*
N.S.I.	G. A. Cooke, *A Text-book of North-Semitic Inscriptions* (1903).
O.B.L.	Orientalia et Biblica Lovaniensia.
O.T.S.	Old Testament Studies.
O.T.S.	*Oudtestamentische Studiën.*
P	The Priestly narrative (*or* code), or the Priestly school.
P.E.Q.	*Palestine Exploration Quarterly.*
Pr.J.B.	*Preußische Jahrbücher.*
R.A.	*Revue d'assyriologie et d'archéologie orientale.*
R.B.	*Revue Biblique.*
R.G.G.	*Die Religion in Geschichte und Gegenwart,* 1st edition, ed. F. M. Schiele and L. Zscharnack (1909–13), 2nd edition, ed. H. Gunkel and L. Zscharnack (1927–32), 3rd edition, ed. K. Galling (1957–65).
R.H.P.R.	*Revue d'histoire et de philosophie religieuses.*
R.H.R.	*Revue de l'histoire des religions.*
S	The Syriac Version (Peshiṭta).
S.A.T.	Die Schriften des Alten Testaments in Auswahl.
S.B.	La Sainte Bible, texte latin et traduction française d'après les textes originaux avec un commentaire exégétique et théologique.
S.B.D.A.W.	Sitzungsberichte der Deutschen Akademie der Wissenschaften zu Berlin, Klasse für Sprachen, Literatur und Kunst.
S.B.J.	La Sainte Bible traduite en français sous la direction de l'École Biblique de Jérusalem.
S.N.	Supplements to *Numen.*
S.N.V.A.O. II	Skrifter utgitt av Det Norske Videnskaps-Akademi i Oslo, II. Hist.-filos. Klasse.
S.T.	*Studia Theologica.*
S.V.T.	Supplements to *Vetus Testamentum.*
T	Targum.
T.C.A.A.S.	Transactions of the Connecticut Academy of Arts and Sciences.
T.D.N.T.	See s.v. *Th.W.N.T.*

Principal Abbreviations

T.L.B.	*Theologisches Literaturblatt.*
T.L.Z.	*Theologische Literaturzeitung.*
T.S.	*Theological Studies.*
T.U.	Tekst en Uitleg.
T.Z.	*Theologische Zeitschrift.*
Th.W.N.T.	*Theologisches Wörterbuch zum Neuen Testament,* ed. G. Kittel and G. Friedrich (1933–); E.T. (= *T.D.N.T.*) by G. W. Bromiley, *Theological Dictionary of the New Testament* (1964–).
U.U.Å.	Uppsala Universitets Årsskrift.
V	The Vulgate.
V.K.A.W.A.	Verhandelingen der Koninklijke Akademie van Wetenschappen te Amsterdam. Afdeeling Letterkunde.
V.S.G.T.R.	Sammlung gemeinverständlicher Vorträge und Schriften aus dem Gebiet der Theologie und Religionsgeschichte.
V.T.	*Vetus Testamentum.*
V.Th.	*Vox Theologica.*
W.O.	*Die Welt des Orients.*
Z.A.W.	*Zeitschrift für die alttestamentliche Wissenschaft.*
Z.D.M.G.	*Zeitschrift der deutschen morgenländischen Gesellschaft.*
Z.D.P.V.	*Zeitschrift des deutschen Palästina-Vereins.*
Z.S.	*Zeitschrift für Semitistik und verwandte Gebiete.*
Z.T.K.	*Zeitschrift für Theologie und Kirche.*

SACRAL KINGSHIP IN
ANCIENT ISRAEL

WE may begin our study with two incidents of unmistakable authenticity, taken from the lives of the first and last Davidic kings in Jerusalem. In the first case the scene is laid somewhere in the lowlands to the west of Judah, and the date must be towards the beginning of the tenth century B.C. The air is filled with the sound of battle between Israelites and Philistines, and at one point David himself, the Messiah or 'Anointed' of Yahweh,[1] is hard pressed by a powerful adversary; but, fortunately for him and for his followers, Abishai springs to the rescue and beats the king's opponent to the ground. Now the noise of battle is over, and the king is safe once more in the comparative security of the camp; but amongst David's followers there is manifest a strong sense of closely averted tragedy which at length finds expression in words, for, we are told,[2]

David's men swore unto him, saying, 'Thou shalt not go out to battle with us again, lest thou quench the lamp of Israel.'

Our second picture brings us to the first half of the sixth century B.C., when the Southern Kingdom, like that of the apostate north, has become a thing of the past. Jerusalem, its capital, is now humbled to the dust. The stones of the holy city litter its streets; and on every hand one may see the horrors of famine in starving and dying children, in the discoloured skin and protuberant bones even of the upper classes, and, worst feature of all, in grim acts of cannibalism on the part of those who not long before had known all the compassion of motherhood. Moreover, the king himself, who should have proved to be the guardian of his people's welfare, has been driven from his citadel

---

[1] Cf. 2 Sam. v. 3, 17; and see below, p. 14, n. 2.
[2] 2 Sam. xxi. 17.

and trapped like some poor creature of the wild. In fact, as the poet says who has left us this grim picture,[1]

> The breath of our nostrils, the Messiah of Yahweh,
>   Was caught in their pits,
> Of whom we had said, 'In his shadow
>   We shall *live* (i.e. flourish)[2] amid the nations.'

The import of these two pictures is clear. Four centuries have passed by, but from first to last the king or, to be more precise, the ruling member of the House of David is regarded in some way as the light or life of his people.

To reach anything like a true appreciation of the implications which are wrapped up in this conception of the king's supremely important place in the social order it is necessary to bear in mind that in Israelite thought, as in that of the so-called 'primitive' peoples of our own day, there is a vivid sense of what has been called 'corporate personality'.[3] In other words, the individual is regarded as a centre of power which extends far beyond the contour of the body and mingles with that of the family and the family property, the tribe and the tribal possessions, or the nation and the national inheritance, to form a psychical whole; and, what

---

[1] Lam. iv. 20.

[2] For the significance of √חיה (חיי), 'to live', see the writer's monograph *The Vitality of the Individual in the Thought of Ancient Israel* (1949), pp. 94 ff., 2nd edit. rev. (1964), pp. 95 ff.

[3] i.e. by H. W. Robinson, e.g. in 'Hebrew Psychology', in *The People and the Book*, ed. A. S. Peake (1925), 353–82, particularly pp. 375 ff.; and 'The Hebrew Conception of Corporate Personality', in *Werden und Wesen des Alten Testaments*, ed. J. Hempel, B.Z.A.W. 66 (1936), pp. 49–62. For a critical elaboration of this point with reference to the Old and the New Testaments, see now J. de Fraine, *Adam et son lignage. Études sur la notion de 'personnalité corporative' dans la Bible* (1959); but, as in the case of the same author's work, *L'Aspect religieux de la royauté israélite. L'institution monarchique dans l'Ancien Testament et dans les textes mésopotamiens*, A.B. 3 (1954), the reader should compare carefully what one says with what is attributed to one. Indeed, while I am on this point, a stronger warning of the same kind must be addressed to the reader in connexion with the views ascribed to me by K. H. Bernhardt, *Das Problem der altorientalischen Königsideologie im Alten Testament unter besonderer Berücksichtigung der Geschichte der Psalmenexegese dargestellt und kritisch gewürdigt*, S.V.T. viii (1961).

is more, such a psychical whole has an extension in time as well as space, so that the mystic bond which unites society may be conceived retrospectively as regards its ancestors and prospectively with regard to future generations.[1] The smallest unit, of course, is the family (i.e. in the narrower sense conveyed by the term 'household'), which finds its focus in the father; and, as we learn from the well-known story of Achan, if he should commit an offence against the sanctions of the wider sphere, represented by the tribe or the nation, then his 'household', like a festering sore interfering with the successful function of the social body, may be involved with him in remedial measures.[2] In the same way the royal family finds its temporary focus in the reigning king, who, like Ahaz, may be referred to or addressed quite simply as 'House of David';[3] so that it is altogether in keeping that the nation as a psychical whole should also be seen to have its focus in the royal house and, at any given time, in the reigning monarch.[4] Thus it is that any violent disturbance of the

[1] Cf. J. Pedersen, *Israel I–II: Sjaeleliv og Samfundsliv* (1920), 2nd edit. rev. (1933), 3rd edit. (1958), pp. 203 ff., E.T., *Israel: its Life and Culture I–II* (1926), 2nd edit. (1959), pp. 261 ff.; O. Eissfeldt, *Der Gottesknecht bei Deuterojesaja* (1933), E.T. in *E.T.* xliv (1932–3), pp. 261–8; S. A. Cook, *The Old Testament: A Reinterpretation* (1936), pp. 115 ff.; J. Hempel, *Das Ethos des Alten Testaments*, B.Z.A.W. 67 (1938), 2nd edit. enlarged (1964), pp. 32 ff. Perhaps I should add that J. R. Porter, 'The Legal Aspects of the Concept of "Corporate Personality" in the Old Testament', *V.T.* xv (1965), pp. 361–80, arouses afresh in me the doubts which I have long felt with regard to the employment of the terms 'personality' in 'corporate personality' and 'psychical' in 'psychical whole', as there is obviously a danger that the modern reader may find these expressions implying more than is intended. Nevertheless I can think of no more suitable terminology for conveying the significance of the phenomena under consideration. The words 'corporate personality' and 'psychical whole' do suggest, for example, an emotional involvement which is lacking in such expressions as 'social solidarity' or 'corporate whole'. Correspondingly one does not expect these emotional aspects to appear in legal records which are simply concerned with the working out of the implications of such solidarity.

[2] Joshua vii (basically JE).

[3] Isa. vii. 2, 13 (cf. verse 17).

[4] Cf., for example, J. Pedersen, *Israel III–IV: Hellighed og Guddommelighed* (1934), 2nd edit. rev. (1960), pp. 65 ff., E. T., *Israel: its Life and Culture III–IV* (1940), 2nd edit. with additions (1959), pp. 81 ff.

national life, such as that caused by a prolonged drought or an outburst of plague, may be attributed to the fact that the king himself has violated the sanctions of the group; and the whole royal house or the very nation itself may be involved with him in the condemnation which follows upon any such trespass.[1] Correspondingly, if the nation is to prosper, the king must act as the embodiment of 'righteousness' (צֶ֫דֶק, צְדָקָה). That is to say, it is first and foremost his concern to see that the behaviour of society at large is thoroughly 'righteous' (צַדִּיק) and that, to this end, the sanctions of the group, particularly the nation's laws, are uniformly observed throughout the different strata of society; for it is only in this way, when the individual is restrained from doing 'what is right in his own eyes',[2] that the well-being (שָׁלוֹם) of the nation, in fact its life or vitality (חַיִּים), can be assured.[3] Thus the king is the supreme 'ruler' or 'judge' (שֹׁפֵט), to whom one may go in any matter of dispute for a final 'ruling' or 'judgement' (מִשְׁפָּט) which, ideally at least, will also be an act of 'justice' (מִשְׁפָּט).[4] What is more,

---

[1] 2 Sam. xxi. 1–14, xxiv. 10–25: cf. 2 Sam. iii. 28 f., xiv. 9; Jer. xv. 4; also Gen. xii. 17 (J), xx. 3 f., 9, 17 f. (E); 1 Kings xviii. 18 (vide xvii. 1, xviii. 1). While the principle underlying the story in 2 Sam. xxi. 1–14 is clear enough, its exact implications remain subject to discussion. Cf. for example, A. Malamat, 'Doctrines of causality in Hittite and Biblical Historiography: a parallel', *V.T.* v (1955), pp. 1–11; A. S. Kapelrud, 'King and Fertility. A Discussion of II Sam. xxi: 1–14', in *Interpretationes ad Vetus Testamentum pertinentes* (S. Mowinckel *Festschrift*) = *Nor. T. T.* lvi (1955), pp. 113–22, also 'King David and the Sons of Saul', in *The Sacral Kingship: La regalità sacra*, S.N. iv (1959), pp. 294–301, esp. 298 ff.; H. Cazelles, 'David's Monarchy and the Gibeonite Claim (II Sam. xxi, 1–14)', *P.E.Q.* (May–Oct. 1955), pp. 165–75.

[2] Cf. Judges xvii. 6, xxi. 25.

[3] The writer hopes that the justification of this and the ensuing statements to the end of the paragraph, although presented in part in the following pages, may ultimately appear in an extended form in a monograph entitled *The Vitality of Society in the Thought of Ancient Israel*. Cf. *The Vitality of the Individual in the Thought of Ancient Israel*, p. 84, n. 1, and p. 103, n. 2, 2nd edit., p. 82, n. 1, and p. 104, n. 5.

[4] For an early illustration of the royal concern with justice, see 2 Sam. xv. 1–6. Cf., too, the right of appeal to the king which belonged to the widow and the orphan, as illustrated by 2 Sam. xiv. 1–20 and, probably, 2 Kings viii. 1–6; the principle involved in the description of Solomon's wisdom in (*Footnote 4 continued on pages 5, 6, and 7.*)

1 Kings iii. 4–28; and the tradition underlying the story of the measures taken by Jehoshaphat to deal with the administration of justice in 2 Chron. xix. 5–11, together with the interesting parallel afforded by the decree of Haremhab (*c.* 1340–1310 B.C.), in which measures were prescribed for the reform of the Egyptian judiciary, as discussed by W. F. Albright, 'The Judicial Reform of Jehoshaphat', in *The Alexander Marx Jubilee Volume*, ed. S. Lieberman (1950), pp. 61–82. Note also the repeated comment on the lawless conditions in Israel prior to the monarchy, Judges xvii. 6, xxi. 25.

For many years the standard illustration of such royal responsibility for justice in the wider sphere of the ancient Near East has been that furnished by the great law-code of Hammurabi (*c.* 1728–1686 B.C.), e.g.:

Prologue i. 27 ff.

At that time Anu and Enlil called me by name
to promote the welfare of the people,
me, Hammurabi, the worshipful, god-fearing prince;
to display justice in the land,
to destroy the wicked and the evil,
to stay the strong from oppressing the weak,
to rise like the sun upon the black-headed people,
and to shed light over the land.

Prologue v. 15 ff.

When Marduk sent me to give the people justice,
to bring order to the land,
I established right and justice within the land,
promoting the welfare of the people.

Epilogue rev. xxiv. 59 ff.

To stay the strong from oppressing the weak,
to give justice to the orphan and the widow,
in Babylon, the city whose head Anu and Enlil raised on high,
in Esagila, the temple whose foundations are firm as heaven and earth,
to enact judgement for the land,
to effect decrees for the land,
to give justice to the oppressed,
I inscribed my precious words on my stele,
And set them up in the presence of my image 'King of Justice'.

See especially A. Deimel, *Codex Hammurabi*, 3rd edit. by E. Bergmann, A. Pohl, and R. Follet (1950–); the translation by T. J. Meek in *Ancient Near Eastern Texts relating to the Old Testament*, ed. J. B. Pritchard (1950), 2nd edit. rev. (1955), pp. 163–80; and the translation and commentary in G. R. Driver and J. C. Miles, *The Babylonian Laws*, ii (1955), pp. 1–304. For wider references in this field see the valuable discussion of the whole question by L. Dürr, *Ursprung und Ausbau der israelitisch-jüdischen Heilandserwartung* (1925), pp. 76 ff.; also R. Labat, *Le Caractère religieux de la royauté assyro-babylonienne* (1939), pp. 221–33.

Now, however, with the discovery of the Ras Shamra tablets (fourteenth century B.C.), it is unnecessary to go beyond the borders of Canaan for evidence of a king's responsibility for justice which is far earlier than any afforded by the Israelite monarchy, e.g.:

The youth Yṣb departs,
   He enters his father's presence,
   He raises his voice and cries.
'Hearken, I pray thee, Keret the noble,
   Listen, and incline thine ear.

· · · · · · · ·
· · · · · · · ·

Thou dost not judge the case of the widow,
   Or adjudicate in the cause of the wretched,
   Or drive away those who oppress the poor;
Thou dost not feed the orphan before thy face
   Or the widow behind thy back.
Inasmuch as thou art brother to a sick-bed,
   Companion to a bed of pain,
Descend from the kingship that I may be king,
   From thy dominion that I may posses it.'

Cf., for example, H. L. Ginsberg, *The Legend of King Keret. A Canaanite Epic of the Bronze Age*, B.A.S.O.R., Supplementary Studies 2–3 (1946), KRT C, col. 6, 39–54; C. H. Gordon, *Ugaritic Handbook* (1947) or *Ugaritic Manual* (1955) or *Ugaritic Textbook* (1965), 127, 39–54, and *Ugaritic Literature* (1949), pp. 82 f.; G. R. Driver, *Canaanite Myths and Legends*, O.T.S. 3 (1956), K II, vi 39–54; J. Gray, *The Krt Text in the Literature of Ras Shamra. A Social Myth of Ancient Canaan*, D.M.O.A. v, 2nd edit. rev. (1964), pp. 28 f.; A. Herdner, *Corpus des tablettes en cunéiformes alphabétiques découvertes à Ras Shamra-Ugarit de 1929 à 1939 = Mission de Ras Shamra* X (1963), 16, vi 39–54. Indeed, further evidence is now afforded (*a*) by the way in which Niqmepa, one of the kings of Ugarit, is described *inter alia* as *b'l ṣdq* ('lord of righteousness'); and (*b*) by the contracts and decrees drawn up in Accadian in the names of various kings, including that of Niqmepa, which have been found in the royal palace of Ugarit. Cf. (*a*) Ch. Virolleaud, *Le Palais royal d'Ugarit II. Textes en cunéiformes alphabétiques des archives est, ouest et centrales = Mission de Ras Shamra* VII (1957), 7, 4 (= Gordon, *Ugaritic Textbook*, 1007, 4): (*b*) J. Nougayrol, *Le Palais royal d'Ugarit III. Textes accadiens et hourrites des archives est, ouest et centrales = Mission de Ras Shamra* VI (1955), pp. 22–176.

Similar evidence is also afforded by the Phoenician epigraphic texts; for the inscription of Yeḥimilk, king of Byblos, which is at least as early as the tenth century B.C., contains a plea that his days and years may be prolonged on the ground that he is 'a righteous and upright king' (מלך צדק ומלך ישר). Cf. M. Dunand, *R.B.* xxxix (1930), pp. 321–31; and now *K.A.I.* 4, and the translation by F. Rosenthal, in Pritchard, op. cit., 2nd edit., p. 499. This example is particularly interesting because of the close parallel afforded some five centuries later by the well-known inscription of Yeḥawmilk of Byblos, in which a similar plea is based upon the claim that Yeḥawmilk is 'a righteous king' (מלך צדק). See *N.S.I.* 3, supplemented by M. Dunand, *B.M.B.* v (1941), pp. 57–85, A. Dupont-Sommer, *Semitica* iii (1950), pp. 35–44, and now *K.A.I.* 10, and the translation by Rosenthal, op. cit., p. 502.

See also, for a general introduction to the data which need to be examined in order to appreciate the development of this conception within the context of the ancient Semitic world as a whole, W. W. Graf Baudissin, *Kyrios als*

it is in Yahweh, the God of Israel, that these laws find their substantiation, for in the ultimate it is from Yahweh, as the great 'Giver of Life', that the nation derives its vitality; and, this being the case, it is to Yahweh that the king is finally responsible and, indeed, upon Yahweh that he is ultimately dependent for the exercise of justice (מִשְׁפָּט) and the consequent right ordering of society, i.e. its righteousness (צֶדֶק, צְדָקָה), which alone can ensure fullness of life for his people.

Happily some indication of the ideas which were associated with this conception of the king's supremely important place in the social order is preserved for us in Psalm lxxii, which is one of the more famous of the so-called royal psalms.[1] The parallelism of the opening line makes it clear

Gottesname im Judentum und seine Stelle in der Religionsgeschichte, ed. O. Eissfeldt (1928), iii, pp. 379–463, esp. pp. 398–428; and similarly, for the thought of ancient Egypt, J. H. Breasted, *The Dawn of Conscience* (1934), *passim*, supplemented by J. A. Wilson in H. and H. A. Frankfort, J. A. Wilson, T. Jacobsen, and W. A. Irwin, *The Intellectual Adventure of Ancient Man. An Essay on Speculative Thought in the Ancient Near East* (1946), pp. 82 ff. and 104 ff., and in *The Burden of Egypt* (1951), e.g. pp. 47–50 and 114–24.

Finally, cf. now the far-seeing discussion of this and related issues by N. W. Porteous, 'Royal Wisdom', in *Wisdom in Israel and in the Ancient Near East* (H. H. Rowley *Festschrift*), ed. M. Noth and D. W. Thomas, S.V.T. iii (1955), pp. 247–61; also the summary but careful discussion of the king's judicial powers in R. de Vaux, *Les Institutions de l'Ancien Testament*, i (1958), pp. 231 ff., E.T. by J. McHugh, *Ancient Israel: Its Life and Institutions* (1961), pp. 150 ff.

[1] For the theory of royal psalms and the question as to what light they may throw on the cultic role and social significance of the king, see H. Gunkel, 'Die Königspsalmen', *Pr.J.B.* clviii (1914), pp. 42–68; *R.G.G.*[1, 2] iv, 'Psalmen', § 9; H. Gunkel and J. Begrich, *Einleitung in die Psalmen*, H. K. (1933), pp. 140–71: S. Mowinckel, *Kongesalmerne i Det Gamle Testamente* (1916); *Psalmenstudien II. Das Thronbesteigungsfest Jahwäs und der Ursprung der Eschatologie*, S.N.V.A.O. II, 1921, No. 6 (1922), pp. 297 ff.; *Psalmenstudien III. Kultprophetie und prophetische Psalmen*, S.N.V.A.O. II, 1922, No. 1 (1923), pp. 78 ff.; *Offersang og sangoffer. Salmediktningen i Bibelen* (1951), pp. 51–91, E.T. by D. R. Ap-Thomas, *The Psalms in Israel's Worship* (1962), i. pp. 42–80; *Han som kommer. Messiasforventningen i Det Gamle Testament og på Jesu tid* (1951), pp. 42–68, E.T. by G. W. Anderson, *He That Cometh* (1956), pp. 52–95: H. Birkeland, *Die Feinde des Individuums in der israelitischen Psalmenliteratur* (1933); *The Evildoers in the Book of Psalms*, A.N.V.A.O. II, 1955, No. 2 (1955): A. Bentzen, *Det sakrale kongedømme. Bemærkninger i en løbende diskussion om de gammeltestamentlige Salmer* (1945): J. de Fraine, *L'Aspect religieux de la royauté israélite* (as cited above, p. 2, n. 3): K. H.

that we are here concerned with no simple portrayal of some future eschatological figure (although this is not to say that the psalm is in no way eschatological),[1] but with a prayer for the ruling member of an hereditary line of kings which bears every appearance of having been composed for use on his accession to the throne; and the whole psalm admirably depicts the literally vital role which it was hoped that he might play in the life of the nation. The key words are 'righteousness' (צֶדֶק, צְדָקָה) and 'justice' (מִשְׁפָּט); and the basic thought throughout is that the king may watch carefully over the rights of his subjects, and so ensure, in particular, that the weaker members of society may enjoy his protection and thus have justice done to them according to their need. What is more, it is clear from the outset that the king is both dependent upon and responsible to Yahweh for the right exercise of his power; for his subjects, whatever their status in society, are one and all Yahweh's people. It is to be observed, too, that the opening lines make passing reference to a basic principle which is expressed at length towards the close of the psalm, i.e. that it is only as the earthly king ensures a sound moral order by means of his righteous rule that one can be sure of a corresponding stability in the realm of nature with all that

Bernhardt, *Das Problem der altorientalischen Königsideologie im Alten Testament* (as cited above, p. 2, n. 3); and the more general discussion by E. Lipiński, 'Les Psaumes de la royauté de Yahwé dans l'exégèse moderne', in *Le Psautier. Ses origines. Ses problèmes littéraires. Son influence*, ed. R. de Langhe, O.B.L. iv (1962), pp. 133–272. See also the present writer's earlier work in this field, i.e. 'The Rôle of the King in the Jerusalem Cultus', in *The Labyrinth. Further Studies in the Relation between Myth and Ritual in the Ancient World*, ed. S. H. Hooke (1935), pp. 71–111; 'Living Issues in Biblical Scholarship. Divine Kingship and the Old Testament', *E.T.* lxii (1950–1), pp. 36–42; 'The Psalms', in *The Old Testament and Modern Study. A Generation of Discovery and Research*, ed. H. H. Rowley (1951), pp. 162–209: and now (i.e. since the publication of the first edition of this monograph) 'Old Testament Exegesis, Imaginative and Unimaginative', *E.T.* lxviii (1956–7), pp. 178 f.; 'Hebrew Conceptions of Kingship', in *Myth, Ritual, and Kingship. Essays on the Theory and Practice of Kingship in the Ancient Near East and in Israel*, ed. S. H. Hooke (1958), pp. 204–35, to which the reader may be referred for other studies, notably those of the so-called Uppsala School, which touch on this subject.   [1] See below, Parts V–VI.

this implies for the economic well-being of the people. The
first few verses, then, may be rendered as follows:[1]

> O God, give Thy judgements to the king,
> And Thy righteousness to this member of the royal line;[2]
> May he judge Thy people with righteousness
> And Thy humble followers with justice.
> Through righteousness let the mountains and hills
> Bring welfare (EVV. 'peace')[3] to the people.
> May he grant justice to the humble among the people,
> Saving[4] the children of the needy and crushing the oppressor.
> ⌜May he also continue⌝[5] as long as the sun,
> And, like the moon, through all generations.
> May his rule be[6] like rain upon the crop,[7]
> Like showers that water the earth.
> May righteousness[8] flourish in his days,
> And welfare (EVV. 'peace') abound till the moon be no more.

[1] vv. 1–7. What appears to be the requisite distinction between jussive
and indicative forms of the imperfect of the verb has been obscured at different points in M.T.; and the rendering of this psalm offered above in the
text is based throughout upon whichever form of the consonantal text seems
to be required by the context, the *matres lectionis* being ignored where necessary. Cf. the somewhat similar cases offered by the other readings adopted
in verses 5 and 7.

lit. 'a (*or* the) king's son'.

[3] i.e. שָׁלוֹם. Cf. the writer's monograph, *The Cultic Prophet in Ancient
Israel* (1944), p. 44, n. 1, 2nd edit. rev. (1962), p. 49, n. 1; and see further
G. von Rad, 'שָׁלוֹם im A.T.', in *Th.W.N.T.* ii (1935), s.v. εἰρήνη, pp. 400–5,
= *T.D.N.T.* ii. (1964), pp. 402–6.

[4] See below, p. 19, n. 2.

[5] Reading יַאֲרֵךְ (cf. LXX) for יִרְאוּךְ, i.e. a simple case of metathesis
prior to the introduction of the *matres lectionis*. Compare the use of the
corresponding verb in the Phoenician royal inscriptions with reference to
the 'prolonging' of the days and years of the reigning king, i.e. in the inscriptions of Yeḥimilk (as cited above, p. 4, n. 4), Šapaṭbaʿal or Šiptibaʿal
(as cited below, p. 41, n. 8), and Elibaʿal (ed. R. Dussaud, *Syria* vi (1925),
pp. 101–17), all of which are probably to be dated within the twelfth to the
ninth centuries B.C., and that of Yeḥawmilk (as cited above p. 4, n. 4), which
belongs to the fifth or, perhaps, the fourth century B.C.

[6] lit. 'May he rule', i.e. vocalizing the consonantal text as יֵרְךְ (√רדה):
cf. verse 8.

[7] גֵּז appears to have been used, like the corresponding English terms
'fleece' and 'crop', to denote such animal or vegetable growth either before
or after being cut.

[8] Reading צֶדֶק for צַדִּיק with three MSS., LXX, S, and Jerome.

The psalmist then allows his thoughts to reach out beyond
the confines of his own land to the world at large, and prays
in equally picturesque terms that this earthly king may
come to enjoy so complete and so universal a sway that all
the kings of the earth may pay him tribute and all the nations
submit to his rule.[1]

> May he rule also from sea to sea,
> And from 'The River' to the ends of the earth.
> May the creatures of the wild[2] bow down before him,
> And his enemies lick the dust.
> May the kings of Tarshish and the coastal lands
> Render tribute.
> May the kings of Sheba and Seba
> Bring their gifts.
> Yea, may all kings make obeisance to him,
> All nations serve him.

It is commonly thought that the allusion to 'The River' in
the first metrical line is a reference to the Euphrates,[3] and,
as a result, the poet's language has been taken as an indication that he has been influenced by the court style of the
Babylonian world.[4] Such a view, however, fails to do justice
to the central importance which Jerusalem came to enjoy
in Hebrew cosmology.[5] At a later stage in our discussion
we shall see reason to believe that the reference, far from

---

[1] vv. 8–11.   [2] Or (as LXX) 'Ethiopians'.

[3] Cf., for example, Gen. xxxi. 21 (E); Exod. xxiii. 31 (E); Num. xxii. 5 (E);
Joshua xxiv. 2 (E); 2 Sam. x. 16; 1 Kings v. 1 (EVV. iv. 21), xiv. 15; 2
Chron. ix. 26; Isa. xxvii. 12: also, without the article, Ps. lxxx. 12 (EVV. 11);
Isa. vii. 20; Jer. ii. 18; Mic. vii. 12.

[4] Cf., for example, H. Gressmann, *Der Ursprung der israelitisch-jüdischen
Eschatologie*, F.R.L.A.N.T. 6 (1905), p. 254, *Der Messias*, F.R.L.A.N.T. 43
(1929), p. 19; Mowinckel, *Kongesalmerne i Det Gamle Testamente*, pp. 39 f.:
and see further the extended discussion of this verse by H. Gross, *Weltherr-
schaft als religiöse Idee im Alten Testament*, B.B.B. 6 (1953), pp. 11–18.

[5] Cf., for example, R. Patai, *Man and Temple: In Ancient Jewish Myth and
Ritual* (1947), pp. 83 ff.: and, for an introduction to the wider questions involved, see A. J. Wensinck, *The Ideas of the Western Semites concerning the
Navel of the Earth*, V.K.A.W.A., N.R. xvii. 1 (1916); J. Jeremias, *Golgotha* =
ΑΓΓΕΛΟΣ Beihefte, i (1926), pp. 43 ff., 66 ff.; E. Burrows, 'Some Cosmo-
logical Patterns in Babylonian Religion', in *The Labyrinth*, pp. 43–70, esp.
pp. 53 ff.

being an allusion to the Euphrates, is really an allusion to the current of the great cosmic sea which nourishes the holy city,[1] i.e. that of which the psalmist speaks when he says:[2]

> As for 'The River', its streams make glad the city of God,
> The most sacred abode of the Most High.[3]

Similarly the expression 'from sea to sea', far from denoting, say, the Mediterranean and the Persian Gulf,[4] is really an allusion in general terms to the all-embracing cosmic sea[5] and, taken in conjunction with the expression 'from "The River" to the ends of the earth', points to the thought of a sovereignty covering the wide circle of the earth.[6]

This, however, is a matter to which we shall return; and, continuing our reading of the psalm, we have now to note that, after this ambitious vision of a world sovereignty exercised from the citadel on Mount Zion, the poet reverts to the thought of the king as the guardian of the humble and the needy, the weak and the helpless. In fact the anticipated realization of this hope is now offered as the ground for his being permitted such universal dominion.[7]

> For he will deliver the needy when he crieth,
> And the humble when he hath no helper.

[1] See Isa. viii. 6, 'the waters of Shiloah that go softly'; Ezek. xlvii, i.e. the vision of the stream which issues from beneath the Temple and, gathering volume, becomes a great river flowing with fertilizing power in the direction of the Jordan valley and the Dead Sea. Cf. G. A. Cooke, *The Progress of Revelation* (1910), pp. 41 f. Note also the important parallel to Ps. lxxii. 8 which is to be found in Zech. ix. 9 f., especially as the latter passage may ultimately be found all the more striking in view of the argument of these pages as a whole.

[2] Ps. xlvi. 5 (EVV. 4). The omission of the article in the case of נָהָר is to be compared with the similar omission in the passage under discussion, as well as those passages which are cited above, p. 10, n. 3 *ad fin.*, where the reference is to the Euphrates.

[3] Or, reading קֹדֶשׁ מִשְׁכְּנוֹ עֶלְיוֹן, on the basis of LXX and V, 'Which the Most High hath sanctified as His abode'.

[4] Cf., for example, Gressmann, loc. cit., Mowinckel, loc. cit.

[5] Cf., for example, H. Gunkel, *Die Psalmen*, H. K. (1926), *in loc.*; Pedersen, *Israel III–IV*, p. 327, E.T., p. 433.

[6] Cf. Job xxii. 14; Prov. viii. 27; Isa. xl. 22: also Job xxvi. 10 (following S and T).   [7] vv. 12–14.

He will have pity on the lowly and the needy;
Yea, the lives[1] of the needy will he save.
He will protect[2] their life from oppression and violence,
And their blood will be precious in his eyes.

These lines lead in turn to a plea for the economic prosperity which is to be expected as a result of righteous or just government on the part of the king; and this is to be reflected in such rich revenue from abroad and such abundant harvests at home that his name is to be in constant use for all time and amongst all peoples as the pattern of the highest blessing.[3]

So may he *live* (i.e. flourish)[4] and be given
Of the gold of Sheba.
So may one pray for him continually,
And bless him all the day long.
May there be a wealth[5] of corn in the land
To the tops of the mountains.
May their fruit be as plenteous[6] as Lebanon;
May they flower on the summit[7] like the grass of the earth.
May his name endure for ever,
May his name continue[8] as long as the sun;
Yea, may [all the families of the earth][9] bless themselves by him,
May all nations acknowledge his happiness.

[1] It is, perhaps, hardly necessary to point out that the use of the plural form of נֶפֶשׁ in this line affords no argument for a late date. Cf., for example, 2 Sam. xxiii. 17, which bears every appearance of being an early passage.

[2] See the writer's paper, 'The Primary Meaning of √גאל', S.V.T. i (1953), pp. 67–77.

[3] vv. 15–17. The doxology which follows is no part of the original psalm; it simply marks the close of Book II of the Psalter.

[4] Cf. the familiar salutation יְחִי הַמֶּלֶךְ (EVV. 'God save the king'; mgn. 'Heb. *Let the king live*'), as in 1 Sam. x. 24: 2 Sam. xvi. 16; 2 Kings xi. 12; 2 Chron. xxiii. 11; and (in an expanded form) 1 Kings i. 25, 31, 34, 39: also Neh. ii. 3. See further *The Vitality of the Individual in the Thought of Ancient Israel*, pp. 96 f., 2nd edit., pp. 97 f.

[5] Cf. G. R. Driver, *H.T.R.* xxix (1936), pp. 185 f.

[6] Cf. G. R. Driver, *J.T.S.* xxxiii (1931–2), p. 43.

[7] Vocalizing the consonantal text as מְעִיר on the analogy of the Arabic غِير as used of a 'ridge' or similar prominence. Cf. E. W. Lane, *An Arabic–English Lexicon* (1863–6), s.v.

[8] The original idea underlying the verb (cf. נִין, 'offspring') appears to be that of the continuation of the male line—with all that this implies for the preservation of one's name. Cf. the writer's monograph, *The One and the Many in the Israelite Conception of God* (1942), pp. 7 f., 2nd edit. (1961), pp. 3 f.   'So LXX.

Thus the basic principle underlying the thought of this psalm is clear enough; and it is that the national prosperity of Israel is conditioned by the behaviour of society as a whole. That is to say, as we have already observed, the moral realm and the realm of nature are regarded as one and indivisible. What is more, however, such an effective communal life is ultimately dependent upon the character of the king, whose function it is to maintain law and order. Accordingly he must be careful to guarantee justice for all, and thus show a constant concern for the weaker and more helpless members of society. The nation cannot be expected to be righteous and therefore prosperous, if the king does not prove to be righteous; and, as we learn from the opening line of the psalm, he cannot do this in his own strength, but is ultimately dependent upon Yahweh (or 'The Eternal'[1]), who is clearly 'the enduring power, not ourselves, which makes for righteousness'.[2]

The question therefore arises as to what exactly was the relationship between the king and Yahweh; for it is obvious that it must have been regarded as one of a most intimate kind. Indeed this conclusion is reinforced by the fact that the king is not only found leading his people in worship with the offering of sacrifice and prayer on important occasions in the national life,[3] but throughout the four

---

[1] Cf. *The Vitality of the Individual in the Thought of Ancient Israel*, p. 106, n. 7, 2nd edit., p. 108, n. 4.

[2] This, of course, is the familiar language of Matthew Arnold, *Literature and Dogma. An Essay towards a better Apprehension of the Bible* (1873). The use of this famous phrase with approval, however, is not to be understood as involving an acceptance of the content which Arnold gave to it. If it is to form a true definition of the Israelite conception of Yahweh (or 'The Eternal', to use Arnold's own language again), it must carry with it the thought of a *personal* and indeed, in modern terms, a *supra-personal* Power.

[3] See 1 Sam. xiii (although, as is pointed out by M. Noth, *Z.T.K.* xlvii (1950), p. 185, n. 1, now reprinted in *Gesammelte Studien zum Alten Testament* (1957), 2nd edit. enlarged (1960), p. 221, n. 37, this is a somewhat doubtful example); 2 Sam. vi (1 Chron. xiii, xv, xvi), xxiv. 18–25 (1 Chron. xxi. 18–xxii. 1); 1 Kings iii. 4, 15 (2 Chron. i. 6), viii (2 Chron. v. 2–vii. 10), ix. 25 (2 Chron. viii. 12 f.), x. 5 (2 Chron. ix. 4: LXX); 2 Kings xix. 14 ff. (Isa. xxxvii. 14 ff.); 2 Chron. xiv. 8–14 (EVV. 9–15), xx. 1–30: also the obviously tendentious story in 2 Chron. xxvi. 16–20. Cf. too, 1 Kings xii. 32–xiii. 10;

hundred years of the Davidic dynasty, from the time of
David's active concern for the Ark to that of Josiah's
thorough-going reform, himself superintends the organiza-
tion of the cultus in all its aspects.[1] Some indication of this
relationship is to be seen, of course, in the familiar rite of
anointing by which the king was installed in office and in
virtue of which he enjoyed the title of 'Messiah' (מָשִׁיחַ);[2]
for, the sacred commission having come in the ultimate from
Yahweh and having been communicated by His messenger,
whether prophet or priest,[3] the king was not merely 'the

---

[2] Kings x. 18–28, xvi. 10–18 (2 Chron. xxviii. 22–25): and see now the writer's
additional comments in 'Hebrew Conceptions of Kingship' (as cited above,
p. 7, n. 1, *ad fin.*), pp. 211 ff.

[1] See 2 Sam. vi (1 Chron. xiii, xv, xvi), xxiv. 18–25 (1 Chron. xxi. 18–xxii. 1);
1 Kings v. 15 (EVV. v. 1)–viii. 66 (2 Chron. i. 18 (EVV. ii. 1)–vii. 10), xv.
12–15 (2 Chron. xv. 1–18); 2 Kings xii. 5–17 (EVV. 4–16) (2 Chron. xxiv.
4–14), xviii. 4 (2 Chron. xxix. 3–xxxi. 21), xxii. 3–xxiii. 23 (2 Chron. xxxiv.
3–xxxv. 19): and, what is particularly interesting, the Chronicler's emphasis
upon David's preparations for the building of the Temple and his organiza-
tion of the musical side of its worship, 1 Chron. xxii. 2–19, xxv (cf. 1 Chron.
xv. 16 ff.; 2 Chron. xxix. 25 ff.). Cf., too, 1 Kings xii. 26–32 (2 Chron. xi.
14 f.); 2 Kings x. 18–28, xvi. 10–18 (2 Chron. xxviii. 22–25).

[2] See especially (*a*) Judges ix. 7–21; 1 Sam. xvi. 1–13; 2 Sam. ii. 1–7, v.
1–5; 1 Kings i. 28–40; 2 Kings ix. 1–13, xi. 4–20; (*b*) 1 Sam. xxiv. 7, 11
(EVV. 6, 10), xxvi. 9, 11, 16, 23; 2 Sam. i. 14, 16, xix. 22. An early parallel
to this rite is to be found in a letter of the fourteenth century B.C., sent by
Addu-nirari, king of Nuḫashshe, to his overlord, the king of Egypt, in which
he refers to the fact that the latter's grandfather had poured oil upon the
head of his own grandfather, thus conferring the kingship upon him, i.e.:

To the sun, the king, my lord, the king of Egypt,

Addu-nirari thy servant, as follows:

At the feet of my lord I fall.

(Behold), when Manaḫbi(r)ia, the king of Egypt, thy grandfather, established (Taku), my (grandfather), as king in Nuḫashshe, and set oil upon his
head, (he said). . . .

Cf. J. A. Knudtzon, *Die El-Amarna-Tafeln* (1915), and S. A. B. Mercer,
The Tell el-Amarna Tablets (1939), No. 51, 1 ff.: and see now, for a general
discussion of this rite within the context of the ancient Near East, E. Kutsch,
Salbung als Rechtsakt im Alten Testament und im Alten Orient, B.Z.A.W. 87
(1963); also, as regards its use in connexion with the kingship in ancient
Israel, R. de Vaux, 'Le Roi d'Israël, vassal de Yahvé', in *Mélanges Eugène
Tisserant* (1964), i, pp. 119–33. For an important criticism of Kutsch's
treatment of the historical aspects of the O.T. data, see de Vaux, op. cit.,
p. 133, n. 68, and *R.B.* lxxi (1964), pp. 276–8.

[3] Cf. 1 Sam. xvi. 1–13; 1 Kings i. 28–40; 2 Kings ix. 1–13, xi. 4–20
(following LXX in verse 12: cf. 2 Chron. xxiii. 11): and, for both prophet

Messiah' but 'the Messiah of Yahweh'.[1] Indeed it seems clear that, as a result, he was now thought to be a channel for the operation of the divine 'Spirit' (רוּחַ); and, this being the case, it may well be that for the Israelites the symbolic action was eloquent of the power with which he was to be imbued and which should henceforward govern his behaviour.[2] Be that as it may, a special endowment of the Spirit is clearly associated with the rite in question, when it is said of the founder of the Davidic dynasty that, on his being chosen for this high office,[3]

> Samuel took the horn of oil, and anointed him in the midst of his brethren; and the Spirit of Yahweh burst upon David from that day forward.

Whatever the date of this passage,[4] there can be no reasonable doubt that the picture which it gives is in line with popular tradition, for it corresponds so exactly with what we are told in the obviously early stories about the exploits of the great heroes of Israel in the period immediately prior to the foundation of the monarchy and indeed the exploits of David's predecessor Saul.[5] What is more, it should be borne in mind that from the first the activity of the Spirit, which, as an extension of the Personality of Yahweh, was certainly not thought of as an impersonal

and priest as Yahweh's messengers, see *The One and the Many in the Israelite Conception of God*, pp. 36 f., 2nd edit., pp. 32 f.; also *The Cultic Prophet in Ancient Israel*, pp. 10 f., 48 f., 2nd edit., pp. 8 f., 57 f.

[1] Cf., for example, 1 Sam. xxiv. 7, 11 (EVV. 6, 10), xxvi. 9, 11, 16, 23; 2 Sam. i. 14, 16, xix. 22 (EVV. 21).

[2] Cf. the language of Isa. xliv. 3; Ezek. xxxix. 29; Joel iii. 1f. (EVV. ii. 28 f.): also Isa xxxii. 15; Zech. xii. 10.

[3] 1 Sam. xvi. 13.

[4] Cf., for example, (*a*) K. Budde, K.H.C. (1902), pp. 113 ff.; W. Nowack, H.K. (1902), p. 79; P.(E.) Dhorme, E.B. (1910), pp. 145 f.; H. Gressmann, S.A.T. ii. 1, 2nd edit. rev. (1921), pp. 63 ff.; R. Kittel, *H.S.A.T.* (1922), p. 431; W. Caspari, K.A.T. (1926), pp. 187 ff.; A. F. Kirkpatrick, C.B., 2nd edit. rev. (1930), pp. 130 f.; (*b*) H. P. Smith, I.C.C. (1899), p. 143; A. R. S. Kennedy, Cent. B. (n.d.), p. 116; H. W. Hertzberg, A.T.D. (1956), pp. 104 ff., 3rd edit. (1965), pp. 107 ff., E.T. (of the 2nd edit. rev. (1960)) by J. S. Bowden (1964), pp. 135 ff.

[5] See esp. (*a*) Judges vi. 34 ff., xi. 29 ff., xiii. 25, xiv. 6, 19, xv. 14; (*b*) 1 Sam. x. 1, 6 ff., xi. 6 ff. (cf. xvi. 14).

force,¹ was by no means restricted to exhibitions of physical prowess,² but might include the foresight of an administrator like Joseph and the organizing ability of a potential king such as Gideon.³ All in all, therefore, it is obvious that David, like the divine 'Angel' or 'Messenger' (מַלְאָךְ) with whom he could henceforward be compared for his insight,⁴ must himself have been regarded as a potent extension of the divine Personality.⁵ Accordingly it is little wonder that the king's person should have been regarded as sacrosanct; i.e., as we learn already from the way in which David spared Saul's life, that one should beware of stretching forth one's hand against Yahweh's Messiah,⁶ and that the cursing of a king could be brought into line with the cursing of God.⁷

Nevertheless the peculiar bond existing between the Davidic king and Yahweh is also expressed in other terms than this, as one may see from the short poem commonly known as 'The Last Words of David'.⁸ It is, of course, a matter of dispute as to whether or not this poem was actually the work of David; and, if it was, one is still left with the question as to whether or not it represents anything like his last words, for it seems to owe its citation in this way to an editorial desire to give David a 'testament' similar to those which have been ascribed to Jacob and Moses.⁹ At the same time it must be said that no conclusive

¹ Cf. *The One and the Many in the Israelite Conception of God*, pp. 17 ff., 2nd edit., pp. 13 ff.
² e.g. Judges xiii. 25, xiv. 6, 19, xv. 14.
³ Gen. xli. 38 (J/E); Judges vi. 34 ff. (cf. viii. 22 f.). Cf. Judges iii. 10, xi. 29 ff.; 1 Sam. xi. 6 ff.: also Isa. xi. 1 ff., lxi. 1, to which the writer hopes to return in a subsequent work. See also *The Vitality of the Individual in the Thought of Ancient Israel*, pp. 28 ff., 2nd edit., pp. 24 ff.
⁴ 2 Sam. xiv. 17, 20, xix. 28 (EVV. 27): cf. 1 Sam. xxix. 9.
⁵ Cf. *The One and the Many in the Israelite Conception of God*, pp. 32 ff., 2nd edit., pp. 28 ff.
⁶ 1 Sam. xxiv. 7, 11 (EVV. 6, 10), xxvi. 9, 11, 23; 2 Sam. i. 14, 16.
⁷ 1 Kings xxi. 10, 13: cf. Exod. xxii. 27 (EVV. 28) (E); 2 Sam. xix. 22 (EVV. 21); also Prov. xxiv. 21.   ⁸ 2 Sam. xxiii. 1–7.
⁹ Gen. xlix; Deut. xxxiii. Cf., too, the late work known as *The Testaments of the Twelve Patriarchs*.

evidence has been advanced for denying the Davidic authorship of at least the body of the poem;[1] for there is not the slightest justification for the view that vocabulary, style, and thought prove it to be of comparatively late date.[2] Happily, however, a decision on this point is not important for our present purpose. It is sufficient to note (a) that the poem is of a piece with the royal psalms, (b) that, like Psalm lxxii, it reveals the lofty ideal of righteousness which was associated with the House of David, and (c) that this ideal of a righteous kingship is rooted in a 'covenant' (בְּרִית), carefully and securely drawn up, between David as the founder of the dynasty and Yahweh as the national God.

The language of the introduction, with its repeated reference to the oracular nature of David's words, emphasizes the prophetic character of what follows; and this is in keeping with David's own claim (or the claim made in the name of David) that what he is about to say has come to him directly through the Spirit of Yahweh. This, of course, is in harmony with the tradition which we have already noticed, i.e. that David, in virtue of his being anointed and thus becoming the Messiah of Yahweh, came powerfully under the influence of Yahweh's Spirit. The poem as a whole may be rendered thus:

[1] Cf. O. Procksch, 'Die letzten Worte Davids', in *Alttestamentliche Studien Rudolf Kittel zum 60. Geburtstag dargebracht*, B.W.A.T. 13 (1913), pp. 112–25: also Gunkel–Begrich, *Einleitung in die Psalmen*, p. 146 (David himself as author); Gressmann, op. cit., pp. 184 ff. (a contemporary of David as author); Kittel, op. cit., p. 488 (probably time of David); A. Causse, *Les Plus Vieux Chants de la Bible*, E.H.P.R. xiv (1926), pp. 152 ff. (David or a court poet). Cf. now, too, R. de Vaux, S.B.J., 2nd edit. rev. (1961); Hertzberg, op. cit., p. 324, 3rd edit., pp. 329 f., E.T., pp. 399 f.

[2] Cf., for example, Smith, op. cit., pp. 381 ff.; Budde, op. cit., pp. 315 ff.; Nowack, op. cit., p. 251; Dhorme, op. cit., pp. 447 f.: and especially S. Mowinckel, ' "Die letzten Worte Davids" II Sam 23^1–7', *Z.A.W.* xlv (1927), pp. 30–58 (cf. G.T.M.M.M. ii (1935), pp. 296 ff.), which suffers from (a) a radical scepticism with regard to the text, (b) an undue emphasis upon the supposedly gnomic character of the resultant poem, and (c) an interpretation of Yahweh's covenant with David in a way which proves to be without justification, when the thought of these lines is compared with that of Pss. lxxxix and cxxxii, both of which are recognized by Mowinckel himself as being connected in some way with the poem under discussion.

Oracle of David, the son of Jesse,
  And oracle of the man who was raised on high,[1]
The Messiah of the God of Jacob
  And the hero of Israel's psalms.[2]

The Spirit of Yahweh speaketh through me,
  And His utterance[3] is upon my tongue;
The God of Israel hath said,
  To me the Rock of Israel hath spoken.

'A ruler of men must be righteous,
  Ruling in the fear of God[4]
And like the light of morning, at sunrise,
  A cloudless morning which maketh the grass
  Glisten[5] from the earth after rain.'

Nay, but[6] is not that how my house stands with God,
  Since He hath granted me an everlasting covenant,

[1] In view of the writer's subsequent argument it would be pleasant to accept the suggestion that עַל is here a divine name, corresponding to the familiar עֶלְיוֹן ('Most High'), and that הֻקַם should be read as הֵ(י)קִם, thus securing the rendering:

Oracle of David, the son of Jesse,
  And oracle of the man whom the Most High raised up,
The Messiah of the God of Jacob
  And the hero of Israel's psalms.

Cf. H. S. Nyberg, *Studien zum Hoseabuche*, U.U.Å. 1935: 6 (1935), pp. 57 ff., and 'Studien zum Religionskampf im Alten Testament. I. Der Gott 'Al: Belege und Bedeutung des Namens', *A.R.W.* xxxv (1938), p. 378; G. R. Driver, *E.T.* l (1938–9), pp. 92 f. As is pointed out by J. A. Bewer, *J.B.L.* lxi (1942), pp. 47 f., it may hardly be claimed that this suggestion is confirmed by LXX[B]; but, even so, it remains a possibility and may well be right. It has not been adopted here, however, as the writer is anxious to avoid using any argument in support of his thesis which, in his opinion, admits the possibility of doubt. See further p. 50, n. 4.

[2] Cf. Ps. xcv. 2 and the royal psalms discussed below, in Parts V–VI, which are so intimately concerned with David and the House of David.

[3] The time has gone by when the presence of an 'Aramaism' in a work could be regarded without more ado as an indication of a late date. Cf., for example, G. R. Driver, *J.T.S.* xxxvi (1935), pp. 294 ff., *Problems of the Hebrew Verbal System*, O.T.S. 2 (1936), pp. 98 ff., 151 f., 'Hebrew Poetic Diction', S.V.T. i (1953), pp. 26–39; D. W. Thomas, in *Record and Revelation*, ed. H. W. Robinson (1938), pp. 386 f.; and now M. Noth, *Die Ursprünge des alten Israel im Lichte neuer Quellen*, A.F.L.N.W. 94 (1961), e.g., pp. 28 f., 34 ff.

[4] Cf. Gen. xx. 11 (E).

[5] Vocalizing מִנֹּגַהּ as מְנַגַּהּ. Cf. for example, Budde, op. cit., *in loc.*

[6] Cf. Ruth i. 10; 1 Sam. x. 19.

Set forth in detail with proper safeguard?[1]
Yea, doth He not bring to growth
My complete salvation (יֵשַׁע)[2] and every wish?

Whereas evil must be like thistles, all running wild,[3]
For these are not removed[4] by hand,
But the man who cometh into touch with them
Must be complete with iron and spear-shaft,
And they must be burned with fire on the spot.[5]

Comment is superfluous; such vivid, pictorial language speaks for itself.

This theme of a covenant between Yahweh and the House of David occurs again in Psalm cxxxii, which clearly comes within the category of the royal psalms and, as such, appears to have as its original *Sitz im Leben* a dramatic commemoration or liturgical re-enactment of the bringing of the Ark to Jerusalem and the consequent foundation of the Jerusalem cultus in close association with the Davidic dynasty.[6] It falls clearly into two parts: (*a*) a hymn beseeching Yahweh's continued favour to the royal house, and (*b*) a response of an oracular kind in which the worshippers are assured that Yahweh will preserve His covenant with the House of David, i.e. the 'everlasting covenant' to which the preceding poem referred, although this carries with it corresponding obligations on the part of David's

[1] Cf., for example, S. R. Driver, *Notes on the Hebrew Text and the Topography of the Books of Samuel*, 2nd edit. rev. (1913), *in loc.*

[2] i.e. as 'freedom' from whatever interferes with fullness of life. Cf. *The Vitality of the Individual in the Thought of Ancient Israel*, pp. 94 ff., 2nd edit., pp. 95 ff. For the wide range of meaning which √ישׁע came to admit see Driver, op. cit., pp. 118 f.

[3] *lit.* 'the whole of them being allowed to wander'. The suffix of כֻּלְּהָם refers back to the collective noun קוֹץ (i.e. *constructio ad sensum*).

[4] Vocalizing יְקָחוּ as יֻקָּחוּ. Cf., for example, Budde, op. cit., *in loc.*, although this is not absolutely necessary (cf. Driver, op. cit., *in loc.*).

[5] Hebrew בַּשֶּׁבֶת = *in situ*. The writer cannot find the slightest reason for questioning the text; and the removal of the expression on the ground that it has arisen from confusion with the corresponding set of consonants in the next verse (cf., for example, Driver, op. cit., *in loc.*) merely succeeds in robbing the simile of much of its force.

[6] 2 Sam. vi: cf. 1 Chron. xiii, xv, xvi.

successors upon the throne. Thus its liturgical character
seems clear. The hymn begins with a striking appeal to
Yahweh to remember on David's behalf 'all his humility'.[1]
This is a quality which we find stressed repeatedly in the
Psalter as the characteristic attitude which Yahweh requires of all His followers, king and subjects alike;[2] and its
use in the present connexion is then explained in terms of
David's reverent concern for the Ark and his untiring
determination to find a suitable home for this important
cultic object, which was the guarantee of Yahweh's presence
with His people, and was famous in Israelite history as a
potent and indeed, even for Yahweh's own worshippers, a
somewhat dangerous extension of the divine Personality.[3]
The home in view is obviously the Temple, for which
David was primarily responsible even if Solomon was its
builder; and, as the Ark is lifted into its place, Yahweh is
implored to show favour to His followers, specifically the
priests and general assembly of worshippers, and, above all,
to be gracious to the reigning king for the sake of his ancestor David.[4]

> O Yahweh, remember for David
>   All his humility;
> How he swore to Yahweh,
>   How he vowed to the Mighty One of Jacob,
> 'I will not enter the tent which is my dwelling,
>   Nor ascend the couch which is my bed,
> I will not give sleep to mine eyes

---

[1] i.e. reading עֱנוֹתוֹ with LXX and S. The vocalization of M.T. (cf. T)
is supposed to refer to all the trouble which David underwent in the service
of Yahweh, especially in the case of the incident under discussion. Cf., for
example, A. F. Kirkpatrick, C.B. (1902), *in loc.* To the present writer, however, this is unlikely for the reason given above in the text.

[2] See below, for example, pp. 79 f., 91, 111 ff., and 120 f.

[3] Cf. 1 Sam. iv. 1b–vii. 1; 2 Sam. vi. 6 f.: and see further *The One and the
Many in the Israelite Conception of God*, pp. 23 ff., 2nd edit., pp. 19 ff. See
also, for the cultic background to the stories of the Ark in 1 Sam. iv–vii
and 2 Sam. vi, L. Rost, *Die Überlieferung von der Thronnachfolge Davids*,
B.W.A.N.T. 42 (1926), pp. 4–47.

[4] vv. 1–10. See also 2 Chron. vi. 41 f. for a slightly different text in the case
of the last three lines (i.e. vv. 8 ff.).

Or slumber to mine eyelids,
Until I find a place for Yahweh,
A dwelling for the Mighty One of Jacob.'
Lo, we heard of it in Ephrathah;
We came across it in the countryside of ⸢Jair⸣.[1]
Let us enter His dwelling,
Let us make obeisance before His footstool.

[1] A.V.: 'Lo, we heard of it at Ephrath: we found it in the fields of the
wood.'
R.V.: 'Lo, we heard of it in Ephrathah (mgn. '*Or* Ephraim'):
We found it in the field of the wood (mgn. '*Or* Jaar').'
R.S.V.: 'Lo, we heard of it in Ephrathah,
we found it in the fields of Jaar.'

O. Eissfeldt, 'Psalm 132', *W.O.* ii 5/6 (1959), pp. 480–3, like Kirkpatrick,
op. cit., follows Franz Delitzsch, *Biblischer Kommentar über die Psalmen*,
5th edit. rev. by Friedrich Delitzsch (1894), E.T. of the 4th edit. by D. Eaton
(1887–9), in holding that the reference in each stichos is to the locating of
the Ark at Kiriath-jearim; but, despite such strong support for Delitzsch's
theory, it seems to me that this well-known *crux interpretum* remains un-
solved; for the ingenious attempt to prove that in this instance the name
Ephrathah denotes the district in which Kiriath-jearim lay (cf. 1 Chron. ii.
19, 50 f., iv. 4) is governed by the common but highly questionable assumption that 'Jaar' is here employed as a poetical variant of 'Kiriath-jearim'.
The rendering given in the text, which merely involves the vocalizing of יַעַר as
יָעִ(י)ר, is offered, therefore, as another attempt at a solution of the problem.
This reading is suggested by the theory that David's original name was
'Elhanan ben Jair' (cf. 1 Sam. xvii, 2 Sam. xxi. 19, and what appears to be
the harmonizing gloss in 1 Chron. xx. 5, as referred to below, p. 51, n. 1);
and, if this suggestion be sound, the reference in the case of both 'Ephrathah'
and 'the countryside of Jair' must be to the district of Bethlehem (cf. Ruth
iv. 11; 1 Sam. xvii. 12; Mic. v. 1 (EVV. 2)). The suffixes of שְׁמַעֲנוּהָ and
מְצָאנוּהָ may then be taken as having neuter force and referring, not to the
Ark (cf. the customary citation of 1 Sam. iv. 17 and 2 Chron. viii. 11 in support of the feminine forms of these suffixes), but to the early evidence for
David's humility as expressed in the foregoing vow, which was first 'heard
of' (√שׁמע) or 'come across' (√מצא) as a piece of oral tradition concerning
the creator of the Davidic dynasty which was found current in the district
in which Elhanan had been brought up. Finally, if it be objected that there is
no evidence to warrant the view that √מצא could be used of 'finding' in
the sense of 'lighting upon' such oral tradition (cf., for example, Gunkel,
H.K., *in loc.*, with reference to H. Kessler, K.K., 2nd edit. (1899)), it must
be said that, if one might use this Hebrew verb of coming across someone
when on one's travels (e.g. Gen. xxxvii. 15 (J); 1 Sam. ix. 11, xxx. 11; 2 Kings
iv. 29, x. 15) and even of meeting with trouble and sorrow (Ps. cxvi. 3), it is
difficult to see why it could not have been used of happening upon a popular
local story of the kind suggested, especially when it may be held that the
actual meaning of the term in this particular context is already indicated by
the use of √שׁמע in the parallel stichos.

> Rise up now, O Yahweh, to Thy home,[1]
> Thou and Thy powerful Ark.
> Let Thy priests be clothed with righteousness,
> And let Thy votaries[2] rejoice.
> For the sake of David, Thy Servant,
> Turn not back the face of Thy Messiah.

The exact form taken by the oracular response is difficult to determine. It is conceivable, for example, that the whole psalm was sung antiphonally by the Temple choirs. On the other hand, the second half is so clearly a definite response to the prayer offered in the earlier part of the psalm that it seems more reasonable to infer that it was uttered by an appropriate member of the Temple personnel. In that case one may think of a priest or, as this seems a little unlikely in view of the somewhat detached attitude to the priesthood suggested by both parts of the psalm, a cultic prophet of the type which we find associated with the musical side of the Temple worship.[3] For the rest, the wording of the response is so straightforward that little is required in the way of comment, and it may be rendered as follows:[4]

> Yahweh hath sworn to David,
> A pledge from which He will not turn back.
> 'Of the fruit of thy body
> Will I set upon thy throne.
> If thy sons keep My covenant
> And My testimony (*or* testimonies) that I shall teach them,
> Their sons too, for ever,
> Shall sit upon thy throne.'
> For Yahweh hath chosen Zion;
> He hath desired it for His abode.

---

[1] *lit.* 'resting-place'; but see, for example, Ruth i. 9.

[2] In the writer's opinion the nearest English equivalent to the term חֶסֶד (EVV. 'mercy', 'kindness', 'lovingkindness') is 'devotion'; and, correspondingly, the term חָסִיד (EVV. 'saint', 'holy', 'godly', 'merciful' etc.) denotes one who is 'devoted', i.e. a 'devotee' or 'votary' or, in certain contexts, one who is 'devout'. See now my discussion of the use of these terms in *Interpretationes ad Vetus Testamentum pertinentes* (S. Mowinckel *Festschrift*) = *Nor. T.T.* lvi (1955), pp. 100–12.

[3] Cf. *The Cultic Prophet in Ancient Israel*, pp. 59 ff., 2nd edit., pp. 69 ff.

[4] vv. 11–18.

This is My home for ever;
Here will I dwell, for I have desired it.
I will bless her with abundant provision;
I will satisfy her poor with bread.
I will clothe her priests with salvation;[1]
And her votaries shall greatly rejoice.
There I will make a horn shoot up for David,
I have prepared a lamp for My Messiah.
His enemies I will clothe with shame,
While on himself his crown shall sparkle.

The only question of interpretation is that which is raised by the reference to the 'testimony' (*or* 'testimonies'[2]), which Yahweh is to teach David's descendants. As the parallelism shows, this must be a comprehensive term for the duties, involved in the acceptance of the covenant, which each must learn to carry out on ascending the throne. It is an allusion to the conditions whereby each successive king will be entitled to wear, in the language of the psalm, the 'sparkling crown' which will be the symbol of his office; and it is important because it throws light upon a passage in the account of the coronation of the boy king Jehoash which has been seriously questioned, i.e. the statement that he was invested with 'the crown and the testimony (*or* testimonies)'.[3] The Hebrew of the latter term has been found so odd that it is commonly emended so as to read 'the bracelets'[4] or 'the insignia';[5] but the fact surely is that

---

[1] See above, p. 19, n. 2.

[2] The vocalization of M.T. (עֵדֹתִי) points to an uncertainty as to whether one should read a singular form, 'My testimony' (עֵדוּתִי), or the plural, 'My testimonies' (עֵדֹתַי). See further, p. 67, n. 2.

[3] אֶת־הַנֵּזֶר וְאֶת־הָעֵדוּת (*or* הָעֵדוֹת). 2 Kings xi. 12: cf. 2 Chron. xxiii. 11.

[4] הַצְּעָדוֹת. Cf., for example, J. Wellhausen, *Die Composition des Hexateuchs und der historischen Bücher des Alten Testaments*, 3rd edit. (1899), p. 292, n. 2: and I. Benzinger, K.H.C. (1899); R. Kittel, H.K. (1900); C. F. Burney, *Notes on the Hebrew Text of the Books of Kings* (1903); J. Skinner, Cent.B. (n.d.), alternatively; H. Gressmann, S.A.T. ii. 1, 2nd edit. rev. (1921); O. Eissfeldt, *H.S.A.T.* (1922); S. Landersdorfer, H.S.A.T. (1927); E. R. Goodenough, *J.B.L.* xlviii (1929), p. 190; S. Mowinckel, in G.T.M.M.M. ii (1935), but see the more recent work cited below, p. 24, n. 2; L. Waterman, in *The Bible: an American Translation*, ed. J. M. P. Smith and E. J. Good-

(*Footnotes 4 and 5 continued on next page.*)

the king was made to wear, not merely the royal crown, but a document embodying the basic terms of Yahweh's covenant with the House of David, i.e. in much the same way as the devout Jew, generation after generation, has to learn the words of the Shema (the basic principle underlying the Sinaitic covenant as defined in the book of Deuteronomy)[1] and wear them, bound on the arm and the brow, at morning prayer.[2] Thus the conditions for the continua-

speed (1935); R. Patai, *H.U.C.A.* xx (1947), p. 195, alternatively; A. Causse and C. Jaeger, in *La Bible du Centenaire*, ii (1947); R. de Vaux, S.B.J. (1949), but see now the qualification, op. cit., 2nd edit. rev. (1958), and especially the more recent work cited below, n. 2, *ad fin.*; N. H. Snaith, I.B. (1954); E. Dhorme, *B.P.(A.T.)*, i (1956); A. van den Born, B.O.T. (1958).

5 e.g. הָעֵדְיוֹת. Cf., for example, A. Klostermann, K.K. (1887), *in loc.*; Skinner, loc. cit., alternatively; *The Holy Scriptures*, Jewish Publication Society of America (1917), *in loc.*; G. R. Driver, *J.T.S.* xxxvi (1935), pp. 293 f.; Patai, loc. cit., alternatively.

---

[1] vi. 4 f.

[2] Something of the true significance of this passage was realized by W. E. Barnes, C.B., 2nd edit. rev. (1928), *in loc.*, and T. H. Robinson, in W. O. E. Oesterley and T. H. Robinson, *A History of Israel* (1932), i, p. 351, both of whom rightly refrained from an attempted emendation of the text. The same holds good of G. Widengren, *Psalm 110 och det sakrala kungadömet i Israel*, U.U.Å. 1941: 7, 1 (1941), pp. 19 f. (followed by G. Östborn, *Torā in the Old Testament: a Semantic Study* (1945), pp. 76 ff.), *The Ascension of the Apostle and the Heavenly Book = King and Saviour III*, U.U.Å. 1950: 7 (1950), pp. 24 ff., *The King and the Tree of Life in Ancient Near Eastern Religion=King and Saviour IV*, U.U.Å. 1951: 4 (1951), pp. 39 f., and now 'King and Covenant', *J.S.S.* ii (1957), pp. 5 ff.; but in the present writer's opinion he makes the mistake of accepting the traditional view which sees in the term עֵדוּת a reference to the Mosaic 'Tablets of the Law'. Another step in the right direction is that of G. von Rad, in 'Das judäische Königsritual', *T.L.Z.* lxxii (1947), cols. 211–18=*Gesammelte Studien zum Alten Testament* (1958), pp. 205–13 (followed, for example, by Mowinckel, *Offersang og sangoffer*, pp. 73 f., E.T., i, p. 62; G. Fohrer, 'Der Vertrag zwischen König und Volk in Israel', *Z.A.W.* lxxi (1959), pp. 11 f.), who in partial dependence upon Ps. ii. 7 (cf. also Ps. cv. 10) sees in the reference to the עֵדוּת, not the conditions which the king undertakes to observe (as the present writer maintains), but the promises to which Yahweh commits Himself in fulfilment of the covenant, i.e.: 'In diesem Königsprotokoll spricht Jahwe in direkter Rede den König an, nennt ihn Sohn, belehnt ihn mit der Herrschaft, nennt seine Thronnamen usw.' Again, however, it seems to the writer that the language of Ps. cxxxii. 12 (cf., too, verse 18b) requires the interpretation given in the text. See also in general H. G. May, *J.B.L.* lvii (1938), p. 181; J. A. Montgomery and H. S. Gehman, I.C.C. (1951), *in loc.*: and now, in support of the view advanced above in the text, J. Gray, *I & II Kings* (1964),

tion of the Davidic dynasty were explicit enough, and, no doubt, they were so framed in order to remind David's successors of the responsibilities of their office; but, as we have already had occasion to note and as we shall see again presently, there remains the underlying thought that David has an '*everlasting* covenant' with Yahweh, so that failure at any point to fulfil the conditions, while it must meet with suitable punishment, will not be allowed to annul the promise which was originally made to the founder of the royal house.

This thought comes clearly to the fore in Psalm lxxxix, where the covenant between Yahweh and David is referred to at such length that we are able to complete our picture of the intimate relationship which was held to exist between Yahweh and the successive kings of the Davidic dynasty. The poem itself, which belongs to the class of royal psalms, is a perfectly organic whole; for the variation in metre and theme, which is so commonly regarded as an indication of different authorship,[1] is simply due to its liturgical background. In other words, it is a perfectly straightforward work which reveals sufficiently clearly of itself the circumstances which have called it into being. Disaster has overtaken the royal forces or, at least, the

pp. 518 f., who, unlike Widengren, op. cit., p. 6, n. 2, *ad fin.*, rightly distinguishes this interpretation of the text in question from that advanced by von Rad; R. de Vaux, 'Le Roi d'Israël, vassal de Yahve', in *Mélanges Eugène Tisserant* (1964), i, pp. 127 f.

[1] Cf., for example, B. Duhm, K.H.C., 2nd edit. rev. (1922); W. Staerk, S.A.T. iii. 1, 2nd edit. rev. (1920); R. Kittel, K.A.T., 5th and 6th edit. (1929), possibly; H. Gunkel, H.K. (1926); H. Schmidt, H.A.T. (1934); J. Calès, *Le Livre des psaumes* (1936), probably; M. Buttenwieser, *The Psalms: Chronologically treated with a New Translation* (1938); W. O. E. Oesterley, *The Psalms* (1939); F. Nötscher, Echt. B. (1947), 2nd edit. rev. (1959), possibly; E. Podechard, *Le Psautier. Traduction littérale, explication historique et notes critiques*, ii (1954). See, however, (a) the emphatic rejection of this view by E. König, *Die Psalmen* (1927); F. M. Th. Böhl, T.U. ii (1947): and (b) the suggestion of a common background of cultic tradition which is more strongly emphasized by Mowinckel, *Psalmenstudien III*, pp. 34 ff.; E. A. Leslie, *The Psalms: Translated and Interpreted in the Light of Hebrew Life and Worship* (1949); A. Weiser, A.T.D. (1950), 5th edit. rev. (1959), E.T. by H. Hartwell (1962); and now H. J. Kraus, B.K.A.T., 2nd edit. rev. (1961).

king has suffered some deep humiliation; and the trouble is
attributed to the anger of Yahweh. Accordingly the repre-
sentatives of the people, under the leadership of the king
himself, have assembled in the Temple in order to implore
the divine favour. The opening lines form a hymn of
praise celebrating the supremacy of Yahweh, as the 'Holy
One' of Israel, and His power in Creation;[1] and this is
followed by an equally lengthy passage in which Yahweh
is reminded of His former promises to David and, in David,
to his descendants upon the throne of Jerusalem. It is this
passage which is our immediate concern, i.e.:[2]

> Of old Thou didst speak by a prophet[3]
> To Thy votaries,[4] and saidst—
> 'I have bestowed aid[5] upon a manly one,

---

[1] vv. 2–19 (EVV. 1–18), as below, pp. 106 ff.

[2] vv. 20–30 (EVV. 19–29). It is commonly held that these and the en-
suing lines, i.e. verses 20–38 (EVV. 19–37), are a poetic paraphrase of
Nathan's prophecy in 2 Sam. vii. 1–17 (= 1 Chron. xvii. 1–15). Cf., for
example, F. Baethgen, H.K. (1892), 3rd edit. rev. (1904); A. F. Kirkpatrick,
C.B. (1902): and the following, all op. cit., Duhm, Staerk, Kittel, Calès,
Oesterley, Böhl; also B. Bonkamp, *Die Psalmen nach dem hebräischen
Grundtext* (1949). It is much more likely, however, that the author of 2 Sam.
vii. 1–17 was himself dependent upon the cultic tradition of the Jerusalem
Temple, of which this poem is a typical product. Cf. the remarks of H.
Gressmann, S.A.T. ii. 1, 2nd edit. rev. (1921), p. 139; Mowinckel, *Psalmen-
studien III*, pp. 34 ff.; G. von Rad. *T.L.Z.* lxxii (1947), col. 214 = *Gesam-
melte Studien &c.*, p. 210; and the following, all op. cit., Gunkel, Schmidt,
Leslie, Weiser. See also p. 110, n. 2 for recent works offering a fuller discussion of this question.

[3] EVV. 'in vision'. See, however, *The Cultic Prophet in Ancient Israel*,
pp. 13 ff., 33 ff., 2nd edit., pp. 11 ff., 35 ff.

[4] See above, p. 22, n. 2.

[5] The term עֵזֶר ('aid') has often been viewed with suspicion, and it has
been usual to regard it as a corruption of נֵזֶר ('crown'). Cf., for example,
Duhm, Staerk, Kittel, Gunkel, Schmidt, Buttenwieser, Oesterley, Nötscher,
Böhl, Leslie, Weiser (1st edit. (1950), but see below), Podechard, all op. cit.;
also A. Bertholet, *H.S.A.T.* (1923); H. Herkenne, H.S.A.T. (1936); L.
Randon, *La Bible du Centenaire*, iii (1947); R. Tournay and R. Schwab, S.B.J.
(1950), but subsequently abandoned (cf. 3rd edit. rev. (1964)). On the other
hand, the reading עָזוּר has been defended on the ground that it corresponds
to the Ugaritic *ġzr* ('youth'), the suggestion being that one should render the
passage:
> 'I have placed a youth above the mighty man;
> I have raised a young man above the people.'

I have exalted a youth from among the people.
I have found David, My Servant;
  With My holy oil I have anointed him,
So that My Hand shall be his constant support,
  Mine Arm also shall strengthen him.
No enemy shall oppress him,
  Nor shall the wrongdoer afflict him;
But I will beat down his adversaries before him,
  And I will smite them that hate him.
My faithfulness and My devotion[1] shall be with him,
  And through My Name shall his horn be lifted up.[2]
I will lay his hand also upon the sea,
  And his right hand upon the ocean currents.[3]
He shall cry unto Me, "Thou art my Father,
  My God and the Rock that is my salvation."[4]
I on My part will make him My first-born,
  The highest of earthly kings.
I will always preserve for him My devotion,
  Always keep My covenant true for him.
I will make his seed to endure for ever
  And his throne as the days of heaven.'

These lines are not to be taken at their face value, as if they
refer merely to the individual whom we know as David;

See W. F. A. Albright, *The Archaeology of Palestine* (1949), p. 233, 4th edit.
rev. (1960), p. 234. This seems possible, and it has now been accepted by
Weiser, op. cit., 5th edit. (1959), E.T. (1962); but it also seems to the writer
that the traditional interpretation (cf. LXX) is supported by the analogous
construction in Ps. xxi. 6 (EVV. 5), which, like Ps. lxxxix, may be classed as
a royal psalm. Cf. R. Tournay, *R.B.* lviii (1951), p. 617, n. 2; and see below,
pp. 132 f.   [1] See above, p. 22, n. 2.

[2] For the significance of this picturesque idiom and some indication of its
importance for our understanding of the Psalter, see *The Cultic Prophet in
Ancient Israel*, 2nd edit., p. 70, n. 3.

[3] It is usually assumed that the reference in this line must be to the
Mediterranean and the Euphrates, the plural form נְהָרוֹת (EVV. 'rivers'),
being explained either as a poetic generalization or as denoting the Euphrates
and its canals. Cf. Deut. xi. 24; Pss. lxxx. 11, cxxxvii. 1; and see further, for
example, Kirkpatrick, op. cit., *in loc.* However, it should be borne in mind
that the term נְהָרוֹת is also used of the 'currents' of the cosmic sea (e.g.
Pss. xxiv. 2, xciii. 3, as below, pp. 65 f. and 72 f.); so that here again the thought
appears to be one of a dominion extending over the wide circle of the earth,
i.e. as in the expression 'from sea to sea' in Ps. lxxii. 8, as above, pp. 10 f. Cf.
already Pedersen, *Israel III–IV*, p. 496, E.T., p. 655.

[4] See above, p. 19, n. 2.

they must be read in the light of what we know about
Israelite ideas of corporate personality.[1] When this is done,
they are seen to imply that the line of David is to issue in
one who shall be something more than 'The Messiah of
Yahweh'. He and, in him, his ancestor David[2] will be the
accepted 'Son' of the national deity, and, what is more, in
virtue of this fact he will hold sway as 'the highest of earthly
kings'. As we shall see, these two complementary promises,
(*a*) that the Messiah[3] will ultimately be, not merely the
Servant, but the 'Son' of the national deity, and (*b*) that
he shall thus have supremacy over all earthly kings, are of
the first importance and recur elsewhere in the Psalter.
Meantime, however, it is to be observed that in the light
of the covenant background the promise of 'Sonship' is
simply one of adoption, which carries with it certain attendant conditions so far as David and his descendants are
concerned.[4] Moreover, as the oracle goes on to show,
failure to observe these conditions must bring strict
discipline in its train;[5] but even so, whatever an individual
member of the ruling dynasty may do and however he may
fare as a result, Yahweh's covenant with David is valid for
all time, for, as we have seen, it is an '*everlasting* covenant'.[6]

'If his children forsake My law,
    And walk not according to My judgements (*or* rulings),
If they violate My statutes,
    And do not keep My commandments,
I will attend to their rebellion with a rod
    And their iniquity with blows.
But My devotion will I not break off from him,

---

[1] Cf. 2 Sam. vii. 14; 1 Chron. xxii. 10, xxviii. 6: and see above, pp. 2 ff.

[2] Cf. such passages as 1 Kings viii. 66, xi. 36, xii. 16: also (although this
is to anticipate a proposed sequel to the present work) Jer. xxx. 9; Ezek.
xxxiv. 23 f., xxxvii. 24 f.; Hos. iii. 5.

[3] Cf. v. 21b (EVV. 20b); also vv. 39, 52 (EVV. 38, 51).

[4] For the somewhat remote parallels to this form of divine 'sonship'
which are furnished by Mesopotamian thought, see, for example, Labat,
Le Caractère religieux de la royauté assyro-babylonienne, pp. 63 ff.; H. Frankfort, *Kingship and the Gods. A Study of Ancient Near Eastern Religion as the
Integration of Society and Nature* (1948), pp. 299 ff.

[5] Cf. 2 Sam. vii. 14.   [6] vv. 31–38 (EVV. 30–37).

Nor will I be untrue to My faithfulness.
I will not violate My covenant,
Nor alter that which hath passed My Lips.
Once for all have I sworn by My Holiness,
To David I will not lie;
His seed shall endure for ever,
And his throne like the sun before Me,
Like the moon, which shall continue for ever,
A faithful witness in the sky.'

As we shall have occasion to note again later, it is this important promise which is made the ground of appeal in the last part of the liturgy; for the psalm concludes with a plea, in which the king himself takes part, begging that in the present hour of need Yahweh may not forget His sworn devotion to the House of David.[1] For the present, however, enough has been said to make it evident that the Davidic Messiah, as the 'Son' of the national deity, is to possess only a limited monarchy, and that in the last resort he will be responsible to Yahweh for the right administration of his office. Indeed it may be observed that, despite this reference to David's 'Sonship', the oracle does not conceal but rather emphasizes the king's essential humanity with the opening reference to the founder of the dynasty:[2]

'I have bestowed aid upon a manly one,
I have exalted a youth from among the people.'

For that matter, the same is true of the poem which we know as 'The Last Words of David', where there is an unmistakable emphasis upon the fact that the founder of the dynasty was 'the son of Jesse' and 'the man who was raised on high'. Accordingly, despite David's promised elevation to the rank of Yahweh's 'Son' and despite the

---

[1] vv. 39–52 (EVV. 38–51), as discussed below, pp. 111 ff. Verse 53 (EVV. 52) is no part of the original psalm, but marks the close of Book III of the Psalter.

[2] Verse 20b (EVV. 19b). The statement made above in the text remains true even if one accepts the alternative rendering which is refered to above, p. 26, n. 5, i.e.:

'I have placed a youth above the mighty man;
I have raised a young man above the people.'

gift of the divine 'Spirit' from the 'Holy One' of Israel (with
all that this may imply in terms of Father, Son, and holy
Spirit), we must beware of exaggerating the importance of
the fact that in Israelite thought the Davidic king is poten-
tially so closely related to God. Although, in theory at least,
he may be on such intimate terms with Yahweh and
powerfully subject to His influence, he is by nature a man;
and, so far as his subjects are concerned, he is no more
than *primus inter pares.*[1]

[1] There is no real conflict between the statement made above in the text
and Ps. xlv. 7 (EVV. 6), even if it be the case that this obviously royal psalm
was composed in honour of a member of the House of David. The context,
of course, requires that it should be the king, not Yahweh (as EVV. 'O God'),
who is being addressed in this verse; but it is a misunderstanding of Hebrew
syntax which has led to the claim that the first stichos must be rendered
'Thy throne, O God, is for ever and ever', and that, as a result, we have here
a clear indication of a belief in 'divine kingship'. The fact is that the construction in question is analogous to that of עֵינַיִךְ יוֹנִים (Song of Sol.
i. 15, iv. 1), *lit.* 'Thine eyes are doves', i.e. 'Thine eyes are like those of
doves'; and the passage means no more than 'Thy throne is like that of God
(*or* a god)—for ever', i.e. 'Thy throne is everlasting like that of God (*or* a
god).' See the valuable discussion of this passage by C. R. North, 'The
Religious Aspects of Hebrew Kingship', *Z.A.W.* l (1932), pp. 29 ff.; also
the earlier treatment by G. R. Driver, in *The Psalmists*, ed. D. C. Simpson
(1926), p. 124.
   Since the foregoing words were first written J. R. Porter, in *J.T.S.* N.S. xii
(1961), pp. 51–53, has advocated afresh the view that in Ps. xlv. 7 (EVV. 6)
the term אֱלֹהִים should be regarded as a vocative, and that one should think of
an Israelite king as indeed being addressed as 'God'. Porter seeks to meet
the common objection that such a conception is out of keeping with Old
Testament thought by citing the way in which David is compared with the
'Angel' of God (2 Sam. xiv. 17, 20, xix. 28 (EVV. 27), as above, p. 16); but
this will not serve, for it must be borne in mind that what we have in the
passages cited is no more than a clearly expressed *comparison*, the point of
the comparison being the common quality of insight. Further, when Porter
goes on to argue that the point of the comparison in Song of Sol. i. 15 and
iv. 1 is the 'whiteness' of doves rather than the 'softness and innocence' of
their eyes, he clearly recognizes that a comparison of some kind is intended,
so that on his view the Hebrew of both passages would be rendered quite
suitably by saying 'Thine eyes are dove-like'; and, this being the case, the
Hebrew of Ps. xlv. 7 (EVV. 6) could be held to mean 'Thy throne is god-like',
the point of the comparison being made explicit in this case through the
addition of the words עוֹלָם וָעֶד ('for ever and ever'), which thus serve to
indicate the quality of durability as common to the royal throne and God
(*or* a god). For that matter, however, one might read כְּיוֹנִים ('like doves': cf.
Song of Sol. v. 12) and כֵּאלֹהִים ('like God' or 'like a god') in the passages

II

Straightforward as all this is, however, it leaves us with one outstanding question which is prompted by the statement made in the oracular section of Psalm cxxxii:[1]

> Yahweh hath chosen Zion;
> He hath desired it for His abode.

In short, we have to ask what there was about Mount Zion that it should have grown to such importance, inviting

under discussion on the familiar and perfectly justifiable ground of haplography; and in that case we should arrive quite simply at the same conclusion. All in all, therefore, and independently of the point which is made in the final sentence of the next paragraph, the view that in Ps. xlv. 7 (EVV. 6) we have evidence for a belief in 'divine kingship' has little to support it.

Again, the supposed analogy in the name אֵל גִּבּוֹר (A.V. 'The mighty God', R.V. 'Mighty God'), as applied to the Davidic Messiah in Isa. ix. 5 (EVV. 6), which is cited, for example, by R. Kittel, K.A.T., 5th and 6th edit. (1929), H. Gunkel, H.K. (1926), A. Bentzen, *Fortolkning til de gammel-testamentlige Salmer* (1939), in connexion with Ps. xlv. 7 (EVV. 6), again appears to be the product of a too literal approach to Hebrew idiom; for, *pace* H. Wildberger, in *T.Z.* xvi (1960), pp. 315 ff., the expression in question (like פֶּלֶא יוֹעֵץ, 'Wonderful Counsellor', *lit.* 'a wonder of a counsellor') need mean no more than 'Mighty Warrior', *lit.* 'a god of a warrior'; and we may compare the way in which English permits one to speak of 'a devil of a fellow'. In other words, it seems to me that we must beware of jumping to the understandable but somewhat hasty conclusion that the grammatical construction in this expression is similar to that which is used of Yahweh in Deut. x. 17, Neh. ix. 32, and Jer. xxxii. 18, for in every one of these three passages we have an example of asyndeton which ought not to be overlooked. Correspondingly, the recurrence of the expression אֵל גִּבּוֹר in Isa. x. 21 with reference to Yahweh may imply, not that He is the 'Mighty God', but simply that He is the Warrior *par excellence*, i.e. in much the same way as He is described in Exod. xv. 3 as אִישׁ מִלְחָמָה (EVV. 'a man of war'). Moreover, it seems worthy of note in this connexion that, even if it could be shown conclusively that in Ps. xlv. 7 (EVV. 6) an Israelite king is being addressed as a 'god', this would not of necessity carry with it the implication that he was actually regarded as divine—any more than the fact that Yahweh could be referred to as 'a man of war', as in the passage just cited, carries with it the implication that He was thought to be human.

Finally, if Ps. xlv is to be traced in origin to the Northern, rather than the Southern, Kingdom, we should also bear in mind the conception of kingship which comes to the fore in the story of the healing of Naaman the leper by Elisha; i.e. when we are told that the king of Israel, having read the appeal addressed to him on Naaman's behalf by the king of Syria, asks in consternation, 'Am I God (*or* a god) to cause to die and to make to live?' (2 Kings v. 7).

[1] Verse 13.

another psalmist to begin his hymn of praise and thanksgiving with the words:[1]

> God is renowned in Judah,
> His Name is great in Israel.
> His covert is to be found in Salem,
> And in Zion hath He made His lair.

The answer to this question is usually given, of course,
in terms of David's military and political foresight.[2] It is
pointed out, for example, that this stronghold, which
David succeeded in capturing only by a ruse, occupied an
almost impregnable site at the southern end of the easterly
of the two hills over which the city of Jerusalem subse-

---

[1] Ps. lxxvi. 2 f. (EVV. 1 f.). Mowinckel, *Psalmenstudien II*, pp. 57 ff.,
126 ff., stresses the first word of verse 4 (EVV. 3), i.e. שָׁמָּה, on the ground
that it points to the use of some form of dramatic symbolism within the sacred
precincts of the city itself, i.e.:

> *There* He hath shattered the bow's bright missile,
> Shield and sword in war's encounter.

Cf. Schmidt, Bentzen, Leslie, op. cit., *in loc.* Although the present writer
thinks that in principle the suggestion of a ritual drama or the like may be
sound (see below, pp. 85 ff.), he cannot but agree with T. W. Davies,
Cent.B. (n.d.), *in loc.*, that on metrical grounds the form in question should
be read as שָׁמָּה and construed as the last word of verse 3 (EVV. 2), i.e.
somewhat more literally than above:

> And as for His lair, in Zion hath He set it.

On the ground of style this reading, which involves one's regarding מְעוֹנָתוֹ
as a *casus pendens*, seems more likely than שָׁמָה (or שָׁמָּה), which is
favoured by C. A. Briggs, I.C.C. (1906–7) and T. H. Robinson, in Oesterley,
op. cit. In any case it is obvious that the form שָׁמָּה may not be pressed in
support of the theory of a ritual drama or some corresponding form of
dramatic symbolism.

[2] Cf., for example, H. P. Smith, *Old Testament History* (1903), pp. 142 ff.;
R. Kittel, *Geschichte des Volkes Israel*, ii, 6th edit. rev. (1925), pp. 116 ff.;
A. Alt, 'Jerusalems Aufstieg', *Z.D.M.G.* lxxix (1925), pp. 1–19, now
reprinted in *Kleine Schriften zur Geschichte des Volkes Israel*, iii (1959),
pp. 243–57; A. Lods, *Israël des origines au milieu du VIIIᵉ siècle* (1930),
pp. 418 ff., E.T. by S. H. Hooke (1932), pp. 360 ff.; W. O. E. Oesterley and
T. H. Robinson, *A History of Israel* (1932), i, pp. 214 ff.; H. W. Robinson,
The History of Israel: its Facts and Factors (1938), pp. 62 ff.; M. Noth, *Das
System der zwölf Stämme Israels*, B.W.A.N.T. 52 (1930), pp. 116 ff., *Geschichte Israels* (1950), pp. 165 f., 2nd edit. rev. (1954), pp. 175 f., E.T., 2nd
edit., rev. by P. R. Ackroyd (1960), pp. 189 ff.; J. Bright, *A History of Israel*
(1960), pp. 178 f.

quently spread; and, what is more, it lay immediately above the spring Gihon, with which it was connected by means of a shaft and tunnel excavated in the rock, so that it was possible for the inhabitants to draw water without going outside the city walls.[1] Further, it was situated in a safely remote but reasonably strategic position on the backbone of the central range of hills. Indeed, it was so placed that David could not hope to unify the rival tribes of north and south in anything like an effective way while it remained in Jebusite hands. Finally it occupied neutral ground between these northern and southern tribes, and therefore could give neither group reason to be jealous of the sovereign claims of the other; and, allied to this, it had no prior religious associations for any of the tribes, and so, by housing the Ark, seemed readily adaptable as the chief cultic centre of the tribal brotherhood of Israel in its new role as a united kingdom. All this is true, of course, but it may be questioned if it gives us the whole of the picture.[2] Although this Canaanite city had no religious associations for any of the Israelite tribes, it cannot have been without its own cultic traditions; and the question therefore arises as to whether or not it may have had a contribution to make along these lines to its growth in importance as the city of David and the earthly abode of the heavenly King.

This is no idle question, for it seems clear that David, on capturing the city, made no attempt to exterminate its inhabitants, but actually went out of his way to conciliate

---

[1] Cf., for example, J. Simons, *Jerusalem in the Old Testament: Researches and Theories* (1952), pp. 162 ff.; L.-H. Vincent and A.-M. Steve, *Jérusalem de l'Ancien Testament: Recherches d'archéologie et d'histoire*, i (1954), pp. 260 ff.; and now the important results of the current series of excavations at Jerusalem as reported by K. M. Kenyon, *P.E.Q.*, Jan.–June, 1962, pp. 72–89, Jan.–June, 1963, pp. 7–21, Jan.–June, 1964, pp. 7–18, and *B.A.* xxvii (1964), pp. 34–52. See also, for the early and continuing cultic importance of this spring, A. von Gall, 'Über die Herkunft der Bezeichnung Jahwes als König', in *Studien zur semitischen Philologie und Religionsgeschichte* (Wellhausen Festschrift), ed. K. Marti (1914), pp. 156 ff.

[2] Cf. M. Noth, 'Gott, König, Volk im Alten Testament', *Z.T.K.* xlvii (1950), pp. 182 ff. = *Gesammelte Studien zum Alten Testament*, pp. 218 ff. (See above, p. 13, n. 3.)

them and secure their good will, if we give what appears to be due weight to the fact that he did not seize Araunah's threshing-floor as by right of conquest, when he required it as the site of an altar to Yahweh, but was willing to purchase it at a fair price from its Jebusite owner.[1] Further, this city, which David captured but obviously did not destroy, must already have witnessed a thousand years of history, to say the least, for its name occurs in Egyptian execration texts which apparently date from the closing years of the twelfth dynasty (c. 2000–1780 B.C.).[2] Five hundred years later it is well represented in the Tell el-Amarna tablets of the late fifteenth and early fourteenth centuries B.C. by the half-dozen letters of its ruler Abdi-Ḫiba; and it is obvious, both from Abdi-Ḫiba's own statements and from the references made to him by his ally and former enemy Šuwardata, that at this time it was an important and comparatively powerful city-state dominating a large part of the surrounding hill-country.[3] Indeed these data from the archaeological field simply reinforce the picture presented by the Old Testament itself. Thus another four hundred years after the time of David it was

---

[1] Cf. 2 Sam. xxiv, esp. verses 16 ff.; 1 Chron. xxi. 1–xxii. 1.

[2] See K. Sethe, *Die Ächtung feindlicher Fürsten, Völker und Dinge auf altägyptischen Tongefäßscherben des Mittleren Reiches*, A.P.A.W. 1926: 5 (1926), p. 53; G. Posener, *Princes et pays d'Asie et de Nubie. Textes hiératiques sur des figurines d'envoûtement du Moyen Empire* (1950), p. 86. The texts published by Sethe were found on fragments of clay bowls and jars, and contained the names of neighbouring peoples and rulers, as well as individuals in Egypt itself, who were regarded as planning war, fomenting rebellion, or similarly plotting mischief of some kind against the state. It seems clear that, after the bowls and jars in question had been inscribed with these names, they were smashed in symbolic fashion and probably with magical intent as a means of bringing these plans to nought. The texts published by Posener, which are of a slightly later date, were inscribed for the most part on clay figurines rudely fashioned to represent prisoners in a kneeling position with their arms bound by the elbows behind their backs; and, while a similar purpose probably underlies their construction, it is questionable in this case if such damage as they have suffered was intentional, and, therefore, a direct result of the magical design which brought them into being.

[3] Cf. Knudtzon, *Die El-Amarna-Tafeln*, Nos. 280 and 285–90; Mercer, *The Tell el-Amarna Tablets* Nos. 280 and 285–90a: and, as regards the name Abdi-Ḫiba, Knudtzon, op. cit., pp. 1333 f.

still possible for Ezekiel to begin his scathing picture of the city's failure to live up to its high calling by saying:[1]

> Thine origin and birth were of the land of the Canaanite;
> Thy father was an Amorite, and thy mother a Hittite.

Moreover, a tradition was current which reached far back into this early period and told of the friendly treatment Abram had received at the hands of Melchizedek, king of Salem;[2] and, finally, there was a full and graphic account of the way in which Joshua had found in Adoni-zedek, king of Jerusalem, the determined leader of a Canaanite coalition which sought in vain to stem the tide of invasion.[3]

Now it is a striking fact about the names of these traditional kings of Jerusalem that each is compounded from the root which in Hebrew gives us the term צֶ֫דֶק, 'righteousness'; and this is made the more interesting by the fact that Abdi-Ḫiba himself, although employing Accadian as the medium of his correspondence with the Egyptian court, actually makes use of the cognate term ṢADUḲ (ṢA-DU-UḲ), which is clearly a Canaanite word, in order to affirm that he has done or said the right thing in his dealings with the king of Egypt:[4]

> Behold, my lord the king, I am *in the right*
> with regard to the Kaši people.

Further, such an early use of this root in the Canaanite area is well attested outside Jerusalem in the Ras Shamra tablets (i.e. the literary remains of the ancient city of Ugarit in northern Syria which come to us from the early part of the fourteenth century B.C.),[5] where it is used quite clearly to denote the thought of right relationship, as when Keret, the king, is introduced with a passing reference to 'his *rightful* wife' ('*aṭt . ṣdḳh*) and 'his true spouse' (*mtrḫt .*

---

[1] xvi. 3. [2] Gen. xiv. 18–20.

[3] Joshua x. 1–28 (JE/R^D). Cf., probably, Judges i. 5–7, as discussed by G. A. Cooke, C.B. (1913) and C. F. Burney, *The Book of Judges* (1920), *in loc.*

[4] A-MUR ŠARRU BĒLI-IA ṢA-DU-UḲ A-NA IA-A-ŠI
AŠ-ŠUM AMĒLŪTI KA-ŠI-WI.
Cf. Knudtzon, op. cit., Mercer, op. cit., No. 287, 32 f.

[5] See above, p. 4, n. 4.

yšrh).[1] Here the form in use, i.e. the noun *ṣdḳ*, is one which
corresponds to the Hebrew form צֶדֶק, and its employment is wholly in keeping with that which is to be found
a thousand years later in a Phoenician inscription of the
third or second century B.C. from the island of Cyprus,
where it or the corresponding adjective (Hebrew: צַדִּיק)
is used of a man's *'rightful* offspring' (צֶמַח צֶדֶק).[2] What
is even more significant in the present connexion, the
Phoenician epigraphic texts reveal the fact that already in
or about the tenth century B.C. Yeḥimilk, king of Byblos,
like his successor Yeḥawmilk in the fifth century B.C., was
prepared to advance the claim that he should be rewarded
with a long life on the ground that he was 'a *righteous*
king' (מֶלֶךְ צֶדֶק).[3] For the rest, it is really of little
moment that, so far as the names Melchizedek and Adoni-
zedek are concerned, there is no general agreement as to
how the element under discussion is to be construed. The
traditional interpretation, adopted, for example, by the
writer of the epistle to the Hebrews,[4] is that which yields
the meaning 'King of righteousness' and 'Lord of righteousness'.[5] On the analogy of other early names of this type,
however, such a rendering must be regarded as unlikely,
and it has been suggested accordingly that the element in
question should be construed as a divine name, embodying,
so to speak, the ideal which the term implies; and in that
case the names must be held to mean 'My King is Ṣedeḳ'
and 'My Lord is Ṣedeḳ' or (to adopt a simple transcription

---

[1] Cf., for example, Ginsberg, *The Legend of King Keret*, KRT A, 12 f.;
Gordon, *Ugaritic Handbook* or *Ugaritic Manual* or *Ugaritic Textbook*, Krt,
12 f., and *Ugaritic Literature*, p. 67; Driver, *Canaanite Myths and Legends*,
K I, i 12 f.; Gray, *The Krt Text in the Literature of Ras Shamra*, pp. 11,
31 f., *The Legacy of Canaan. The Ras Shamra Texts and their Relevance to the
Old Testament*, S.V.T. v, 2nd edit. rev. (1965), pp. 132 f.; Herdner, *Mission
de Ras Shamra* X, 14, i 12 f. Finally, on this and the following material from
the Phoenician inscriptions which is discussed above in the text, see now the
valuable discussion by J. Swetnam, 'Some Observations on the Background
of צַדִּיק in Jeremias 23, 5a', *Biblica* xlvi (1965), pp. 29–40.

[2] *N.S.I.* 29, 11; *K.A.I.* 43, 11.

[3] (*a*) *K.A.I.* 4, 3 ff. (as above, p. 4, n. 4): (*b*) *N.S.I.* 3, 8 f.; *K.A.I.* 10, 8 f.
(as above, p. 4, n. 4).   [4] vii. 2.   [5] G.K., § 90*l*.

in conformity with the accepted renderings of these names in the Revised Version)[1] 'My King is Zedek' and 'My Lord is Zedek'.[2] This may be so, but we cannot affirm it with certainty;[3] and it is equally possible that it should be construed on the lines of the name Jehozadak ('Yahu is righteous')[4] so as to yield the meaning 'My (*or* The) King is righteous' and 'My (*or* The) Lord is righteous'.[5] In any case the early association of this ideal with the city of Jerusalem is beyond dispute, although, having recognized this, we must beware of making the naïve assumption that the content of the term remained unchanged through the years. It may well be that in Jerusalem at the period under discussion the notion in question gave legal sanction to practices which the invading Hebrews or men of a later generation found incompatible with what they knew of the God of Israel.[6]

---

[1] Cf. Ginsberg, op. cit., pp. 5 f.

[2] Cf., for example, W. W. Graf Baudissin, *Adonis und Esmun. Eine Untersuchung zur Geschichte des Glaubens an Auferstehungsgötter und an Heilgötter* (1911), pp. 71 and 247 f. (alternatively), *Kyrios als Gottesname im Judentum und seine Stelle in der Religionsgeschichte*, iii, pp. 45, n. 1, and 54 (alternatively); von Gall, op. cit., pp. 155 f.; G. Widengren, *The Accadian and Hebrew Psalms of Lamentation as Religious Documents* (1937), pp. 322 f.; Nyberg, *A.R.W.* xxxv (1938), pp. 355 f.; H. Ringgren, *Word and Wisdom. Studies in the Hypostatization of Divine Qualities and Functions in the Ancient Near East* (1947), pp. 83 ff.; W. F. Albright, *J.B.L.* lxix (1950), p. 389; and now J.S. Fitzmyer, '"Now This Melchizedek..." (Heb 7, 1)', *C.B.Q.* xxv (1963), p. 312 ('most likely').

[3] Cf. the similar ambiguity with regard to the Ugaritic personal name *ṣdḳ'il* (Gordon, *Ugaritic Handbook* or *Ugaritic Manual* or *Ugaritic Textbook*, 321, iii 4; Herdner, *Mission de Ras Shamra* X, 119, iii 4), which is held to mean 'Ṣdḳ is (my) god' by F. Thureau-Dangin, *R.A.* xxxvii (1940–1), p. 114, Ringgren, loc. cit., Albright, loc. cit., whereas O. Eissfeldt, *El im ugaritischen Pantheon*, B.V.S.A.W.L. 98, 4 (1951), pp. 48 f., insists that it must be construed so as to yield the meaning "Il is righteous'.

[4] Hag. i. 1, 12, 14, ii. 2, 4; Zech, vi. 11; etc.

[5] Cf. Baudissin, *Adonis und Esmun*, loc. cit. (alternatively), *Kyrios als Gottesname*, loc. cit. (alternatively); Burney, op. cit., pp. 41–43; S. A. Cook, *C.A.H.* ii (1924), p. 397; E. Dhorme, *L'Évolution religieuse d'Israël*, i (1937), p. 330.

[6] See below, p. 45, n. 4: and, for a general discussion of this ideal in its association with the gods of the ancient Near East, particularly as an aid to understanding the association of √צדק with Yahweh, see (with caution) Baudissin, op. cit., pp. 379 ff.; also S. A. Cook, op. cit., pp. 397 ff., in W. R. Smith, *Lectures on the Religion of the Semites*, 3rd edit. rev. (1927), pp. 655 ff., and *The 'Truth' of the Bible* (1938), pp. 108 ff., 140 ff.

These names Melchizedek and Adoni-zedek, however, are instructive in yet another respect, i.e. the elements corresponding to the Hebrew terms מֶלֶךְ ('king') and אָדוֹן ('lord'). As is well known, the latter not only came to be used as an appellation with reference to Yahweh, but could also be employed by itself in what appears to be a suffixed form as virtually a proper name in much the same way as the Accadian term BĒLU ('lord') came to be employed in connexion with the Babylonian pantheon, notably with reference to Marduk, as the name of a deity, i.e. Bel.[1] This, of course, was the form which the Massoretes reproduced as a possible plural of divine majesty, i.e. אֲדוֹנָי or, to adopt another simple transcription, Adonai ('My Lord').[2] Accordingly, in view of the foregoing suggestion that the name Adoni-zedek should be construed as meaning 'My (*or* The) Lord is righteous', it is conceivable that the first component already has the force of a proper name even here, i.e., to adopt a simple transcription once again, 'Adoni is righteous'; and, if we restrict the analogy merely to the term under discussion, we may compare the way in which the Greeks came to know the dying and rising god named Adonis (Ἄδωνις), whose original home seems to have been Phoenicia.[3] It is the term מֶלֶךְ, however, which must engage our attention, for there is reason to believe that even if the term does not occur in a theophorous name with clear reference to Yahweh until the time of Jeremiah,[4] it had long been employed in the liturgy of the royal Temple in Jerusalem as a divine appellation, i.e. that, whether or not the Hebrews entertained the thought of such a divine 'Kingship' at the time of the settlement in Canaan,[5] the

---

[1] Cf. Isa. xlvi. 1; Jer. l. 2, li. 44; *Bel and the Dragon.*

[2] For an introduction to the vexed question of (*a*) the origin of this form, and (*b*) the history of the use of this term in its application to Yahweh, see Baudissin, op. cit. i–ii; and G. Quell, *Th.W.N.T.* iii (1938), pp. 1056 ff., E.T. by H. P. Kingdon, *Lord*, B.K.W. (1958), pp. 36 ff.

[3] Cf. Baudissin, *Adonis und Esmun*, pp. 65 ff., *Kyrios als Gottesname*, iii, pp. 52 ff.   [4] See below, pp. 43 ff.

[5] For the view that the conception of Yahweh as מֶלֶךְ or 'King' is to be traced back to so early a period, see (*a*) E. Sellin, 'Alter, Wesen und Ursprung

worship of Yahweh as מֶלֶךְ or 'King' was certainly no
late development in the religious history of Israel but
dates from at least the early years of the monarchy and, so
far as the House of David was concerned, served as a constant reminder to the earthly king that there was a heavenly
King to whom he was ultimately responsible.[1]

Now, restricting our data for the most part to the
Canaanite area, we may note that the use of the equivalent
term as a divine appellative in theophorous names or even
as a divine name Milku(-i) in its own right is well attested as
early as the fifteenth to the fourteenth centuries B.C.; for it
occurs in the Tell el-Amarna tablets in the personal names
ILU(-I)-MILKU[2] and MILK(I)-ILI (or MILK(I)-ILU),[3] which are
all, perhaps, to be construed as meaning 'Ilu(-i) is (my)

der alttestamentlichen Eschatologie', in *Der alttestamentliche Prophetismus*
(1912), pp. 132 ff., 153 f., 167, 183 ff.: (*b*) with what appears to be an exaggerated emphasis upon the primary meaning of the term מֶלֶךְ as 'counsellor'
or 'leader', M. Buber, *Das Kommende I. Königtum Gottes*, 2nd edit. enlarged (1936), 3rd edit. enlarged (1956), *passim*, supplemented by 'Das
Volksbegehren', in *In Memoriam Ernst Lohmeyer*, ed. W. Schmauch (1951),
pp. 53–66, which was to have been published as the first chapter (and now
by 'Die Erzählung von Sauls Königswahl', *V.T.* vi (1956), pp. 113–73,
which is the second chapter) of *Das Kommende II. Der Gesalbte*; also *Moses*
(1946), pp. 78, 105 ff., 113 ff., 137 ff., 157 ff., 170 f.; and 'Het Geloof van
Israel', in *De Godsdiensten der Wereld*, ed. G. van der Leeuw, 2nd edit. (1948),
pp. 193 ff., or, similarly, in a translation from the Hebrew by C. Witton-
Davies, *The Prophetic Faith* (1949), pp. 45 ff.: (*c*) de Fraine, *L'Aspect
religieux de la royauté israélite*, pp. 117–34: (*d*) H. Wildberger, *Jahwes
Eigentumsvolk*, A.T.A.N.T. 37 (1960), pp. 20 ff. The problem really centres,
of course, in the vexed question of the date and historical value of such
passages as Exod. xv. 18, xix. 6 (JE); Num. xxiii. 21 (JE); Deut. xxxiii. 5;
1 Sam. viii. 7, xii. 12; also Judges viii. 23.

[1] Cf. what follows with the theory advanced by von Gall, op. cit., pp. 152–
60; and note, with reference to the Northern Kingdom in the ninth century
B.C., the significance of the picture presented by Micaiah's vision in 1 Kings
xxii. 19. Incidentally, it should be clear from the way in which the foregoing
note is introduced that the writer allows for the possibility that the conception of Yahweh as 'King' already played a part in Israel's worship at an early
cultic centre such as Shiloh, whether or not this was due to Canaanite influence. Cf. W. Schmidt, *Königtum Gottes in Ugarit und Israel*, B.Z.A.W. 80
(1961), pp. 76 ff.

[2] Knudtzon, op. cit., and Mercer, op. cit. 151, 45 (*AN.LUGAL*); 286, 36.

[3] e.g. Knudtzon, op. cit., and Mercer, op. cit., (*a*) 267, 4; 268, 3; 269,
4; 270, 4; 271, 4; 289, 5, 11, 25; (*b*) 249, 16; 290, 6. See also 249, 6; 250, 32,
54; 254, 27, 29; 273, 24; 287, 29

king' rather than 'My god is Milku' and 'Milku(-i) is (my) god';[1] ABI-MILKI (or ABU-MILKI),[2] which may be construed as meaning either '(My) father is (my) king' or '(My) father is Milki';[3] and ABDI-MILKI,[4] which must mean either 'Servant of the king' or 'Servant of Milku(-i)'.[5] Similarly the Ras Shamra tablets of almost the same date reproduce the foregoing personal names in the forms *'ilmlk*,[6] *'abmlk*,[7] and *'abdmlk*[8] along with other such

---

[1] Cf. the corresponding Hebrew forms אֱלִימֶלֶךְ and מַלְכִּיאֵל, as referred to below, pp. 43 f. Baudissin, *Kyrios als Gottesname*, iii, p. 44, followed by O. Eissfeldt, 'Jahwe als König,' *Z.A.W.* xlvi (1928), p. 85 (= *Kleine Schriften* i (1962), p. 175), would restrict the meaning to the first instance given above, i.e.: '"El ist König", nicht "Milk ist Gott", da in kanaanäischen Personennamen, soviel ich sehe, el sonst niemals prädikativ gebraucht wird.' The present writer, however, is not altogether convinced of the soundness of this. Cf. the discussion of the whole problem of the order of subject and predicate in names of this type by M. Noth, *Die israelitischen Personennamen im Rahmen der gemeinsemitischen Namengebung*, B.W.A.N.T. 46 (1928), pp. 15 ff. See below, n. 6; also p. 37, n. 3.

[2] e.g. Knudtzon, op. cit., and Mercer, op. cit., (*a*) 147, 2; 148, 2; 149, 2; 151, 2; 154, 2; (*b*) 152, 55. See also 153, 2 (IABI-MILKI).

[3] Cf. the corresponding Hebrew form אֲבִימֶלֶךְ, as referred to below, p. 44.

[4] Knudtzon, op. cit., and Mercer, op. cit. 123, 37; 203, 3.

[5] Cf. the corresponding Hebrew form עֶבֶד־מֶלֶךְ, as referred to below, p. 45, n. 3.

[6] e.g. Gordon, *Ugaritic Handbook* or *Ugaritic Manual* or *Ugaritic Textbook*, 62, 53; 127, 59 (=Herdner, *Mission de Ras Shamra* X, 6, vi 53; 16, vi 59), which may now be supplemented by *Ugaritic Textbook*, 2015, rev. 1; 2022, 13; 2045, 8. See further Eissfeldt, *El im ugaritischen Pantheon*, p. 47, n. 3, who, as against Thureau-Dangin, *R.A.* xxxvii (1940–1), p. 103, again favours the meaning ''Ilu(-i) is (my) king' rather than '(My) god is Milku(-i)'. See above, n. 1. Cf., too, the parallels in the Accadian texts from Ugarit (corresponding to the above-mentioned ILU(-I)-MILKU of the Tell el-Amarna tablets), e.g. Nougayrol, *Mission de Ras Shamra* VI (as above, p. 4, n. 4), 16. 252, 13, 20, 22; 16. 250, 13; 16. 145, 4; 16. 257+16. 258+16. 126, ii. 3, iii 48; id., *Le Palais royal d'Ugarit* IV. *Textes accadiens des archives sud = Mission de Ras Shamra* IX (1956), 18. 20+17. 371, rev. 15; 19. 70, 8: and see further Eissfeldt, *Sanchunjaton von Beirut und Ilumilku von Ugarit* (1952), pp. 47–57.

[7] e.g. Gordon, op. cit. 323, iv 10 (= Herdner, op. cit. 102, iv 10).

[8] e.g. Gordon, op. cit. 300, 2, 16; 323, iv 8 (= Herdner, op. cit. 82, 2, 16; 102, iv 8); 1006, 9; 1024, 20; 1035, rev. 5; 1081, 6; supplemented by Ch. Virolleaud, *Le Palais royal d'Ugarit* V. *Textes en cunéiformes alphabétiques des archives sud, sud-ouest et du petit palais = Mission de Ras Shamra* XI (1965), 163, iii b 2. Cf. here again the parallels in the Accadian texts from

personal names as *'aḥmlk* (*'iḥmlk*),[1] meaning 'Brother of the king' or 'Brother of Milku(-i)',[2] *'aḥtmlk*,[3] meaning 'Sister of the king' or 'Sister of Milku(-i)',[4] and *mlkn'm*,[5] meaning something like 'The (*or* My) king is a delight' or 'Milku(-i) is a delight';[6] and here the possibility that the term under discussion may in some instances have the force of a proper name becomes more of a probability in view of the fact that it appears to occur in a list of gods as just such a personal name in a form which corresponds to the foregoing MILKU (-I) with mimation, i.e. *mlkm* or, as it is probably to be vocalized, Milkum.[7] Further, from as early as the tenth century B.C. or thereabouts, when it appears in the form יחמלך i.e. Yeḥimilk ('May Milk live'),[8] the

Ugarit, e.g. Nougayrol, *Mission de Ras Shamra* VI, 16. 356, 5, 7, 11, 16; 16. 283, 6, 10, 13; 15. 154+164, rev. 8; 15. 155, 16, 23; 16. 204, rev. 4, 7; 16. 154, 4, 18; 16. 205+192, 7, 11, 14, 23; 16. 257+16. 258+16. 126, iv 13.

[1] e.g. Gordon, op. cit., 1060, B 3 (restored); 2011, 33 (restored); 20. 68, 22 (*'iḥmlk*). Cf. again the parallels in the Accadian texts from Ugarit, e.g. Nougayrol, op. cit. 15. 120, 20, 23; 16. 154, 19; 16. 139, 6; 16. 125, 2; 15. 09, B i 8.

[2] Cf. the corresponding Hebrew form אֲחִימֶלֶךְ, as referred to below, p. 44.

[3] e.g. Gordon, op. cit. 95, 4 (= Herdner, op. cit. 51, 4). Cf. again the parallels in the Accadian texts from Ugarit, e.g. Nougayrol, op. cit. 15. 89, 8, 11, 18; 16. 197, 16; 16. 146+161, 1: *Mission de Ras Shamra* IX, 17. 352, 6.

[4] Cf. the corresponding Hebrew form אֲחִתְמֶלֶךְ, D. Diringer, *Le inscrizioni antico-ebraiche palestinesi* (1934), pp. 219 f.

[5] e.g. Gordon, op. cit. 326, i? 2 (= Herdner, 123, A 2); 1116, 5; 2039, 3; 2097, 15.

[6] Cf. the Hebrew proper names אֲבִינֹעַם (Judges iv. 6, 12, v. 1, 12), אֲחִינֹעַם ((*a*) 1 Sam. xiv. 50, (*b*) 1 Sam. xxv. 43, xxvii. 3, etc.: cf. Diringer, op. cit., pp. 24 f., 27), and אֶלְנַעַם (1 Chron. xi. 46), as discussed by G. B. Gray, *Studies in Hebrew Proper Names* (1896), pp. 80 ff., and especially Noth, op. cit., pp. 16, 18, 166.

[7] e.g. Gordon, op. cit. 17, 11 (= Herdner, 29, rev. 11): but, for an element of doubt about this vocalization, see now R. de Vaux, *Studies in Old Testament Sacrifice* (1964), pp. 86 f. = *Les Sacrifices de l'Ancien Testament*, C.R.B. 1 (1964), p. 78.

[8] i.e. (*a*) in the inscription of Yeḥimilk, as cited above, p. 4, n. 4; (*b*) in the inscription of Šaḍaṭba'al (*or* Šiḍṭiba'al: cf. W. F. Albright, *J.A.O.S.* lxvii (1947), p. 154, n. 15, *J.B.L.* lxix (1950), p. 389), published by M. Dunand, *Byblia Grammata* (1945), pp. 146–51: cf. now *K.A.I.* 7. For the dating of these texts, see G. R. Driver, *Semitic Writing*, 2nd edit. rev. (1954), pp. 104 ff., 231, supplemented in the second case by R. de Vaux, *R.B.* liii (1946), pp. 463 ff.; and now *K.A.I.*, loc. cit.

term under discussion frequently recurs in just such a personal form as a component of theophorous names in Phoenician and, later, Punic epigraphic texts,[1] while the god Milḳart (מלקרת) or, to use a more familiar form, Melqart (cf. Μελκάθρος and Μελκάρθος),[2] who figures so prominently in the life of Tyre, owes his name to the fact that he was originally regarded as 'King of the city' (מלך קרת);[3] and in the light of the Ugaritic texts it is

---

[1] e.g. יחומלך, 'May Milk grant life' (*C.I.S.* i. 1 = *N.S.I.* 3, *K.A.I.* 10, as above, p. 4, n. 4), מלכיתן, 'Milk hath given' (e.g. *C.I.S.* i. 10 = *N.S.I.* 12, *K.A.I.* 32); יתנמלך, id. (e.g. *C.I.S.* i. 244); חמלך, corresponding to the Hebrew אֲחִימֶלֶךְ (as noticed above, p. 41, n. 2, and below, p. 44: cf. J. Friedrich, *Phönizisch-Punische Grammatik* (1951), § 94), 'Brother of Milk' (e.g. *C.I.S.* i. 143 = *N.S.I.* 40, *K.A.I.* 66: common in the Punic votive inscriptions); חתמלך, corresponding to the Hebrew אֲחתמלך (as noticed above, p. 41, n. 4; cf. Friedrich, loc. cit.), 'Sister of Milk' (e.g. *C.I.S.* i. 429); עבדמלך, corresponding to the Hebrew עֶבֶד־מֶלֶךְ (as noticed above, p. 40, n. 5, and below, p. 45, n. 3), 'Servant of Milk' (e.g. *C.I.S.* i. 46 = *N.S.I.* 16, *K.A.I.* 35); אמתמלך, 'Handmaid of Milk' (*C.I.S.* i. 1371); גרמלך, 'Protégé of Milk' (*C.I.S.* i. 50); עזמלך, 'Milk is (my) strength' (M. Lidzbarski, *Handbuch der nordsemitischen Epigraphik* (1898), i. p. 418 = *N.S.I.* 8: common in the Punic votive inscriptions); מלכרם, 'Milk is exalted' (*N.S.I.* 150, 1).

[2] e.g. Eusebius, *Praeparatio Evangelica*, i. 10, 27. Cf. C. Clemen, *Die phönikische Religion nach Philo von Byblos*, M.V.A.G. xliii. 3 (1939), p. 28.

[3] i.e. *milk ḳart*. Cf., for example, *C.I.S.* i. 122 = *N.S.I.* 36, *K.A.I.* 47: also such proper names as עבדמלקרת, 'Servant of Melqart' (e.g. *C.I.S.* i. 14: especially common in the Punic votive inscriptions); אמתמלקרת, 'Handmaid of Melqart' (e.g. *C.I.S.* i. 446); גרמלקרת, 'Protégé of Melqart' (e.g. *C.I.S.* i. 47 = *N.S.I.* 17, *K.A.I.* 36); בדמלקרת, 'Client of Melqart' or, more likely perhaps, 'By means of (i.e. Thanks to) Melqart' (*C.I.S.* i. 139 = *N.S.I.* 39, *K.A.I.* 64: frequent in the Punic votive inscriptions. Cf., for example, Z. S. Harris, *A Grammar of the Phoenician Language* (1936), p. 85; Friedrich, op. cit., § 80 (*a*); also Eissfeldt, *El im ugaritischen Pantheon*, p. 49). See also (*a*) the remarkable stele, bearing a relief of Melqart accompanied by an inscription in Aramaic, which appears to date from the ninth century B.C. Cf. M. Dunand, 'Stèle araméenne dédiée à Melqart', *B.M.B.* iii (1939), pp. 65–76; W. F. Albright, 'A Votive Stele erected by Benhadad I of Damascus to the god Melcarth', *B.A.S.O.R.* 87 (Oct. 1942), pp. 23–29: and see further A. Herdner, in *Syria* xxv (1946–8), pp. 329 f., and now *K.A.I.* 201. (*b*) the possible occurrence of the name Melqart (in the form MI-IL-ḲAR-TU) in the record of a treaty effected in the seventh century B.C. between Ba'al of Tyre and Esarhaddon of Assyria. Cf. S. Langdon, 'A Phoenician Treaty of Assarhaddon', *R.A.* xxvi (1929), pp. 189–94; E. F. Weidner, *A.f.O.* viii (1932–3), pp. 29–34; and now R. Borger, *Die Inschriften Asarhaddons Königs von Assyrien*, *A.f.O.*, Beiheft 9 (1956),

obvious that all this is in keeping with early Canaanite tradition. Moreover, the national deity of the Ammonites, Israel's neighbours in Transjordan, was clearly worshipped under this name in the form which the Massoretes reproduce as מִלְכֹּם (EVV. 'Milcom');[1] and there is little reason to doubt that this corresponds to the fore-mentioned Milkum of the Ras Shamra tablets. So far as the Hebrew field itself is concerned,[2] we must, of course, recognize that the appearance of the name Malchiel (מַלְכִּיאֵל) as that of a grandson of Asher in the genealogical lists of P and the Chronicler offers doubtful testimony to the use of this term in theophorous names prior to the settlement, despite the fact that it corresponds to the MILK(I)-ILU(-I) of the Tell el-Amarna tablets, for it is still difficult to know what value to place on these lists;[3] and a similar doubt as to its authenticity must be admitted for the analogous form

pp. 107–9. It is usually assumed that Melqart (qua 'King of the city') was so named as being the tutelary god of Tyre; but in Albright's opinion (loc. cit.) the occurrence of this name in the foregoing Aramaic inscription affords strong support for his view that the element *ḳart* ('city') is here used of the underworld, and that the name Melqart thus reflects the cosmic character of this god. Cf., originally, *A.J.S.L.* liii (1936–7), p. 11: also *Archaeology and the Religion of Israel*, 3rd edit. (1953), pp. 81, 196, and 226 f.; *From the Stone Age to Christianity*, 2nd edit. (1946), pp. 235 and 333, id. with a new introduction (1957), p. 307. While the present writer agrees that Melqart was probably a cosmic deity, he finds it difficult to believe that the element *ḳart* here refers to the underworld. Cf. G. Levi Della Vida, 'Some Notes on the Stele of Ben-hadad', *B.A.S.O.R.* 90 (Apr. 1943), pp. 30 ff., together with the reply by Albright, op. cit., pp. 32 ff.; and now Comte du Mesnil du Buisson, 'Origine et évolution du panthéon de Tyr,' *R.H.R.* clxiv (1963), pp. 133–63, specifically p. 157: and see below, p. 86, n. 6. Finally, on Melqart in general, see R. Dussaud, 'Melqart', *Syria* xxv (1946–8), pp. 205–30, and now 'Melqart, d'après de récents travaux', *R.H.R.* cli (1957), pp. 1–21; also H. Seyrig, *Syria* xxiv (1944–5), pp. 62–80, esp. pp. 69 ff.

[1] 1 Kings xi. 5, 7 (cf. LXX), 33; 2 Kings xxiii. 13; Jer. xlix. 1 (LXX, S, V), 3 (LXX, S, V); Zeph. i. 5 (LXX^mss, S, V): also, perhaps, 2 Sam. xii. 30 (cf. LXX) = 1 Chron. xx. 2 (cf. LXX, V); and, more doubtfully, Amos i. 15 (cf. S and Jer. xlix. 3).

[2] Cf. Gray, op. cit., pp. 115 ff., 146 ff.; Noth, op. cit., pp. 114 ff.

[3] Gen. xlvi. 17 (P); Num. xxvi. 45 (P); 1 Chron. vii. 31. Cf., too, 1 Chron. viii. 35 (LXX^BL) and ix. 41 (LXX^L), where Malchiel is given as the name of a great-grandson of Jonathan, a reading which is the more remarkable because of the occurrence of the name Malchi-shua as that of a brother of Jonathan. See below, p. 45, n. 2.

Elimelech (אֱלִימֶלֶךְ), which appears in what is the somewhat late, if not post-exilic, book of Ruth as the name of
Naomi's husband in the period of the Judges,[1] even though
it too has an early parallel in the Tell el-Amarna tablets in
the form ILU(-I)-MILKU as also in the Ugaritic texts in the
form *'ilmlk*. On the other hand, the name Abimelech
(אֲבִימֶלֶךְ), which also has its parallels in both series of
tablets in the forms ABU(-I)-MILKI and *'abmlk*, is found in
relatively early Israelite sources as that of a Canaanite
king of Gerar in the patriarchal period and as that of the
son of Gideon who in the period of the Judges early left his
mark on Israelite history as one who sought royal power
over Shechem and its neighbourhood.[2] Similarly the name
Ahimelech (אֲחִימֶלֶךְ), which has its parallel in the Ugaritic
texts under the form *'aḥmlk*, is well attested as that borne by
two of David's contemporaries, i.e. the head of the priestly
community at Nob who befriended David when he was a
fugitive from the court of Saul and, equally remarkable, a
Hittite who was his companion during his flight;[3] and it
finds ample archaeological support at least as early as the
time of Jeroboam II (*c.* 786–746 B.C.), if not that of Ahab
(*c.* 869–850 B.C.), in the ostraca which have been recovered
from the ruins of Samaria.[4] Finally, it is to be noted that

---

[1] Ruth i. 2, 3, ii. 3, iv. 3, 9. On the question of the date of the book of
Ruth, see now W. Rudolph, K.A.T. (1962), pp. 26–29.

[2] (*a*) Gen. xx. 1–18 (E), xxi. 22–32 (E), xxvi. 1–33 (J): (*b*) Judges viii. 31,
ix. 1–x. 1; 2 Sam. xi. 21. The appearance of this name in the heading to
Ps. xxxiv, where the incident which is there referred to Abimelech appears
to be that which is told of Achish of Gath in 1 Sam. xxi. 11 (EVV. 10)–xxii
2, is a matter of dispute. Cf., for example, E. Podechard, *Le Psautier: Notes
critiques*, i (1949), and E. Pannier, *Les Psaumes*, S.B., ed. H. Renard (1950),
in loc. Further, its occurrence in 1 Chron. xviii. 16, i.e. 'Abimelech the son
of Abiathar', is usually recognized to be a mistake for 'Abiathar the son of
Ahimelech': see the following note.

[3] (*a*) 1 Sam. xxi. 2–10 (EVV. 1–9), xxii. 6–23, xxiii. 6, xxx. 7; Ps. lii. 2
(EVV. title). Cf., too, 2 Sam. viii. 17, where one should probably read
'Abiathar the son of Ahimelech' for 'Ahimelech the son of Abiathar' (cf. S),
followed by 1 Chron. xviii. 16 (with the further mistake of reading 'Abimelech' for 'Ahimelech': cf. LXX, V), xxiv. 3, 6, 31. See, for example,
A. F. Kirkpatrick, C.B., 2nd edit. rev. (1930), on 2 Sam. viii. 17. (*b*) 1 Sam.
xxvi. 6.

[4] Cf., for example, Diringer, op. cit., pp. 21–68; Albright, *Archaeology*

the term under discussion also comes to the fore in Hebrew circles at this time in the name Malchi-shua (מַלְכִּי־שׁוּעַ), meaning either 'My king (= Yahweh?) is salvation' or 'Milku(-i) is salvation',[1] which was given by Saul to one of his sons.[2] In short, so far as our comparatively meagre evidence goes, the use of names of this type, whether the term under discussion be regarded as an appellative or as a proper name, was as common at the beginning of the monarchy as at its close;[3] and, what is more important in the present connexion, it already had a long history behind it so far as the land of Canaan was concerned.[4]

and the Religion of Israel, p. 214. See also S. Moscati, *L'epigrafia ebraica antica 1935–1950* (1951), pp. 52, 58, 63, 76, for its occurrence on Hebrew seals. In Phoenician circles it must have enjoyed considerable popularity, for it appears frequently in Punic in the abbreviated form חמלך, as noticed above, p. 42, n. 1.

[1] Cf. Noth, op. cit., p. 154, n. 2 (also p. xviii).

[2] 1 Sam. xiv. 49, xxxi. 2; 1 Chron. viii. 33, ix. 39, x. 2.

[3] Cf. Nathan-melech (נְתַן־מֶלֶךְ, corresponding to the Phoenician (Punic) יתנמלך, referred to above, p. 42, n. 1), a court official of the time of Josiah, 2 Kings xxiii. 11; Ebed-melech (עֶבֶד־מֶלֶךְ, corresponding to the forms ABDI-MILKI and 'abdmlk, discussed above, p. 40), an Ethiopian court official of the time of Zedekiah, Jer. xxxviii. 7–13, xxxix. 15–18; Malchiram (מַלְכִּירָם, corresponding to the Phoenician מלכרם, referred to above, p. 42, n. 1), a son of Jehoiachin, 1 Chron. iii. 18; and, if the text be sound, Regem-melech (רֶגֶם־מֶלֶךְ), meaning originally, perhaps, 'Milk hath spoken' (cf. Ugaritic *rgm*, 'to say', and Hebrew names of the type Amariah ((וּ)אֲמַרְיָה, 'Yah(u) hath spoken', e.g. 1 Chron. xxiv. 23, Zeph. i. 1)), a member of a deputation sent to the Temple in Jerusalem shortly after the Return, Zech. vii. 2.

[4] According to Lev. xviii. 21 (H), xx. 2–5 (H); 2 Kings xxiii. 10; Jer. xxxii. 35 (cf. Isa. xxx. 33), it would seem that, at least during the later monarchy, the valley of Hinnom at Jerusalem was the scene of child sacrifices which were made to a god Molech (מֹלֶךְ) or, rather, Milk (the consonantal text having been vocalized, we are told, in order to suggest the term בֹּשֶׁת (*bōšeṯ*, 'shame'); and opinion has differed as to whether this worship was indigenous (as may well seem likely in view of what is said above with regard to the Jerusalem cultus in pre-Israelite days) or had been introduced from abroad, e.g. Phoenicia. Cf., for example, G. F. Moore, 'Molech, Moloch', *E.B.* iii (1902), cols. 3183–91. However, O. Eissfeldt, *Molk als Opferbegriff im Punischen und Hebräischen und das Ende des Gottes Moloch* (1935), has given reason to believe that the term מֹלֶךְ (*mōlek*) may correspond to the Punic מלך (*mlk*), which appears to have been used as a technical term for a sacrifice made, perhaps, in fulfilment of a vow; and the reference in the

As it happens, there is no clear evidence for the explicit association of this term with Yahweh as the component of a theophorous name until the appearance of the form Malchiah or Malchijah ((וֹ)מַלְכִּיָּה), 'My king is Yah(u)' or 'Yah(u) is (my) king', towards the end of the seventh century B.C.[1] Thereafter it figures prominently in the genealogical lists of the Chronicler,[2] as also in the books of Ezra[3] and Nehemiah.[4] Indeed, in the case of the Chronicler it is given very early authority, for it appears *inter alia* as the name of an ancestor of Asaph, the reputed founder of one of the three musical guilds established by David,[5] and as that of the head of one of the divisions or courses of priests similarly in-

above-mentioned passages must then be construed as the sacrificing of children, not 'to Molech (*mōlek*),' but 'as a *mōlek*'. This being the case, all reference to the name of a god seems to disappear. The argument is attractive and, on the whole, convincing; but, while Eissfeldt adopts the view that the Hebrew *mōlek* (= Punic *mlk*) is to be associated with the Syriac ܡܠܟ, 'to counsel' in its secondary sense 'to promise', and thus made to yield the meaning 'promise' or 'vow', it seems more likely that the term in question should continue to be associated with the worship of Milk (= 'king'), and interpreted in terms of what we should call a 'royalty'. Cf. Albright, *Archaeology and the Religion of Israel*, pp. 162 ff., who recognizes that the idea of a 'vow' may have been derived from the divine name Muluk (= Malik, corresponding to Milk), which is well attested for the region of the Middle Euphrates *c.* 1800 B.C. This seems more probable than the view advanced by J. G. Février, *R.H.R.* cxliii (1953), pp. 8 f., following A. Alt, *W.O.* iv (1949), pp. 282 f., that the Punic מלך may be connected with the Yiph'il of √הלך, as used in the Phoenician inscriptions from Karatepe (G. II, 19 = *K.A.I.* 26, II 19) with reference to the offering (or, rather, providing) of sacrifice; for, as Alt himself recognized, it is difficult to reconcile this with the vocalization of the Punic term in the construct state as *molk*, which is attested by the form of its transliteration in the Latin inscriptions on which the whole argument is based (i.e. in the first element of *molchomor*, *morchomor*, and *mochomor*, interpreted as meaning 'sacrifice of a lamb'). Cf. Friedrich, op. cit., §193. Finally, for a valuable survey of the whole question and full bibliographical references, see now H. Cazelles, art. 'Molok', *D.B.S.* v (1957), cols. 1337–46, and de Vaux, *Studies in Old Testament Sacrifice*, pp. 73–90 (= *Les Sacrifices de l'Ancien Testament*, pp. 67–81).

[1] (*a*) the father of Pashhur, one of Zedekiah's advisers, Jer. xxi. 1, xxxviii. 1: (*b*) a prince of the royal house, Jer. xxxviii. 6.

[2] 1 Chron. vi. 25 (EVV. 40), ix. 12 (cf. Neh. xi. 12), xxiv. 9.

[3] Ezra x. 25 (*bis*), 31 (= Neh. iii. 11).

[4] Neh. iii. 11 (= Ezra x. 31), 14, 31, viii. 4, x. 4 (EVV. 3), xi. 12 (cf. 1 Chron. ix. 12), xii. 42.

[5] 1 Chron. vi. 25 (EVV. 40).

stituted by David;[1] but, as already observed in the case of
the analogous form Malchiel,[2] it remains a difficult matter
to determine the precise historical value of the genealogical
lists of P and the Chronicler.[3] In any case, with all the foregoing evidence before us, there is no reason to doubt that
the name Melchizedek correctly points to the fact that a
term *milku(-i)*, corresponding to the Hebrew מֶלֶךְ ('king'),
was used as a divine appellative if not a proper name in the
pre-Israelite worship of Jerusalem. Indeed, in the light of
the foregoing discussion and in view of what was said earlier
with regard to the meaning of the name Adoni-zedek, it may
well be that the name Melchizedek, if it means at basis 'My
(*or* The) King is righteous', should be thought of, rather, as
'Milki is righteous'. In any case, while we must again be prepared to find a revision of opinion as to what is involved in
this notion of divine 'Kingship', there is obviously every
reason to accept its early association with the notion of
'rightness' or 'righteousness' so far as the pre-Israelite
city of Jerusalem is concerned.

The story of Melchizedek, however, teaches us something
more than this about the pre-Israelite worship of Jerusalem,
for we are told that, while Abram was returning from his
victory over the coalition of kings who had plundered
Sodom and Gomorrah,[4]

---

[1] 1 Chron. xxiv. 9.   [2] See above, p. 43.
[3] Cf., for example, 1 Chron. ix. 12 and Neh. xi. 12 with (*a*) 1 Chron.
xxiv. 9, and (*b*) Jer. xxi. 1, xxxviii. 1.
[4] Gen. xiv. 18–20. In the light of Ps. lxxvi. 3 (EVV. 2), as discussed above,
p. 32, where Salem is obviously synonymous with Zion, and Ps. cx, as
discussed below, pp. 130 ff., where Melchizedek is quite clearly associated with
Zion, there is no reason to doubt that Salem is here to be identified with
Jerusalem. See further, for example, F.-M. Abel, *Géographie de la Palestine*,
ii (1938), pp. 441 f., where reference will also be found to the attempts to
locate Salem elsewhere which have been made from quite early in the
Christian era, and L.-H. Vincent and A.-M. Steve, *Jérusalem de l'Ancien
Testament*, ii–iii (1956), pp. 611 ff. Incidentally, it has now been suggested
that the translation '(king) of Salem' is due to a misunderstanding, and that
שָׁלֵם should be (i) read as שְׁלֹמֹה (on the ground of haplography) so as to
yield the supposed meaning 'a king allied to him', or (ii) construed as an
adjective with the supposedly resultant force of 'a submissive king'. Cf. (i)
W. F. Albright, 'Abram the Hebrew: A New Archaeological Interpretation',

Melchizedek, the king of Salem, who was priest to God Most High, had brought forth bread and wine, and had greeted him and said:

> 'Blessed[1] be Abram by God Most High,
> Owner (*or* Creator)[2] of heaven and earth!
> Blessed be God Most High,
> Who hath delivered thy foes into thy hand!'

And he had given him a tenth of everything.

B.A.S.O.R. 163 (Oct. 1961), p. 52; (ii) R. H. Smith, 'Abram and Melchizedek (Gen 14[18–20])', *Z.A.W.* lxxvii (1965), p. 145. However, apart from the debatable connotation which is thus claimed for the terms שָׁלוֹם and שָׁלֵם (and, if the first suggestion is at least ingenious, the second is highly questionable), the simple perusal of any respectable Hebrew concordance to the Old Testament, s.v. מֶלֶךְ, will suffice to show how unlikely it is that we have here a reference to a king who is described vaguely as an ally or vassal emerging from some unspecified quarter, rather than a king who is defined by means of a following genitive as ruling over a particular territory or people, i.e. with a resultant indication of the district in (or from) which he makes his appearance upon the scene.

¹ Cf. Pedersen, *Israel I–II*, p. 153, E.T., p. 199; also, for valuable comparative material, E. Westermarck, *Ritual and Belief in Morocco* (1926), i pp. 35–261.

² Cf., perhaps, Deut. xxxii. 6 (and 8); Ps. cxxxix. 13; Prov. viii. 22: and see further, for example, H. G. May, *J.B.L.* lx (1941), p. 118, n. 11. Cf. the similar uncertainty in the case of the corresponding expression אל קן ארץ which occurs in the Phoenician inscriptions from Karatepe (G. III, 18 = *K.A.I.* 26, III 18) and in a Neo-Punic inscription from Leptis Magna in Tripolitania (G. Levi Della Vida, *Libya* 3 (1927), pp. 105–7, No. 13 = *K.A.I.* 129, 1), and may be held to mean either "El, owner of the earth (*or* land)' or "El, creator of the earth'. Cf., for example, (*a*) Levi Della Vida, *J.B.L.* lxiii (1944), pp. 4 ff. (also p. 1, n. 1); T. H. Gaster, *Thespis: Ritual, Myth and Drama in the Ancient Near East* (1950), p. 312, 2nd edit. rev. (1961), p. 375; J. Obermann, *New Discoveries at Karatepe*, T.C.A.A.S. 38 (1949), p. 36 (alternatively): (*b*) A. Alt, *W.O.* iv (1949), p. 284; Obermann, loc. cit. (alternatively). Cf., too, the use of the Ugaritic √*ḳny*, as in the expression *ḳnyt 'ilm*, which is used as an appellation of Asherah of the Sea (Gordon, op. cit. 51, i 23 = Herdner, *Mission de Ras Shamra* X, 4, i 23, etc.) and may be held to mean either 'mistress of the gods' (e.g. Gaster, op. cit., pp. 163 ff., 2nd edit. rev., pp. 174 ff.; G. R. Driver, *Canaanite Myths and Legends*, pp. 92 ff.) or 'creatress (= mother) of the gods' (e.g. Gordon, op. cit., p. 479 (2249), as in *Ugaritic Literature*, pp. 28 ff.; J. Aistleitner, *Wörterbuch der ugaritischen Sprache*, ed. O. Eissfeldt, B.V.S.A.W.L. 106, 3 (1963), p. 279 (2426); Driver, op. cit., p. 93, n. 2 (alternatively). For a discussion of the Hebrew terminology see P. Humbert, '"Qânâ" en hébreu biblique', in *Festschrift für Alfred Bertholet* (1950), pp. 259–66 = *Opuscules d'un hébraïsant*, M.U.N. xxvi (1958), pp. 166–74; and, with special reference to Proverbs viii. 22, W. A. Irwin, 'Where shall Wisdom be found?', *J.B.L.* lxxx (1961), pp. 133–42.

This story of Abram's deference towards the sacral king of a Canaanite city, coupled with the emphatic and repeated reference to 'Ēl 'Elyôn (אֵל עֶלְיוֹן) or 'God Most High' (cf. R.V., R.S.V.) is quite remarkable. If it is not historical (and this is much disputed),[1] the only satisfactory explanation of its existence would seem to be that it is an aetiological myth designed to justify the pre-Israelite worship of Jerusalem in the eyes of those who were worshippers of Yahweh; and, as such, it would be most suitably assigned to the reign of David.[2] Now, until recently the only evidence outside the general stream of Biblical tradition for the use of the epithet 'Elyôn as a divine name was that offered by Philo of Byblos (A.D. 64–161), who knew of a god 'Elioun called Most High' (Ἐλιοῦν καλούμενος Ὕψιστος) who had once been worshipped in the neighbourhood of that city;[3] but striking evidence for the existence of this divine name outside Israel is now to be found in the formal expression קדם אל ועלין, corresponding to the Hebrew for 'in the presence of 'Ēl and 'Elyôn', which occurs in the record of a treaty, inscribed in Aramaic and dating from the middle of the eighth century B.C., which has

---

[1] While the historical value of Genesis xiv remains uncertain, it is becoming increasingly clear that the names of the kings to which it refers are quite authentic for the first half of the second millenium B.C. Cf., for example, R. de Vaux, 'Les Patriarches hébreux et les découvertes modernes' (*suite*), *R.B.* lv (1948), pp. 326 ff. = *Die hebräischen Patriarchen und die modernen Entdeckungen* (1961), pp. 33 ff.

[2] Cf., for example, H. S. Nyberg, 'Studien zum Religionskampf im Alten Testament. I. Der Gott 'Al: Belege und Bedeutung des Namens', *A.R.W.* xxxv (1938), pp. 351, 363 f. (see above, p. 18, n. 1), followed by Th. C. Vriezen, *V. Th.* xv (1944), pp. 83 f., *Oud-israëlietische Geschriften* (1948), pp. 108 f.; H. H. Rowley, 'Zadok and Nehushtan', *J.B.L.* lviii (1939), p. 125, supplemented by 'Melchizedek and Zadok (Gen. 14 and Ps. 110)', *Festschrift für Alfred Bertholet* (1950), p. 466. See also G. von Rad. A.T.D. 2–4 (1949–53), 6th edit. (1961), pp. 150–2, E.T. by J. H. Marks (1961), pp. 174–6; and now, in general, A. H. J. Gunneweg, *Leviten und Priester. Hauptlinien der Traditionsbildung und Geschichte des israelitisch-jüdischen Kultpersonals*, F.R.L.A.N.T. 89 (1965), pp. 100 ff.

[3] Eusebius, *Praeparatio Evangelica*, i. 10, 14–15. Cf. Clemen, *Die phönikische Religion nach Philo von Byblos*, pp. 24 f.; also O. Eissfeldt, *Ras Schamra und Sanchunjaton* (1939), p. 114; *Taautos und Sanchunjaton*, S.B.D.A.W. 1952: 1 (1952), pp. 40 f.

been found near Aleppo.[1] The importance of this discovery
lies, not merely in the fact that it offers much earlier testimony of an extra-Biblical kind to the use of this divine
name in northern Syria, but also in the fact that it serves to
confirm what the Old Testament itself leads one to suspect,[2]
i.e. that in the expression 'Ēl 'Elyôn ('God Most High') two
divine names 'Ēl ('God') and 'Elyôn ('Most High'), which
were originally distinct, have been fused together so as to
suggest one supreme God.[3] All in all, therefore, there is no
reason to doubt that, so far as Jerusalem was concerned, the
term 'Elyôn ('Most High') was just what the epithet itself
implies, i.e. an appellation of the high god who had been
worshipped in this ancient Canaanite city prior to its capture by David.[4]

[1] Cf., originally, P. S. Ronzevalle, 'Notes et études d'archéologie orientale
(Deuxième série, II). Fragments d'inscriptions araméennes des environs
d'Alep', *M.U.S.J.* xv. 7 (1931), pp. 237–60. See further, for example, H.
Bauer, *A.f.O.* viii (1932–3), pp. 1–16; J. Hempel, *Z.A.W.* l (1932), pp. 178–
83; and now, with an extensive bibliography, *K.A.I.* 222 (–224).

[2] Cf., for example, Num. xxiv. 16 (JE); and see below, pp. 74 ff.

[3] The fact that in the foregoing Aramaic inscription the preposition קדם is
not repeated before עלין makes it clear that a similar fusion of these two
terms was under way in northern Syria in the eighth century B.C., as will be
seen if the expression is read in its immediate context. G. Levi Della Vida,
"El 'Elyon in Genesis 14, 18–20', *J.B.L.* lxiii (1944), pp. 1–9, followed by
J. Morgenstern, 'The Divine Triad in Biblical Mythology', *J.B.L.* lxiv
(1945), pp. 15–37, thinks it possible to distinguish a god El, who was the
lord of earth, and a god 'Elyon, who was the lord of heaven (i.e. 'the astral
sky, the seat of sun, moon and stars' as opposed to 'the atmospheric or
meteoric sky, where storms are formed').

[4] It is possible that one should recognize the survival of a corresponding
divine name 'Al or 'Elî in a number of Old Testament passages, e.g. Deut.
xxxiii. 12; 1 Sam. ii. 10; 2 Sam. xxiii. 1 (as noticed above, p. 18, n. 1); Ps. vii.
9 (EVV. 8). Cf., for example, the Ugaritic *'ly* (|| *b'l*) in KRT C, col. 3, 6 and
8 (= Gordon, *Ugaritic Textbook*, 126, iii. 6 and 8, and Herdner, *Mission de
Ras Shamra* X, 16, iii 6 and 8); and especially the name *yḥw'ly* (יחועלי,
'May *'ly* grant life') which occurs in the ostraca from Samaria (Diringer, op.
cit., pp. 35 f., 46: cf. Noth, op. cit., pp. 129, 206), and the familiar Old
Testament name 'Ēlî or Eli (1 Sam. i–iv, xiv. 3; 1 Kings ii. 27). See further
Nyberg, op. cit., *passim*, also *Studien zum Hoseabuche*, pp. 57 ff.; Albright,
Archaeology and the Religion of Israel, pp. 201 f., *C.B.Q.* vii (1945), p. 31,
n. 89; F. M. Cross jr. and D. N. Freedman, *J.B.L.* lxvii (1948), pp. 204 f.;
R. Tournay, *R.B.* lvi (1949), pp. 48 ff.; M. Dahood, 'The Divine Name
'Ēlî in the Psalms', *T.S.* xiv (1953), pp. 452–7. Cf. now H. Schmid, 'Jahwe
und die Kulttraditionen von Jerusalem', *Z.A.W.* lxvii (1955), pp. 168–97;

The attempt to discover a more personal name for the high god of this Canaanite city which David made the cultic centre of his kingdom, like the supposed cultic implication of the name 'David' itself,[1] must be regarded as

and note, with reference to R. Lack, 'Les Origines de 'Elyôn, Le Très-Haut, dans la tradition culturelle d'Israël', *C.B.Q.* xxiv (1962), pp. 44–64, that it is obviously no part of the argument of this monograph that the use of the divine appellative 'Elyôn was peculiar to the worship of the Jebusite cultus of Jerusalem and was totally unknown in Israelite circles prior to the time of David.

[1] The view has been advanced that the original name of the founder of the Davidic dynasty was Elhanan or even Baalhanan, and that the name David is derived from an original Dôdô or Dôd, the name of the Palestinian counterpart of the fertility god Tammuz as worshipped in Jerusalem, which was assumed by Elhanan (or Baalhanan) only after the capture of the city. Cf. (*a*) 1 Sam. xvii with 2 Sam. xxi. 19 (as against the harmonizing passage 1 Chron. xx. 5); (*b*) Gen. xxxvi. 38 (P) = 1 Chron. i. 49: and see further A. H. Sayce, 'The Names of the First Three Kings of Israel', *The Modern Review* v (1884), pp. 158–69, esp. pp. 159–63, *Lectures on the Origin and Growth of Religion as illustrated by the Religion of the Ancient Babylonians* (1887), pp. 52 ff.; J. G. Frazer, *The Golden Bough. IV. Adonis, Attis, Osiris*, 3rd edit. rev. (1914), i. pp. 18 ff.; S. A. Cook, *C.A.H.* ii, pp. 393 ff. Indeed, it has also been suggested that the Song of Songs is, at basis, a liturgy belonging to this cult of the god Dôd (cf., for example, the bride's repeated reference to her *dôd* or 'beloved', i. 13, etc.), and that it owes its preservation to the fact that it was Solomon (see below, p. 53, n. 1), rather than Adonijah, who succeeded David on the throne, for this ensured the continuation of his father's efforts at syncretism. Cf., for example, T. J. Meek, 'Canticles and the Tammuz Cult', *A.J.S.L.* xxxix (1922–3), pp. 1–14, 'The Song of Songs and the Fertility Cult', in *The Song of Songs: A Symposium*, ed. W. H. Schoff (1924), pp. 48–79; Schoff, 'The Offering Lists in the Song of Songs and their political significance', ibid., pp. 80–120; and for a critical survey of this and associated theories, see H. H. Rowley, *The Servant of the Lord and other Essays on the Old Testament* (1952), pp. 213 ff., 2nd edit. rev. (1965), pp. 223 ff. On the other hand, while it seems likely that 'David' was, in fact, a regnal name assumed by Elhanan (cf. A. M. Honeyman, 'The Evidence for Regnal Names among the Hebrews', *J.B.L.* lxvii (1948), pp. 23 f.; and see now the vocalization of the Hebrew text of Psalm cxxxii. 6b, as proposed above, p. 21, n. 1), one should not overlook the fact that it may be interpreted as meaning 'Beloved', and, as such, may be etymologically akin to the first element in what appears to be the private name of his son Solomon (cf. Honeyman, op. cit., pp. 22 f.), i.e. Jedidiah, 'Beloved of Yah' (2 Sam. xii. 24 f.); for this suggests that it may be a simple hypocoristicon. Cf. Noth, op. cit., pp. 149, 183 n. 4, 223.

In the first edition of this work I also referred, for the sake of completeness, to the widely current view that the name David might be related to the term DA-WI-DU-Ú-UM (and the like) which had been found to occur quite often in the Accadian texts of the eighteenth century B.C. from Mari and was thought doubtful, although there is some reason to believe that, if the association of a god Ṣedeḳ with Jerusalem remains extremely uncertain,[1] its tutelary deity may have been the god

to refer to a military leader of some kind. Cf., for example, G. Dossin, *A.R.M.* i (1950), Nos. 69, 92, 124; C. F. Jean, *A.R.M.* ii (1950), Nos. 74, 141; Dossin, *A.R.M.* iv (1951), Nos. 33, 40, 41; *A.R.M.* v (1952), Nos. 2, 72; also J. Bottéro and A. Finet, *A.R.M.* xv (1954), p 200 (s.v. *dâwidûm*). However, it now seems clear that the form in question should be regarded, rather, as a variant of *dabdû*, 'defeat'. Cf. H. Tadmor (citing B. Landsberger), in *J.N.E.S.* xvii (1958), pp. 129 ff., followed, for example, by *A.D.* and *A.H.*, s.v. *dabdû*.

Finally, for more recent discussion of the original significance of the name David along much the same divergent lines as those already indicated, see now (a) G. W. Ahlström, *Psalm 89. Eine Liturgie aus dem Ritual des leidenden Königs* (1959), pp. 163 ff., and (b) J. J. Stamm, 'Der Name des Königs David', in *Congress Volume: Oxford 1959*, S.V.T. vii (1959), pp. 165–83, who stresses, as an alternative to the meaning 'Beloved' ('Liebling'), that of paternal 'Uncle' ('Vatersbruder'). In connexion with the latter work, however, I must enter a protest against the fact that the first edition of this monograph is cited (p. 171, n. 1; with the broad reference '*passim*'!) as evidence for the statement that I have taken up and developed the argument of I. Engnell, *Studies in Divine Kingship in the Ancient Near East* (1943), pp. 176 f., who claimed (i) that the term דוד had been used originally in Jebusite Jerusalem as 'an appellative or a proper name of the "vegetation-deity" corporalized in the king', (ii) that it came to be employed in the Old Testament 'simply as a title of the reigning king', and (iii) that, correspondingly, its use in the expression לדוד, which figures so often in the headings to the individual compositions in the Psalter, is to be interpreted as 'an original cultic-liturgical rubric inherited from pre-Israelite Jebusite times with the actual import of "a psalm for the king"'. It should have been clear, both from the statement in the text which has given rise to this footnote and from the wording of this note in its original form, that I was reserving judgement (as, obviously, I still do) on the whole of this highly controversial issue. What is more, the fact that this monograph develops the argument of a work which I published eight years before that of Engnell (see above, in the preface to the first edition) should have been sufficient to show that its thesis owes nothing to any hints which had been dropped by this Swedish scholar. The fact is that, as I have indicated repeatedly elsewhere (see above, p. 7, n. 1), I owe my treatment of the psalms in question to Gunkel's valuable recognition of a class of psalm which he described as 'royal psalms' ('Königspsalmen'), many of which, as it seems to me, have close links with a modified form of Mowinckel's epoch-making treatment of the psalms which celebrate the Kingship of Yahweh.

[1] See above, pp. 36 f. It has also been suggested that the figure of Zadok, a priest of uncertain genealogy, who comes suddenly to the fore as an associate of Abiathar when once David is established in Jerusalem, acquires deeper significance when seen in the light of the Melchizedek tradition; in fact, that he may have been either the earlier Jebusite king of Jerusalem, who, in line with David's general policy of conciliation, had been allowed to

Šālēm.¹ In any case, as we turn in the following pages to an examination of those psalms which are to be our main concern, we shall find reason to believe that, after the capture of Jerusalem, David found in the Jebusite cultus with its worship of the 'Most High' in association with the royal-priestly order of Melchizedek a ritual and mythology which might prove to be the means of carrying out Yahweh's purposes for Israel and fusing the chosen people into a model of national righteousness.²

retain something of his earlier priestly status, or, simply, a priest of this earlier Jebusite cultus. Cf., for example, 2 Sam. viii. 17, xv. 24 ff., xvii. 15, xix. 12 (EVV. 11); 1 Kings i. 1–ii. 35; 1 Chron. v. 30–40 (EVV. vi. 4–14), vi. 35–38 (EVV. 50–53), xviii. 16: and see (*a*) A. Bentzen, *Studier over det zadokidiske præsteskabs historie* (1931), pp. 8–18, following the suggestions of S. Mowinckel, *Ezra den skriftlærde* (1916), p. 109, n. 2 (cf. *Offersang og sangoffer*, p. 135, *The Psalms in Israel's Worship*, i. p. 133), and H. R. Hall, in *The People and the Book*, ed. A. S. Peake (1925), p. 11, and the summary of this work in German by the author, *Z.A.W.* li (1933), pp. 173–6; Nyberg, *A.R.W.* xxxv (1938), p. 375; (*b*) H. H. Rowley, 'Zadok and Nehushtan', *J.B.L.* lviii (1939), pp. 113–41, 'Melchizedek and Zadok (Gen. 14 and Ps. 110)', *Festschrift für Alfred Bertholet* (1950), pp. 461–72; and now C. E. Hauer jr., 'Who was Zadok?', *J.B.L.* lxxxii (1963), pp. 89–94.

¹ It is possible that a divine name Šālēm should be recognized behind the alternative names of the city, Salem (i.e. 'Šālēm') and Jerusalem ('Foundation of Šālēm'?), and the personal names which were given by David to his two favourite sons, Absalom (originally 'Šālēm is father'?) and Solomon (but see in this connexion J. J. Stamm, 'Der Name des Königs Salomo', *T.Z.* xvi (1960), pp. 285–97). Cf. the form *šlm* which occurs unmistakably in the Ras Shamra tablets as the name of a god (Gordon, op. cit., 17, 12; 52, 52 f. = Herdner, 29, rev. 12; 23, 52 f.; see also G. R. Driver, *Canaanite Myths and Legends*, pp. 120 ff.), and the divine names Šalim and Šulmānu which are attested by theophorous names in Accadian texts. See further, for example, J. Lewy, 'Les Textes paléo-assyriens et l'Ancien Testament', *R.H.R.* cx (1934), pp. 60 ff.; 'The Šulmān Temple in Jerusalem,' *J.B.L.* lix (1940), pp. 519–22; also Nyberg, op. cit., pp. 352 ff.; N. W. Porteous, 'Shalem-Shalom', *G.U.O.S.T.* x (1940 and 1941, published 1943), pp. 1–7; J. Gray, 'The Desert God 'Aṭtr in the Literature and Religion of Canaan', *J.N.E.S.* viii (1949), pp. 72–83; and now Vincent and Steve, op. cit., p. 612; G. Fohrer, *Th.W.N.T.* vii (1964), pp. 296 f.

² It has been claimed that kingship as an institution was in decline in Canaan at the time of the Hebrew settlement, and, in particular, that the absence of any reference to a contemporary king of Jerusalem in the account of David's capture of the city (2 Sam. v. 6–8) makes it likely that there was no kingship in existence there at that time. Cf. J. Gray, 'Canaanite Kingship in Theory and Practice', *V.T.* ii (1952), pp. 193–220, following A. Alt, *Die Staatenbildung der Israeliten in Palästina* (1930), pp. 31 f. (= *Kleine Schriften zur Geschichte*

III

The dedication of Solomon's Temple, which adjoined the palace and was first and foremost a royal chapel,[1] took place at the celebration of a great autumn festival.[2] This corresponds to a leading feature of Jeroboam's attempt to consolidate his position in the north, following the disruption of the monarchy and the successful break-away from the House of David; for we learn that he established rival centres of worship at Dan in the north and Bethel in the south of his kingdom, and we are expressly told that, in establishing what was essentially a royal cultus at Bethel as a rival to the similar cultus in Jerusalem (the book of Amos revealing that the sanctuary at Bethel, like that in Jerusalem, was indeed a royal sanctuary),[3] he followed the example of the Southern Kingdom by inaugurating at this particular centre a corresponding autumnal festival.[4] This is important; for it indicates that the festival in question was used in Jerusalem for the important purpose of binding the people in loyalty not only to the national deity but also to the reigning house.[5]

des Volkes Israel, ii (1953), pp. 24 ff.), who thinks in terms of a council of elders. See also J. de Groot, in *Werden und Wesen des Alten Testaments*, ed. J. Hempel, B.Z.A.W. 66 (1936), pp. 191 ff., who suggests a Philistine overlordship. However, such an argument from silence, when the data concerning the capture of Jerusalem are so meagre, is extremely precarious; and, if nothing happens to be said here about a king who may be regarded as a successor of Adoni-zedek, as little is said either here or anywhere else about there ever having been a council of elders or, indeed, a Philistine ruler at Jerusalem prior to its capture by David.

[1] Cf. 1 Kings v. 15 (EVV. v. 1)–vii. 51; Ezek. xliii. 7–9: and see further K. Möhlenbrink, *Der Tempel Salomos. Eine Untersuchung seiner Stellung in der Sakralarchitektur des alten Orients*, B.W.A.N.T. 59 (1932), pp. 49–79. As should be clear from the ensuing argument of this monograph, the statement which is made above in the text is not to be construed as implying that the Temple was the king's private chapel. Cf. the careful distinction which is rightly drawn by R. de Vaux, *Les Institutions de l'Ancien Testament*, ii (1960), pp. 158 f., E.T. (as above, p. 4, n. 4), pp. 320 f.

[2] 1 Kings viii. 2: cf. 2 Chron. v. 3, vii. 8–10.

[3] vii. 10–17, esp. verse 13.   1 Kings xii. 26–33.

[5] Cf. N. H. Snaith, *The Jewish New Year Festival: Its Origins and Development* (1947), pp. 47 ff. It is, perhaps, worthy of note in this connexion that, whereas the Northern Kingdom witnessed a succession of dynasties and

Moreover, we learn that the festival under discussion was celebrated in Jerusalem in the month Ethanim, which is then explained as being the seventh month, i.e. the month Tishri (October–November) according to the Babylonian calendar and the numbering of the months from that of Nisan (March–April).[1] In Bethel, on the other hand, it is said to have taken place in the eighth month, i.e. the month Bul or, according to the Babylonian calendar, Marcheshvan (November–December), the variation probably being in keeping with local tradition as well as reflecting the absence of any central control such as that which emerged in close association with the Jerusalem Temple after the Exile.[2] Further, it is generally agreed that the festival in question must have been the last and most important of the three great festivals of the Israelite year,[3] i.e. 'The Feast' *par excellence*,[4] which occurs in the earlier legal codes as 'The Feast of Ingathering' (חַג הָאָסִיף)[5] but ultimately

even isolated rulers, the Southern Kingdom remained faithful to the House of David throughout some four centuries until the kingdom itself was overthrown from outside.

[1] 1 Kings viii. 2.
[2] 1 Kings xii. 32 f. (cf. vi. 38). The argument advanced by J. Morgenstern, *Amos Studies*, i (1941), pp. 146 ff. (cf. *H.U.C.A.* xii–xiii (1937–8), pp. 20 ff.), in an attempt to equate the date of these two festivals in terms of his theory of a triple calendar seems to the present writer to be very strained, and amongst other things overemphasizes the attractions of such a feast at the expense of the traditional rivalry between north and south. Cf., for example, 2 Sam. xix. 41–43, xx. 1; 1 Kings xii. 16. For Morgenstern's theory of a triple calendar, see 'The Three Calendars of Ancient Israel', *H.U.C.A.* i (1924), pp. 13–78; 'Additional Notes on "The Three Calendars of Ancient Israel"', *H.U.C.A.* iii (1926), pp. 77–107; and 'Supplementary Studies in the Calendars of Ancient Israel', *H.U.C.A.* x (1935), pp. 1–148. On the whole, however, Morgenstern's argument is too dependent upon a theory of interpolation to be at all convincing to the mind of the present writer, and no further account of it is taken in connexion with the ensuing discussion; for, even if Morgenstern's theory were to prove true, the writer's general thesis would remain quite unaffected. Finally, note now (i.e. as compared with the time when the foregoing words were written for the first edition of this monograph) that Morgenstern has abandoned this attempt to equate the date of the two festivals: see 'The Festival of Jeroboam I', *J.B.L.* lxxxiii (1964), pp. 109–18.
[3] Cf., for example, J. Skinner, Cent. B. (n.d.), on 1 Kings viii. 2.
[4] Cf. Judges xxi. 19; 1 Kings viii. 2, xii. 32: also John vii. 2.
[5] Exod. xxiii. 16 (E), xxxiv. 22 (J).

appears in the later codes as 'The Feast of Tabernacles' or, better perhaps, 'Feast of Booths' (חַג הַסֻּכּוֹת).[1] According to pre-exilic sources this festival took place 'in the going out of the year' (בְּצֵאת הַשָּׁנָה),[2] or 'at the turn of the year' (תְּקוּפַת הַשָּׁנָה);[3] and a strong case can be made out for the view that the expression 'the going out of the year' denotes the end of the year.[4] Nevertheless it is difficult to escape the impression that the phrase 'the going out of the year' should be regarded as the opposite of the expression 'the return of the year' (תְּשׁוּבַת הַשָּׁנָה), which is defined as the time when military operations might be expected to begin and therefore probably bears reference to the spring.[5] If that should be so, these two contrary expressions may reflect the thought of the dying and reviving year;[6] and, this being the case, the expression 'the going out of the year' should not be stressed as clearly marking, in and of itself, the end of one year or by implication the beginning of the next. In

---

[1] Lev. xxiii. 34–36, 39–44 (H); Deut. xvi. 13–15, 16. Cf. Num. xxix. 12–38 (P); Deut. xxxi. 10–13: also Ezra iii. 4; Neh. viii. 14–18; Zech. xiv. 16–19.

[2] Exod. xxiii. 16 (E).

[3] Exod. xxxiv. 22 (J).

[4] Cf. Snaith, op. cit., pp. 58 ff. (followed by A. Aalen, *Die Begriffe 'Licht' und 'Finsternis' im Alten Testament, im Spätjudentum und im Rabbinismus*, S.N.V.A.O. II, 1951, No. 1 (1951), p. 50), who rightly rejects the theory that the expression in question means 'the begining of the year', as maintained, for example, by G. B. Gray, *Sacrifice in the Old Testament: Its Theory and Practice* (1925), pp. 300 f. See also E. Auerbach, *V.T.* iii (1953), pp. 186 f.; and, for a reiteration of the view that this expression must mean 'the beginning of the year', S. Mowinckel, *Zum israelitischen Neujahr und zur Deutung der Thronbesteigungspsalmen*, A.N.V.A.O. II, 1952, No. 2 (1952), pp. 12–14, and now de Vaux, op. cit., i, p. 289, E.T., p. 190.

[5] 2 Sam. xi. 1 (Q: cf. 1 Chron. xx. 1); 1 Kings xx. 22, 26; 2 Chron. xxxvi. 10. The writer has been unable to accept Snaith's argument, op. cit., pp. 32 ff., that in 2 Sam. xi. 1, 1 Kings xx. 22, 26, the reference cannot be to the opening of hostilities in the spring. The definition of the season as being the time at which the kings 'go forth' does not imply, of course, that hostilities always took place just at that time, but merely that from that particular period of the year onwards they might be expected.

[6] Cf. *The Vitality of the Individual in the Thought of Ancient Israel*, pp. 13 f., 2nd edit., pp. 8 f. Shortly after the publication of the first edition of the present work I found that the suggestion which is made above in the text had already been made by Pedersen, *Israel I–II*, pp. 380 f., E.T., pp. 489 f., and *Israel III–IV*, p. 336, E.T., pp. 444 f.

other words, this expression simply denotes one of the two recognized turning points in the cycle of the year.

On the other hand, some support for the view that the Feast of Ingathering was closely connected with the thought of at least an agricultural New Year is to be found in the so-called Gezer Calendar (possibly as early as the tenth century B.C.), which lists the agricultural operations of the year in their monthly order beginning with that of 'Ingathering' (אֹסֶף);[1] and such a forward look is confirmed by the explicit association of the Feast of Tabernacles with the coming of the rain which would be so necessary if these agricultural operations were to issue in a successful harvest by the end of the ensuing twelve months.[2] Further, it is a noteworthy fact that in the post-exilic period Tishri 1 or the first day of the seventh month was a day of memorial to be celebrated in a special way with the sounding of trumpet or horn,[3] and that in the rabbinical tradition represented by the Mishnah it is expressly stated to be a New Year's Day;[4] for this seems best understood as a reflection of the traditional importance which must have been attached to this season of the year. Moreover, it is to be observed that, whereas this New Year's Day fell on Tishri 1, i.e. at the new moon, the Feast of Tabernacles did not begin its week of celebrations until Tishri 15, i.e. at the full moon;[5] so that the great autumnal festival now came well within the new year marked by this particular New Year's Day.[6]

---

[1] See Diringer, op. cit., pp. 1–20, and Moscati, op. cit., pp. 8–26.

[2] Cf. Snaith, op. cit., pp. 62 ff.; Aalen, op. cit., pp. 52 f.: and see below, p. 59, n. 2.   [3] Lev. xxiii. 24 f. (H); Num. xxix. 1–6 (P).

[4] Rosh ha-Shanah i. 1, e.g. in the translation by H. Danby, *The Mishnah* (1933).

[5] Lev. xxiii. 34, 39 (H); Num. xxix. 12 (P): cf. 1 Kings xii. 32.

[6] It seems possible that in the pre-exilic period each new month began, not with the new moon, but with the full moon; and, this being the case, it may be that the first day of the Feast of Tabernacles or, to use the earlier name, the Feast of Ingathering, since it coincided with the full moon, was originally not only the first day of a new month but also a New Year's Day. Cf. I. Benzinger, *Hebräische Archäologie*, 2nd edit. (1907), p. 169, 3rd edit. (1927), pp. 169 f.; Mowinckel, *Psalmenstudien II*, pp. 87 f.; and esp. Snaith, op. cit., pp. 96 ff., particularly pp. 99–103 with reference to Ps. lxxxi. 4 (EVV.

Unfortunately the Old Testament offers little direct evidence as to the ritual and mythology of this great autumnal festival in any of its forms; and even the little that is available is post-exilic in date. In short, there is the well-known practice of dwelling in 'booths' throughout the seven days of the festival,[1] and there are the regulations concerning the special sacrifices which are to be offered on each successive day;[2] but none of this takes us very far, and it seems extraordinary that so important a festival should have left so little trace. Happily, however, there is a brief but important passage in the post-exilic book of Zechariah which touches on the Feast of Tabernacles and, in so doing, yields a valuable clue to the indirect evidence which is available for the reconstruction of the ritual pattern as it existed in Jerusalem, i.e.:[3]

And it shall come to pass that every one that is left of all the nations which came up against Jerusalem shall go up from year to year to worship the King, Yahweh of Hosts, and to celebrate the Feast of

---

3). Indeed, it is conceivable that in the post-exilic period the celebration of (i) a New Year's Day on Tishri 1, (ii) the Day of Atonement on Tishri 10, and (iii) the Feast of Tabernacles on Tishri 15–21 (22), represents different facets of what had once been a single celebration in the earlier period, when this agricultural New Year began, not with the new moon, but with the full moon. Cf. (i) Rosh ha-Shanah i, 1, as above, n. 4: (ii) Lev. xvi. 29, xxiii. 27 (H); Num. xxix. 7 (P): (iii) Lev. xxiii. 34–36, 39–44 (H); Num. xxix. 12–38 (P): and see further P. Volz, *Das Neujahrsfest Jahwes* (*Laubhüttenfest*), V.S.G.T.R. 67 (1912), p. 18; Mowinckel, op. cit., pp. 206 ff.; and Snaith, op. cit., pp. 89 and 148. Finally, for what may have been a transitional celebration of Tishri 10 as a New Year's Day (cf. Ezek. xl. 1; also Lev. xxv. 9 (H) with reference to the Year of Jubilee), see Snaith, op. cit., pp. 131–41.

[1] Lev. xxiii. 42 f. (H); Neh. viii. 14–18. Various attempts have been made to explain the origin of this practice in terms of the agricultural life of Palestine: for example, (*a*) the practice of camping out in the vineyards at the time of harvest, J. Wellhausen, *Prolegomena zur Geschichte Israels = Geschichte Israels*, i, 2nd edit. (1883), p. 88, E.T. by J. S. Black and A. Menzies, *Prolegomena to the History of Israel* (1885), p. 85; (*b*) a practice corresponding to that of planting Adonis gardens, H. Gressmann, *Tod und Auferstehung des Osiris nach Festbräuchen und Umzügen*, A. O. xxiii. 3 (1923), p. 17; (*c*) a taboo on dwelling indoors at a time of the year when houses were thought to be peculiarly susceptible to demonic visitation, A. J. Wensinck, *Arabic New-Year and the Feast of Tabernacles*, V.K.A.W.A., N.R. xxv. 2 (1925), pp. 25 ff.   [2] Num. xxix. 12–38 (P).   [3] xiv. 16 f.: cf. verse 9.

Tabernacles. Moreover, it shall be that, whoso of all the families of the earth goeth not up to Jerusalem to worship the King, Yahweh of Hosts, upon them the rain shall not come.

It seems reasonable to infer that such an eschatological picture (and for the present writer's argument as a whole this eschatological aspect must be emphasized)[1] is based upon what was already the established complex of ideas associated with this festival in the form which had been current in Jerusalem, i.e. to infer, as a general principle, that the gift of rain was bound up with the celebration of the Feast of Tabernacles (an inference borne out from other sources),[2] and, what is more, that this celebration found its focus in the worship of Yahweh as King and even, perhaps, the universal King.

At this point it is necessary to recall the fact that in Israelite thought the sky is a concrete dome-like structure or 'firmament' which rests upon the circle of the earth, while the earth itself is supported above a part of the all-embracing cosmic sea, in which are sunk the bases of the mountains as the very pillars of heaven. The breaks in the earth's surface, which are caused by the seas and the rivers, the flooded wadies, and the bubbling springs, all reveal the presence of the subterranean waters; and rain is due to the fact that a supply from the upper reaches of this great cosmic sea is released from time to time by Yahweh through the window-like openings of heaven for the service or

---

[1] See below, p. 61, n. 1.
[2] Sukkah iv. 9; Taanith i. 1. Cf., for example, H. St. John Thackeray, *The Septuagint and Jewish Worship* (1921), pp. 62 ff.; Wensinck, op. cit., pp. 27 ff.; G. Dalman, *Arbeit und Sitte in Palästina*, i. 1 (1928), pp. 148 ff.; Patai, *Man and Temple*, pp. 24 ff. For valuable comparative material with regard to the climatic conditions of Palestine including the annual rainfall, see also H. Hilderscheid, 'Die Niederschlagsverhältnisse Palästinas in alter und neuer Zeit', *Z.D.P.V.* xxv (1902), pp. 1–105; F. M. Exner, 'Zum Klima von Palästina', with a foreword by M. Blanckenhorn, *Z.D.P.V.* xxxiii (1910), pp. 107–64; F.-M. Abel, *Géographie de la Palestine*, i (1933), pp. 108–34; M. Noth, *Die Welt des Alten Testaments*, 2nd edit. rev. (1953), pp. 23–28, 4th edit. rev. (1962), pp. 25–30; R. B. Y. Scott, 'Meteorological Phenomena and Terminology in the Old Testament', *Z.A.W.* lxiv (1952), pp. 11–25; and now D. Baly, *The Geography of the Bible* (1957), pp. 40 ff.

destruction of mankind, as He may see fit.[1] Moreover, it seems clear that the 'bronze sea' which figured so prominently in the furnishing of Solomon's Temple was intended as a replica of this cosmic sea, and, as such, must have been designed to play a prominent part in the ritual of the cultus.[2]

Now it is significant to find that in the Psalter there are not a few liturgical works which lay stress upon the fact that Yahweh is King, and, what is more, that He is enthroned as King in virtue of His control over the great cosmic sea and His rule over the more stable world of heaven and earth, of which He is the Creator; for the fact that in the foregoing passage from the book of Zechariah the gift of rain is made dependent upon the celebration of the Feast of Tabernacles and the concomitant worship of Yahweh as King, coupled with the fact that rain is due to Yahweh's power over the cosmic sea, goes far to make it probable that the psalms in question were intended for this great autumnal festival. Moreover, although the passage from the book of Zechariah is of post-exilic date, there is no reason to doubt that it preserves an age-long association of ideas with its roots well back in the pre-exilic period; for cultic thought and practice are notoriously tenacious of existence and quite capable of surviving (even though in a modified form) such a violent upheaval as that of the Babylonian Exile.[3] This is important, for we shall presently

---

[1] Cf., in general, Gen. i. 1 ff. (P), xlix. 25; Exod. xx. 4 (cf. Deut. iv. 18); Deut. xxxii. 22, xxxiii. 13; 2 Sam. xxii. 5 f., 8, 16 f. (corresponding to Ps. xviii. 5 f., 8, 16 f. (EVV. 4 f., 7, 15 f.)); Job xxvi. 10 ff., xxxviii. 4 ff., 16 f.; Ps. xxiv. 1 f., xxxiii. 6 f., lxix. 16 (EVV. 15), lxxi. 20, lxxxviii. 5–8 (EVV. 4–7), cxxxvi. 6; Prov. viii. 24–29; Ezek. xxvi. 19–21; Amos v. 8; Jonah ii. 6 f. (EVV. 5 f.): and, for the lattices or gratings (EVV. 'windows') of heaven, Gen. vii. 11, viii. 2 (P); 2 Kings vii. 2, 19; Isa. xxiv. 18; Mal. iii. 10. See further, on the general question of Israelite cosmology but with special reference to the Underworld (as discussed below, pp. 117 ff.), *The Vitality of the Individual in the Thought of Ancient Israel*, pp. 91 ff., 2nd edit., pp. 90 ff.; and, for the bearing of Israelite cosmology on the conception of rain, E. F. Sutcliffe, 'The Clouds as Water-Carriers in Hebrew Thought', *V.T.* iii (1953), pp. 99–103.

[2] 1 Kings vii. 23–26 (cf. 2 Chron. iv. 2 ff.); 2 Kings xxv. 13. Cf., for example, Albright, *Archaeology and the Religion of Israel*, pp. 148 ff.

[3] In Sukkah (i.e. the Mishnaic tractate on the observance of the Feast of

consider evidence which serves to show that the psalms in question, far from being influenced in some cases by the thought of Deutero-Isaiah as is commonly supposed, are of pre-exilic date, and must be regarded rather as having themselves exerted a powerful influence upon the thought of this great prophet of the Exile.[1]

Tabernacles) no reference is made to this conception of Yahweh as King; but such an omission does not prove that the association of ideas in the book of Zechariah is purely fortuitous, for the tractate is merely concerned with the preservation of traditional material relating to certain practices associated with the festival as celebrated in connexion with the Second Temple or the provincial synagogues, and shows little, if any, interest in the accompanying ideology.

[1] See especially Mowinckel, *Psalmenstudien II*, pp. 190–202, and *Zum israelitischen Neujahr und zur Deutung der Thronbesteigungspsalmen*, pp. 39–53; also the present writer's comments in his essay on 'The Psalms', in *The Old Testament and Modern Study*, ed. H. H. Rowley (1951), pp. 194 f., where it is pointed out (i) that the list of parallels between Psalms xciii, xcv–xcviii and Isaiah xl–lv, drawn up by N. H. Snaith, *Studies in the Psalter* (1934), pp. 66–69 (cf. *The Jewish New Year Festival*, pp. 200 f.) in support of his claim that the former are dependent upon the latter is something of a two-edged sword, for quite the opposite conclusion may be drawn; and (ii) that, if the psalms in question owed their existence to the influence of Deutero-Isaiah, one would expect to find some reference to Yahweh's activity, not only as the universal King, but also as the proven גֹּאֵל (EVV. 'redeemer' or, rather, as argued by the present writer in S.V.T. i (1953), pp. 67–77, 'protector') of His people, for this idea dominates the thought of Isaiah xl–lv from begining to end (cf. (a) xli. 14, xliii. 14, xliv. 6 (גֹּאֵל ‖ מֶלֶךְ), 24, xlvii. 4, xlviii. 17, xlix. 7, 26, liv. 5, 8: (b) xliii. 1, xliv. 22, 23, xlviii. 20, lii. 9); but, as a matter of fact, there is none.

The writer's basic dependence upon Mowinckel's epoch-making work for the ensuing interpretation of the psalms in question is clearly indicated in *The Old Testament and Modern Study*, pp. 196 f., as also in 'Living Issues in Biblical Scholarship. Divine Kingship and the Old Testament', *E.T.* lxii (1950–1), p. 39; and it is again gratefully acknowledged here. Nevertheless, if the writer may be allowed to anticipate the conclusion of his argument at so early a stage as this, it seems desirable to add that, while preparing this series of lectures during the winter of 1950–1 after the forementioned articles had gone to press, he found himself compelled to modify his earlier views at a number of points; and included in these modifications is one change of quite a major character. This is (a) the rejection of the view that the festival under discussion was concerned with the cyclic revival of the social unit, and (b) the recognition that its orientation was not merely towards the following cycle of twelve months but towards a completely new era. That is to say, if ever it had its roots in a complex of myth and ritual which was primarily concerned with the cycle of the year and an annual attempt to secure a renewal of life for a specific social unit, this had been refashioned in

Turning now to the liturgical works which call for consideration, we may begin with Psalm xxix, which is of special importance in that it reveals some close parallels in both language and form with the Ugaritic literature of the latter part of the second millennium B.C., and so may safely be assigned to the pre-exilic period and, indeed, the early pre-exilic period. In fact the parallels with Ugaritic are so close that the psalm has been described as in origin a hymn to Baal which has been but slightly revised in terms of Yahwism;[1] and as such it has been assigned tentatively to the tenth century B.C.[2] This is important, for it admits the possibility that we have here a hymn of the early Jebusite cultus of Jerusalem which was adapted to the worship of Yahweh after the capture of the city by David.[3] The psalm

terms of the Hebrew experience of Yahweh's activity on the plane of history, and the thought in question was really the creation of a new world order and the introduction of an age of universal righteousness and peace. In short, while the writer continues to reject the historical interpretation of these psalms, he now holds, not only that they were cultic in intention from the first, but that their orientation was also eschatological from the first.

The foregoing paragraph (apart from the form of citation in the reference to my own work) has been reproduced, as it stands, from the first edition of this monograph; but the reader may now be referred to my essay on 'Hebrew Conceptions of Kingship', in *Myth, Ritual, and Kingship*, ed. S. H. Hooke (1958), pp. 204–35, for a renewed acknowledgement of my indebtedness to Mowinckel. At the same time, in view of much current misrepresentation of my own line of approach and its conclusions, I must stress the fact, which is there recorded, that I have ventured to differ from him on a number of important points, including this shift of emphasis with regard to the eschatological interpretation of the psalms under discussion.

[1] Cf. H. L. Ginsberg, כתבי אוגרית or *The Ugarit Texts* (1936), pp. 129–31, *Orientalia* v (1936), pp. 180 f., *B.A.* viii (1945), pp. 53 f.: but note that the beginning and the end of the psalm hardly support the view that Yahweh is thought of as riding across the skies from west to east. Cf., too, T. H. Gaster, 'Psalm 29', *J.Q.R.* xxxvii (1946–7), pp. 55–56, *Thespis*, pp. 74–77, 2nd edit., pp. 443 ff.; F. M. Cross jr., 'Notes on a Canaanite Psalm in the Old Testament', *B.A.S.O.R.* 117 (Feb. 1950), pp. 19–21. On the more general question of Ugaritic parallels to the Psalter, see J. H. Patton, *Canaanite Parallels in the Book of Psalms* (1944), and W. F. Albright, 'The Psalm of Habakkuk', in *Studies in Old Testament Prophecy* (T. H. Robinson *Festschrift*), ed. H. H. Rowley (1950), pp. 1 ff., where it is said of this psalm that it 'swarms with Canaanitisms in diction and imagery' (p. 6).

[2] Albright, loc. cit.; also *Archaeology and the Religion of Israel*, p. 129.

[3] Cf. the suggestion advanced in connexion with the Tell el-Amarna tablets, that the somewhat extravagant language which is occasionally used by

itself opens with an exhortation to the lesser members of
the divine assembly or community of the gods (בְּנֵי אֵלִים)¹
to render to Yahweh the praise which is His due:²

Render to Yahweh, O ye gods,
Render to Yahweh glory and strength,
Render to Yahweh the glory due to His Name;
Make obeisance to Yahweh in His holy splendour!

The body of the psalm is then given up to a vivid picture
of thunderstorm and earthquake, described in terms of
Yahweh's powerful and resplendent 'Voice', which echoes
over the many waters,³ shatters the cedars on the mountain slopes, makes Lebanon and Sirion (i.e. Anti-Lebanon)⁴
skip like calves, rends the skies with flashes of lightning,
causes the wilderness of Kadesh to writhe and dance, and
instils terror into the animal world, while in His Temple
the theme on everyone's lips is that of 'Glory!':⁵

the petty rulers of Canaan in addressing their Egyptian overlord may be
drawn from contemporary Canaanite hymnology, and, this being the case,
may be held to indicate the existence of Canaanite prototypes for the
Israelite psalms. F. M. Th. Böhl, 'Hymnisches und Rhythmisches in den
Amarnabriefen aus Kanaan', *T.L.B.* xxxv (1914), cols. 337 ff.: cf. *De
Psalmen*, T.U. i (1946), pp. 25 ff. See also A. Jirku, 'Kana'anäische Psalmen-
fragmente in der vorisraelitischen Zeit Palästinas und Syriens', *J.B.L.* lii
(1933), pp. 108–20.
¹ Cf. Ps. lxxxix. 7 (EVV. 6), as below, p. 108: also, for the corresponding
expression בְּנֵי (הָ)אֱלֹהִים, Gen. vi. 2, 4 (J); Job i. 6, ii. 1, xxxviii. 7. See
further *The One and the Many in the Israelite Conception of God*, pp. 26 ff.,
2nd edit., pp. 22 ff., which may be supplemented by H. W. Robinson, 'The
Council of Yahweh', *J.T.S.* xliv (1943), pp. 151–7, and *Inspiration and
Revelation in the Old Testament* (1946), pp. 166 ff.; also, now, the careful
study by G. Cooke, 'The Sons of (the) God(s)', *Z.A.W.* lxxvi (1964), pp. 22–47,
although I must add that his attempt to distinguish between 'mythological' and 'psychological' sets of ideas (pp. 40 ff.) introduces a false anti-
thesis which must do less than justice to the conception of the divine רוּחַ
or 'Spirit'.   ² vv. 1–2.
³ Cf. H. G. May, 'Some Cosmic Connotations of *Mayim Rabbîm*, "Many
Waters"', *J.B.L.* lxxiv (1955), pp. 9–21.
⁴ Cf. Deut. iii. 9; also, perhaps, 1 Chron. v. 16 (LXXᴮ). In the former
passage 'Sirion' is explained as being the Sidonian, i.e. the Phoenician or
Canaanite, name of Hermon as opposed to the Amorite 'Senir'; and this now
finds confirmation in Ugaritic. Cf. Gordon, *Ugaritic Textbook*, 51, vi 19, 21
= Herdner, *Mission de Ras Shamra* X, 4, vi 19, 21; also Driver, *Canaanite
Myths and Legends*, pp. 98 f.   ⁵ vv. 3–9.

> The Voice of Yahweh soundeth over the waters;
> > The most glorious God hath thundered forth,
> > > Even Yahweh, over the many waters.
> The Voice of Yahweh is full of power;
> > The Voice of Yahweh is full of splendour.
> The Voice of Yahweh shattereth the cedars,
> > Yahweh doth shatter the cedars of Lebanon.
> He maketh Lebanon skip like a calf,
> > And Sirion like the young of the wild-ox.
> The Voice of Yahweh cleaveth flames of fire;
> > The Voice of Yahweh convulseth the wilderness,
> > > Yahweh doth convulse the wilderness of Kadesh.
> The Voice of Yahweh doth make hinds to calve,
> > And causeth the birth of kids in haste,[1]
> > > While all His Temple echoeth the word 'Glory!'

The whole is then brought to a triumphant conclusion in words which make completely clear the ground for such an atmosphere of excitement:[2]

> Yahweh is enthroned over the flood;[3]
> Yahweh is enthroned as King for ever.
> Yahweh will give strength to His people;
> Yahweh will endow[4] His people with welfare (שָׁלוֹם).

To sum up, the theme of this early hymn is obviously that of Yahweh's Kingship over what we should call the realm of nature; and this assurance of His enthronement over the physical universe and, in particular, the chaos of waters or cosmic sea brings with it a guarantee that He can be relied upon to ensure the seasonal rains and the consequent prosperity of His people. In virtue of both its content and its date, therefore, we have good grounds for associating this particular psalm with the occasion under discussion, i.e. Israel's great autumnal festival as celebrated in the Jerusalem Temple during the period of the monarchy.[5]

---

[1] Cf. G. R. Driver, *J.T.S.* xxxii (1930–1), pp. 255 f.   [2] vv. 10–11.

[3] For the cosmic significance of the Hebrew term, see J. Begrich, 'Mabbūl. Eine exegetisch-lexikalische Studie', *Z.S.* vi (1928), pp. 135–53, reprinted in *Gesammelte Studien zum Alten Testament* (1964), pp. 39–54.

[4] *lit.* 'bless'.

It is difficult to resist the impression that Isaiah's vision at the time of his

The foregoing composition acquires added importance, however, in that it now seems to fix the date and interpretation of a number of similar pieces in the Psalter, e.g. Psalm xciii, which may be rendered as follows:

It is Yahweh who is King![1] He is clothed in majesty;
Yahweh is clothed, He is girded with strength!

'call' (vi. 1 ff.) should be seen against this background. Cf., for example, the antiphonal hymn with its emphasis upon the fact that the whole earth is full of Yahweh's 'Glory' (verse 3), the vivid impression of an earthquake in the rocking of the Temple (verse 4), and the final realization, 'Mine eyes have seen the King, Yahweh of Hosts' (verse 5). Cf., in principle, Alt, *Kleine Schriften zur Geschichte des Volkes Israel*, i. pp. 349 ff.

[1] The present writer is not convinced by Mowinckel's argument that the expression מָלַךְ ‎" in this and the other passages to be discussed must mean that Yahweh *has beome* King, and that we should think in terms of an annual enthronement of Yahweh. Cf. *Psalmenstudien II*, pp. 6 ff.; also *Offersang og sangoffer*, pp. 523–6, and now *The Psalms in Israel's Worship*, ii, pp. 222–4 (in reply to O. Eissfeldt, 'Jahwe als König', *Z.A.W.* xlvi (1928), pp. 100 ff.). In the present writer's opinion the thought which dominates these psalms is that of Yahweh's Kingship from the beginning to the end of time, the emphasis lying rather upon the thought that it is Yahweh who *is* King. As will be seen, this is also true of Ps. xlvii. 9 (EVV. 8), despite (*a*) the exception which even Eissfeldt makes in this case, op. cit., p. 101, and (*b*) the stress which is also laid upon this particular passage by H. J. Kraus, *Die Königsherrschaft Gottes im Alten Testament*, B.H.T. 13 (1951), pp. 5 ff. See below, p. 66, n. 3, and p. 77, n. 1: and note indeed that Mowinckel's view is clearly belied by verse 2 of the psalm under discussion.

Since the publication of the first edition of this monograph D. Michel, 'Studien zu den sogenannten Thronbesteigungspsalmen', *V.T.* vi. (1956), pp. 40–68, has rightly stressed the fact that the verb מָלַךְ denotes the *activity* proper to a king, i.e. the function of 'reigning'; and, indeed, this is recognized by the translators of A.V., R.V., and R.S.V. in the passage under consideration. Further, despite the arguments of (i) A. S. Kapelrud, 'Nochmals *Jahwä mālāk*', *V.T.* xiii (1963), pp. 229–31, who maintains that the activity implied by the expression under discussion is 'ingressiv sowohl als durativ', and thinks to translate the Hebrew by 'Jahwe herrscht jetzt aktiv als König', and (ii) E. Lipiński, 'Yāhweh mâlâk', *Biblica* xliv (1963), pp. 405–60, and *La Royauté de Yahwé dans la poésie et le culte de l'ancien Israël* (1965), pp. 336–91, whose citation of supposedly relevant comparative material from Accadian, Egyptian, and Ugaritic sources has, it seems to me, little if any bearing on the question, I find no evidence to show that the form מָלַךְ is ever used in the Old Testament of anything but an existent condition, whatever the temporal circumstances may be. This is not to deny that the form is sometimes used in circumstances which give it an inchoative colouring; but, as I see it, such colouring is not inherent in the form but is due to the light which is shed upon the form by its context. Thus in such a case as מָלַךְ אַבְשָׁלוֹם (2 Sam. xv. 10: cf. 2 Kings ix. 13) the Hebrew simply means

Yea, the world doth continue immovable!
Thy throne was established of old;
Thou Thyself art from ages past!

The currents lift up, O Yahweh,
The currents lift up their voice;
The currents lift up their clamour.

Yahweh in the heights is mightier
Than the voice of the many waters,[1]
Mighty as are the breakers of the sea.

Thy testimonies are strongly supported;
It is seemly that Thy House should be holy,
O Yahweh, who abidest throughout the years![2]

The similarity to Psalm xxix in both form and content is so
marked that there appears to be every justification for the
view that it was intended for the same occasion. The order of
the opening words יְ מָלַךְ, i.e. 'It is Yahweh who is King',
sounds a somewhat polemical note, emphasizing the fact,
as in the case of Psalm xxix, that it is the God of Israel who is
supreme in the general assembly of the gods.[3] Moreover,

'Absalom is king' or, more forcefully, 'Absalom reigneth'; but we gather from
the context that the exercising of this function by Absalom is something
new, the addition of the words 'in Hebron' (as compared with the simple
form of the corresponding statement in 2 Kings ix. 13) indicating the temporary seat of government under what is intended to be a new régime.
On the other hand, the context of the statement מָלַךְ אֱלֹהָיִךְ, meaning quite
simply 'Thy God is King' or, more forcefully, 'Thy God reigneth', with which
the great prophet of the Exile sums up the good news now on its way to
Zion (Isa. lii. 7), does not require one to think in terms of a formal proclama-
tion to the effect that, with the overthrow of Babylon, Zion's God has become
King; rather, it offers Zion the glad assurance that, despite possible appear-
ances to the contrary during the long years of exile, the evidence is now at
hand to prove that Yahweh is still King, the order of the words also showing
the point at issue to be the reality of Yahweh's Kingship rather than any
question as to who among the gods is King (cf. n. 3).

[1] See above, p. 63, n. 3.

[2] The expression לְאֹרֶךְ יָמִים (*lit.* 'for length of days') should be construed
closely with the tetragrammaton. Cf. *The Vitality of the Individual in the
Thought of Ancient Israel*, p. 106, n. 7, 2nd edit., p. 108, n. 4; and observe
how the psalmist thus carries forward the thought of verse 2, *ad fin.*

[3] Cf. the simple statement מָלַךְ אֲדֹנִיָּהוּ, 'Adonijah is king' (1 Kings i.
11) with the inverted form אֲדֹנִיָּה מָלַךְ (verse 18), where stress is clearly

the theme of the psalm is clearly that of Yahweh's power over the primeval ocean with its multitude of waters and its many currents;[1] and this time we are reminded that it was in virtue of His triumph over this cosmic sea that He was able to bring the habitable world into existence, establishing it firmly above the flood. Finally, it is to be observed that the psalm ends, like Psalm xxix, on a note of assurance with regard to the future, based this time upon the thought that Yahweh, who is eternal in being, has the power to fulfil the 'testimonies' or 'promises' (עֵדֹות), to which He is committed under the terms of His covenant with Israel;[2] so that it is but proper that He should enjoy the worship of His people. In the circumstances it seems reasonable to infer that the promises include the all-important one of rain (which was the blessing *par excellence*), and that the thought of Yahweh's control over the cosmic sea, which dominates

being laid upon the fact that, contrary to David's solemn promise that Solomon should succeed him, 'it is Adonijah who is king'. Cf. in general L. Koehler, 'Syntactica III. *IV. Jahwäh mālāk*', *V.T.* iii (1953), pp. 188 f., who is right in his primary inference from the order of the words in the Hebrew expression under discussion but is without justification in the conclusion which he then draws with regard to the dating of this and the corresponding psalms; as against J. Ridderbos, 'Jahwäh Malak', *V.T.* iv (1954), pp. 87–89, with whose further argument I also disagree, in part, for reasons which are sufficiently indicated above, p. 65, n. 1.

[1] For this special sense of the term נָהָר, which is the normal word for 'river', see Ps. xxiv. 2 (as below, p. 73); Jonah ii. 4 (EVV. 3); also, perhaps, Isa. xliv. 27. It now finds illustration in the Ugaritic texts, i.e. in the account of the conflict between Baal and 'Prince Sea' (*zbl ym*) or 'Judge River' (*ṭpṭ nhr*). Cf. Gordon, op. cit., 68, 12 ff. = Herdner, op. cit., 2, iv 12 ff.; also Driver, *Canaanite Myths and Legends*, pp. 81 ff.

[2] The word עֵדָה, which occurs in the Old Testament only in the plural, is traditionally rendered by the word 'testimony'; but it must be borne in mind that it is used in the Old Testament in a specialized sense, i.e. not of that which one testifies to have happened in the past (i.e. evidence) but of that which one protests shall happen in the future (i.e. a solemn promise or pledge), and so, specifically, of the terms of the covenant or, rather, the covenants between Yahweh and His votaries. Accordingly it may be used either (*a*) of Yahweh's promises to His followers, as here, or (*b*) of the undertakings which He requires of them in return, i.e. His 'laws'. Cf., for example, Pss. xxv. 10, cxxxii. 12; and see above, pp. 22 ff. The writer hopes to develop this point more fully in another connexion; see *The Vitality of the Individual in the Thought of Ancient Israel*, p. 88, n. 1, 2nd edit., p. 86, n. 7.

the psalm, is again the assurance that this need can be met. At the same time, in this concluding reference to the covenant relationship between Yahweh and His people, we are carried a step further in our recognition of the way in which the old Canaanite mythology was remodelled in relation to the Hebrew traditions with their focus in the events at Sinai–Horeb.

The last point is important; for another of the so-called enthronement psalms presents us with the other side of the picture, laying stress not on Yahweh's promises to Israel but on Israel's corresponding obligations towards Yahweh. This is Psalm xcv, which opens with a summons to unite in the worship of Yahweh (i) as the great God and King who is also the Creator of the earth, and (ii) as the Maker and Shepherd of His chosen people Israel:[1]

> O come, let us applaud Yahweh,
> Let us acclaim the Rock that is our salvation.
> Let us approach His Person with thanksgiving,
> While we acclaim Him with songs.
> For Yahweh is a great God,
> Even the great King over all the gods;
> In whose Hand are the depths of the earth,
> To whom also the summits of the mountains belong;
> Whose is the sea, which He Himself made,
> And the dry land, which His own Hands moulded.
> Come, let us make obeisance, let us bow down,
> Let us kneel before Yahweh our Maker;
> For it is He who is our God, while we
> Are the people whom He doth shepherd, the flock under
> His Hand.

At this point, however, the course of the utterance undergoes a change. The speaker, instead of acting as the leader of the assembly in a call to worship, now becomes the representative of Yahweh; and as such he administers on this solemn day an equally solemn charge to the worshippers not to be like their disobedient forefathers in the wilderness, but to hearken dutifully to the omnipotent God who has

---

[1] vv. 1–7ab.

led His chosen people so signally into the land which He had selected as His earthly home. He begins with the significant appeal:[1]

> O that *today* ye may hearken to His Voice!

Then the personality of the speaker (possibly a cultic prophet[2]) gives way, as it were, to that of the Godhead; so that, acting as an extension of the divine Personality,[3] he proceeds to address his hearers as Yahweh Himself, and reminds them of this lesson in loyalty from the period of the Wandering:[4]

> 'Harden not your heart as at Meribah (i.e. 'Contention'),
>   As on the day at Massah (i.e. 'Trial') in the wilderness,
> When your fathers put Me on trial,
>   Tested Me, though they had seen what I had done.
> Through forty years I loathed
> [That][5] generation, and said,
> "They are a people errant of heart,
>   A people who ignore My ways."
> Wherefore I swore in My wrath
>   That they should not enter My homeland.'[6]

All this, however, is wholly in line with the fact that, as is now generally recognized, the agricultural festivals of Canaan were taken over by the Hebrews and given an historical interpretation, the dwelling in booths at the Feast of Tabernacles coming to be treated as a reminder of the time when Israel dwelt in tents in the wilderness—the very theme of the present psalm.[7] In other words, the first part of our psalm, with its characteristic emphasis upon Yahweh's universal Kingship and His power in Creation, is mainly a legacy from Canaanite mythology, while the second part, with its emphasis upon the lesson in obedience which is to be drawn from the history of the Wandering, is based upon the Hebrew traditions concerning the great

---

[1] Verse 7c.   [2] See above, p. 22, n. 3.
[3] Cf. *The One and the Many in the Israelite Conception of God*, pp. 36 ff., 2nd edit., pp. 32 ff.   [4] vv. 8–11.   [5] Cf. LXX, Jerome, S.
[6] See above, p. 22, n. 1.
[7] Cf. Lev. xxiii. 42 f. (H): and see above, p. 58, n. 1.

events of the Exodus; and, all in all, we have good reason
to believe that both together formed an important element
in the liturgy of the great autumnal festival as celebrated
in Jerusalem during the period of the monarchy.[1]

In Psalm xcix, another of the so-called enthronement
psalms, we have an obvious companion-piece to the foregoing composition, bringing the sacred story of Yahweh's
dealings with Israel down to the years which saw the rise
of the monarchy and the transference of the Ark to its new
home on Mount Zion. In the first part of the psalm an
eschatological note is clearly sounded, and we are given a
glimpse of that ultimate purpose of Yahweh in choosing
Israel which, as we shall see, is the dominant theme of the
ritual and mythology of this festival which we are attempting
in some measure to reconstruct, i.e.:[2]

> It is Yahweh who is King! The peoples quake.
> He that is seated on the cherubim! The earth trembleth.
> Great is Yahweh, whose home is in Zion;
> He is exalted above all the peoples.
> Let them praise Thy Name as great and terrible,
> One which is mighty in its holiness.[3]

---

[1] Cf. Psalm lxxxi, which offers a remarkable parallel to Psalm xcv in both
form and content, although it appears to stand much closer to the pure
Hebrew tradition. This may well be so, for it seems to have come from the
north; and, what is even more important in the present connexion, there are
ample grounds for believing that it was composed for use at the celebration
of some New Year festival of the pre-exilic period. Cf. Snaith, *The Jewish
New Year Festival*, pp. 99–103. It is possible, too, that the Song of Miriam
(Exod. xv. 1–18, 21) belongs to the same circle of poems; for it links in much
the same way the Hebrew traditions concerning the Exodus, specifically the
miraculous deliverance at the Sea of Reeds, with the celebration of Yahweh's
uniqueness amongst the gods, His settlement in Canaan as His chosen
earthly home, and, finally, the fact that He is the everlasting King. On the
other hand, Psalm c, which has one or two points of contact with Psalm xcv
and is commonly classed with the so-called enthronement psalms (although
there is no explicit reference to Yahweh's Kingship), is really of far too general
a character to be ascribed with any certainty to a particular festival.

[2] vv. 1–5.

[3] *lit.* 'Holy is it—and mighty.' It is difficult to obtain sense from the consonantal text of verses 3 and 4 as vocalized in M.T.; but the meaning of these
lines becomes clear, if the first word of verse 4 is read as וְעֹז and construed
with verse 3. The cause of the trouble is probably the view that we have here
a refrain corresponding to that which occurs in verses 5c and 9c.

> Being a King who loveth justice,
>> Thou hast established equity,
> Thou hast wrought
>> Justice and righteousness in Jacob.
> Extol Yahweh our God,
>> And make obeisance at His footstool;
>>> Such is His holiness!

Thus, as is made clear in the second part of the psalm, we are shown here the ultimate issue of those long years of discipline under the leadership of Yahweh which began with the Exodus, i.e.:[1]

> Moses, and Aaron as His priest,
>> And Samuel as one who calls on His Name
>>> Would cry to Yahweh, and He would answer them.[2]
> In the pillar of cloud He would speak to those
>> Who kept His testimonies and the statute He gave them.
> Thou, Yahweh our God, didst answer them;
>> Thou wast for them a forbearing God,
>>> While punishing their misdeeds.
> Extol Yahweh our God,
>> And make obeisance at His holy hill;
>>> For such is the holiness of Yahweh our God!

The point of view which the psalm reveals is thus perfectly clear, and may be summed up by saying that, after the long vicissitudes of the Wandering and the Settlement, Yahweh is now firmly established in Zion, where, manifesting His presence as 'He that is seated on the cherubim' through the

---

[1] vv. 6–9.

[2] The traditional rendering of this verse, which numbers Moses with Yahweh's priests (e.g. A.V. 'Moses and Aaron among his priests, and Samuel among them that call upon his name'), is due to a misunderstanding of Hebrew syntax. In the first metrical line of the Hebrew there are two examples of the *beth essentiae* in association with a plural of excellence (cf., for example, Ps. cxviii. 7a, as below, p. 125; and see further G.K., §§ 119*i*, 124*g–i*); and the reference is (*a*) to Moses who is in a class by himself, (*b*) to Aaron as Yahweh's priest *par excellence*, and (*c*) to Samuel as His prophet *par excellence*. For the terminology in the last case, see *The Cultic Prophet in Ancient Israel*, pp. 47 ff., 2nd edit., pp. 54 ff. Accordingly there is not the slightest justification for the claim that, as Moses and Samuel are here classed along with Aaron as priests, this harmonizes with the late dating of the so-called enthronement psalms. Cf., for example, Gunkel, H.K., *in loc.*

instrumentality of the Ark,[1] He is to rule over the earth
as the universal King; and, what is more, the achievement of justice and righteousness amongst His own chosen
people is to be the guarantee of His actual presence as a
King who is resolved that His rule shall be just and equi-
table.

Enough has been said to sketch the general background
of our festival, and we may now take a further step in its
attempted reconstruction by observing that in several
psalms we have evidence for a procession in which Yahweh
is again acclaimed as King. The first of these to engage our
attention is Psalm xxiv, which clearly requires us to think
in terms of a scene in which the Ark, as the forementioned
symbol of Yahweh's presence and the focus of His worship,
is being borne in procession up the slopes of Mount Zion
towards the gates of Solomon's Temple. The psalm itself,
which may have something of an antiphonal character,[2]
begins significantly enough with a brief reference to Yahweh's activity in Creation:[3]

[1] Cf. Exod. xxv. 18 ff. (P); 1 Sam. iv. 4; 2 Sam. vi. 2 (cf. 1 Chron. xiii. 6);
2 Kings xix. 15 (cf. Isa. xxxvii. 16); Ps. lxxx. 2 (EVV. 1): and, for a discussion
of the archaeological data now available for our understanding of the symbolism associated with these composite figures so characteristic of the
mythology of the ancient Near East, see P. (E.) Dhorme and L. H. Vincent,
'Les Chérubins', *R.B.* xxxv (1926), pp. 328–58, 481–95; W. C. Graham and
H. G. May, *Culture and Conscience. An Archaeological Study of the New
Religious Past in Ancient Palestine* (1936), pp. 248 ff. See also, for a suggestive
if somewhat speculative attempt to make use of such archaeological data in
order to penetrate behind the work of P to a different origin for this expression in its association with the Ark, O. Eissfeldt, 'Jahwe Zebaoth', *Miscel-
lanea Academica Berolinensia* (1950), pp. 126–50: and now, in general, J.
Trinquet, art. 'Kerub, Kerubim', *D.B.S.* v (1957), cols. 161–86; R. de Vaux,
'Les Chérubins et l'arche d'alliance. Les sphinx gardiens et les trônes divins
dans l'Ancien Orient', *M.U.S.J.* xxxvii (1961–2), pp. 93–124.

[2] It has been argued, on the ground of content and variation in metre, that
Psalm xxiv may be divided up into two or three originally independent
pieces: cf., for example, J. Maier, *Das altisraelitische Ladeheiligtum*, B.Z.A.W.
93 (1965), p. 77. However, we must beware of using such considerations as an
argument for chopping up a composition of this kind in so mechanical a way,
when we ought to be taking into consideration the question of a liturgical
Sitz im Leben with all that this may have involved in terms of (i) ritual
background and corresponding variation in theme, and (ii) musical accompaniment.   [3] vv. 1–2.

> The earth is Yahweh's, and all that filleth it,
>> The world and they that dwell therein;
>> For it is He who founded it upon the seas,
>> And doth maintain it above the ocean currents.[1]

This is followed by a short section, couched in terms of question and answer, in which one is reminded of the moral integrity that Yahweh requires of His worshippers:[2]

> Who may ascend Yahweh's hill?
>> Who may stand in His holy place?
> The clean of hands and the pure of heart,
>> Who hath not made falsity his aim,
>> And sworn with intent to deceive!
> He shall receive blessing[3] from the presence of Yahweh,
>> A due response from the God who is his salvation.
> Such is the lot[4] (*or* circle)[5] of those who look for Him,
>> Those who seek ⌜the Person (*lit.* Face) of the God of⌝ Jacob.[6]

Finally we have the appeal of the worshippers that the gates of the Temple should be opened to admit Yahweh into His sanctuary; and again we note that, as in Psalm xxix, the theme of the song is the actual presence of Yahweh as King in all His attendant 'Glory':[7]

> Lift up your heads, O ye gates;
>> Be lifted up, O everlasting doors;
>>> That the glorious King may enter!

> Who is this—'The glorious King'?
>> Yahweh strong and mighty,
>> Yahweh mighty in battle!

> Lift up your heads, O ye gates;
>> Lift them up, O everlasting doors;
>>> That the glorious King may enter!

---

[1] See above, p. 67, n. 1.   [2] vv. 3–6.   [3] See above, p. 48, n. 1.

[4] Cf. G. R. Driver, *J.B.L.* liii (1934), p. 285.

[5] Cf. F. J. Neuberg, *J.N.E.S.* ix (1950), pp. 216 f.

[6] So LXX. M.T. 'Thy Person (*lit.* Face), O Jacob.'

[7] vv. 7–10. Cf. 1 Sam. iv. 19–22, i.e. the way in which the wife of Phinehas, when she heard that the Philistines had captured the Ark and that her husband as well as her father-in-law was dead, named her new-born child 'Ichabod' (i.e. 'Inglorious'), saying:

> 'Glory is an exile from Israel,
>> For the Ark of God hath been taken.'

> Who *is* this—'The glorious King'?
> Yahweh of Hosts,[1]
> *He* is 'The glorious King'!

Two points stand out in this important psalm, and they must be stressed. In the first place we have to note that, as in the case of the preceding psalm, Yahweh's Kingship is here represented as something more than a sovereignty over the realm of nature. It also includes His sovereign power over what we should call the moral realm; He is, as we shall have further occasion to see, vitally concerned with the way in which men behave. In other words, the divine King is not only worshipped as the Creator; He is also revered as a Judge, who demands that those who would rely upon Him must be able to plead their innocence in both thought and deed and their freedom from all taint of insincerity. The second point to be observed is the emphasis which is laid upon the identification of this King with One who has been proved 'mighty in battle'. That is to say, the procession of this God who is so actively concerned with both the physical and the moral realms is obviously a triumphant one. It is as a victorious warrior that the divine King is now entering His Temple.

A similar situation and indeed the climax of the procession is suggested by Psalm xlvii, in which the Kingship of Yahweh is again an object of emphasis; and this time we have to notice at the outset that, in being acclaimed as King, Yahweh is also addressed as 'Most High', an expression which we have already seen to be the special appellation of the high god worshipped in Jerusalem in pre-Israelite days. That is to say, we have another indication that we are on the right track in seeing in this celebration of Yahweh as King an adaptation of the earlier worship characteristic of this one-time Canaanite city. The psalm itself falls readily into two parts, the first of which begins with a universal summons to hail the heavenly King with

---

[1] Or 'Yahweh Almighty'? Cf., for example, Eissfeldt, loc. cit.; and see in general B. N. Wambacq, *L'Épithète divine Jahvé Seba'ot: Étude philologique, historique et exégétique* (1947).

clapping of hands and loud acclamation.[1] This is followed
by the exultant affirmation that the Kingship of Yahweh is
a universal one which guarantees the supremacy of His
own chosen people over all the other nations; and the
strophe as a whole closes with a word-play on the appellation 'Most High' (עֶלְיוֹן) in the triumphant assertion that
Yahweh has ascended (עָלָה) to His Temple with appropriate acclamation and to the sound of the horn.[2] Accordingly
there seems to be no good reason to doubt that here again,
as in the case of Psalm xxiv, we should think in terms of a
procession which has just ascended to the Temple on Mount
Zion in company with the Ark as the guarantee of Yahweh's
presence in power with His people; and, this being the case,
we are now in a position to see why such emphasis was laid
in Psalm xxiv upon the fact that it is as a victorious warrior
that the divine King enters His sanctuary. As such He is
the guarantor in some way of Israel's ultimate supremacy
over the nations. The first strophe, then, may be rendered
as follows:[3]

> Clap your hands, all ye peoples;
> Make acclamation to God with applauding voice.
> For Yahweh Most High (עֶלְיוֹן) is to be feared,
> The great King over all the earth!

[1] For a valuable discussion of the significance of the corresponding
Hebrew root, which is used again in verse 6, see P. Humbert, *La 'Terou'a':
analyse d'un rite biblique* (1946), although, in the present writer's opinion, he
tends to follow Mowinckel a little too closely in his stress on the supposed
annual enthronement of Yahweh.

[2] For this use of the verb עָלָה with reference to the ascent of Mount Zion,
see Ps. xxiv. 3, as above, p. 73, and Ps. lxviii. 19 (EVV. 18), as below, p. 82);
and, for the subsequent word-play on עֶלְיוֹן, it should be borne in mind
that, just as the Ark is the symbol of Yahweh's Person, so Mount Zion
corresponds to the divine Mount of Assembly, and the Temple itself is the
earthly counterpart of the divine King's heavenly Palace. Cf. Ps. xlviii. 3
(EVV. 2), as below, p. 86; and, for the elaboration of this idea in later Judaism,
see, for example, Patai, *Man and Temple*, pp. 130 ff.

[3] vv. 2–6 (EVV. 1–5). In the ensuing translation of this psalm and its
fellows little attempt has been made to restore the divine name 'Yahweh' in
those cases where it, rather than the present reading 'God', may have been
original. There can be no reasonable doubt that such substitution has been
made in many of the psalms of Books II and III (i.e. Pss. xlii–lxxxix); but it
is difficult to determine every case.

He subdueth[1] the peoples beneath us,
  Yea, the nations beneath our feet,
While our inheritance is of His choosing,
  This proud possession of His beloved Jacob.
God hath ascended (עָלָה) with acclamation,
  Even Yahweh, to the sound of the horn!

The second strophe repeats and expands the thought of the first, emphasizing, to begin with, the universal Kingship of Yahweh and then unfolding its implications as to the supremacy of Israel over the nations, inasmuch as earth's rulers are now all united in subjection to Him. Finally, like the first strophe again, it closes with a word-play on the appellation 'Most High', summing up the theme of the whole psalm in the thought that Yahweh in His universal, sovereign power as the divine King is highly exalted (נַעֲלָה):[2]

Sing the praises of God, sing praises;
  Sing praises to our King, sing praises.
Of a truth He is King throughout[3] the earth;
  Sing the praises of God for His success;[4]
God is King over the nations;
  God is seated on His holy throne.
The princes of the peoples are assembled
  With Him[5] who is the God of Abraham,
For the rulers[6] of earth are subject to God,
  Who is highly exalted (נַעֲלָה)!

---

[1] It may not be without significance that the rare verbal form in this stichos, i.e. the *Hiph'îl* of √דבר, is found elsewhere only once—and then on the lips of the Messiah when he says of the Most High in exactly parallel fashion to the above, 'He hath subdued the peoples beneath me.' Ps. xviii. 48 (EVV. 47), as below, p. 123. For the term itself, see G. R. Driver, *J.T.S.* xxxi (1929–30), pp. 283 f. [2] vv. 7–10 (EVV. 6–9).

[3] Insert עַל with many MSS., and vocalize מֶלֶךְ as מָלַךְ.

[4] *lit.* 'as One who is successful', i.e. the *Hiph'îl* participle of √שׂכל used predicatively: cf. the similar construction in Ps. xcix. 3, as above, p. 70, i.e. 'Let them praise Thy Name as great and terrible.' For the use of this form in an obviously specialized way to denote a discreet and, therefore, successful individual, see 1 Sam. xviii. 14 f.; Job xxii. 2; Pss. xiv. 2, xli. 2 (EVV. 1); Prov. x. 5, 19, xiv. 35, xvi. 20, xvii. 2. Cf., too, Jer. xxiii. 5, where this verb is used to describe the successful ruler who is to issue from the House of David.

[5] Vocalizing עִם as עָם with LXX, S, and V.

[6] LXX: κραταιοί. See further G. R. Driver, *J.T.S.* xxxiii (1931–2), p. 44, and xxxiv (1933), pp. 383 f., followed by K.B., p. 494a.

Clearly Yahweh has returned in triumph to His throne, having asserted His age-long Kingship once and for all by His complete subjection of the nations and their earthly rulers.[1] This graphic description of the kings of the earth as being brought together in subjection to Yahweh is one which we need to bear in mind; for we shall see in due course that they appear to have been formally represented as the captives of this triumphant and victorious King.

The next hymn of this kind to engage our attention is Psalm lxviii, which is extraordinarily graphic and picturesque in its description of the triumphant passage of the divine King into His Temple, and, as a result, succeeds in taking us still further in our attempted reconstruction of the ritual and mythology of this festival. It is also deserving of note, perhaps, that, like Psalm xxix, this hymn is said to offer close parallels to the Ugaritic texts, and for this reason has been similarly assigned to the early years of the monarchy, specifically the tenth century B.C.[2] While the parallels with Ugaritic are apt to be exaggerated, the foregoing discussion has opened the way for us to recognize that the apparent confusion of its thought, which has made it something of a *crux interpretum*,[3] is due to a weaving

[1] Despite the argument of J. Ridderbos, 'Jahwäh Malak', *V.T.* iv (1954), pp. 87–89, the present writer cannot see that, following the analogy of such passages as 2 Sam. xv. 10 and 2 Kings ix. 13, one should regard the normal order of verb–subject in verse 9 (EVV. 8) and again in Isa. lii. 7, *ad fin.*, as requiring the rendering 'Yahweh has become King'. In these passages from Samuel and Kings the expression under discussion need mean no more than 'So-and-so is king', the context serving to show that in these cases the expression has the force of 'So-and-so is (now) king'. See above, p. 65, n. 1, where the foregoing passages are now dealt with at greater length.

[2] Albright, as above, p. 62, nn. 1 and 2.

[3] The apparent lack of connexion within the psalm has led to the suggestion that it is a series of *incipits* or catalogue of hymns from about the time of Solomon. See W. F. Albright, 'A Catalogue of Early Hebrew Lyric Poems (Psalm LXVIII)', *H.U.C.A.* xxiii (1950–1), pp. 1–39, who draws attention to the somewhat similar suggestion made by Schmidt, H. A. T., *in loc.*, and T. H. Robinson, in Oesterley, *The Psalms*, *in loc.* While Albright's article is invaluable for its treatment of individual points, the present writer cannot but regard its main thesis as a counsel of despair. Cf. S. Mowinckel, *Der achtundsechzigste Psalm*, A.N.V.A.O. II, 1953, No. 1 (1953), who defends the unity of the psalm along much the same lines as those offered here.

together, once again, of Hebrew and Canaanite strands of culture and, what is more, to an over-all ideological pattern which is almost wholly strange to the modern Western mind. The psalm opens with an obvious reference to the Ark, which thus appears to be the dominant factor in the actual procession, the language being almost identical with that which was in use when this effective guarantee of Yahweh's presence set out on the different stages of the journey through the wilderness;[1] and this is followed by the thought of Yahweh's power in defence of orphans and widows, the friendless, and those in bondage. Further, it is to be observed that Yahweh's followers are described, somewhat ideally it seems,[2] as the 'righteous' (צַדִּיקִים), while their enemies are referred to categorically as the 'wicked' (רְשָׁעִים) or the 'rebellious' (סוֹרְרִים), and, as such, are condemned to dwell in the arid waste.[3] That is to say,[4]

> When God ariseth, His enemies are scattered,
> They that hate Him flee before Him.
> As smoke is dispersed, so is their dispersal;[5]
> As wax melteth in the presence of fire,
> So do the wicked perish before God.
> The righteous, however, are glad;
> They exult before God,
> Rejoicing for gladness.
> Sing unto God, sing the praises of His Name;
> Extol Him who came riding through the deserts,[6]

---

[1] Num. x. 35 (JE).

[2] Cf. Kirkpatrick, C.B., *in loc.*

[3] Cf. again Zech. xiv. 16 f.; and see further Pedersen, *Israel I–II*, pp. 353 ff., E.T., pp. 453 ff.   [4] vv. 2–7 (EVV. 1–6).

[5] Vocalizing the consonantal text so as to read כְּהִנָּדֵף and תִּנָּדֵף. Cf. Albright, op. cit., p. 17.

[6] It is now commonly maintained that לָרֹכֵב בָּעֲרָבוֹת should be emended to לרכב ערפות so as to make it conform to the expression *rkb ʿrpt*, 'Rider of the Clouds', which appears frequently in the Ugaritic texts as an epithet of Baal. Cf., Gordon op. cit., 51, iii 11, 18, v 122; 67, ii 7; 1 Aqht, 43 f.; 'nt, ii 40; (= Herdner, op. cit., 4, iii 11, 18, v 122; 5, ii 7; 19, 43 f.; 3, ii 40: cf. Driver, *Canaanite Myths and Legends*, pp. 94 f., 98 f., 104 f., 58 f., 84 f.) 2001, rev. 18. See, for example, H. L. Ginsberg, *J.B.L.* lxii (1943), pp. 112 f.; Albright, op. cit., p. 18. The present writer is unconvinced by this suggestion, for it fails to take due notice of the context, which clearly reflects the

Whose Name consisteth of 'Yah',[1] and exult before Him!
God in His holy abode
Is a father of the fatherless and a defender of widows;
God giveth the lonely a home wherein to dwell,
He skilfully[2] setteth free those in bondage;
But (אַך) the rebellious make their home in the arid waste!

The last reference gives the key to the situation, for the ultimate issue in this picturesque statement of the deliverance and well-being vouchsafed to the righteous is clearly one of rain; and this immediately furnishes an occasion to quote somewhat freely a passage from the Song of Deborah which portrays Yahweh less as a god of war than as a god of earthquake and storm. Moreover, this is followed by an explicit forecast of rain as Yahweh's gift to His chosen people, who are now described in obvious contrast to the nation's foes as 'humble' or 'submissive' (עָנִי).[3]

O Yahweh, when Thou wentest forth before Thy people,
When Thou didst march through the desert,
The earth quaked, yea, the heavens were in downpour
Before Yahweh, Him of Sinai,[4]
Before Yahweh, the God of Israel.

Hebrew traditions of the Wandering and the Settlement: cf., again with due regard to the context, Deut. xxxii. 13. It is true that in verse 34 (EVV. 33) Yahweh is referred to as riding through the heavens; but there the context is very different, for it lays stress on Yahweh's universal power.

[1] Despite G.K., § 119*i*N[3], it seems to me that we have here an excellent example of the *beth essentiae*.

[2] The meaning of the Hebrew term is now made abundantly clear by the Ugaritic texts, notably (*a*) in the form *kṯr* (or *kṯr wḫss*), which is the name of the craftsman of the gods, and (*b*) in the form *kṯrt*, which is used of skilled female singers or 'artistes'. Cf., for example, Gordon, op. cit., (*a*) 51, v 103 ff., vii 20 f.; 2 Aqht, v 9 ff., vi 24 (= Herdner, op. cit., 4, v 103 ff., vii 20 f.; 17, v 9 ff.,: vi 24: cf. Driver, op. cit., pp. 98 f., 100 f.; 52 ff.): (*b*) 2 Aqht, ii 26 ff. (= Herdner, op. cit., 17, ii 26 ff.: cf. Driver, op. cit., pp. 50 f.). See further, for example, H. L. Ginsberg, *B.A.S.O.R.* 72 (Dec. 1938), pp. 13 ff.; Albright, *Archaeology and the Religion of Israel*, pp. 81 f.; Gaster, *Thespis*, pp. 89, 154 ff., 277 f., 2nd edit., pp. 161 ff., 338 ff.

[3] vv. 8–11 (EVV. 7–10). In the ensuing translation the name 'Yahweh' has been substituted for 'God' in verses 8–9 (EVV. 7–8), following the Song of Deborah (Judges v. 4–5).

[4] *lit.* 'who is Sinai'. Cf., for example, Pss. lxxiv. 2, lxxviii. 54; Prov. xxiii. 22. Here, as in Judges v. 5 and again in verse 18 (EVV. 17) below, the term

Thou wilt shed[1] a generous rain, O God,
Over Thine inheritance, when it is exhausted,
That which Thou didst found, in which Thy family[2] doth dwell,
Which in Thy goodness Thou wilt keep in order for the humble,
O God.

Then comes what may at first appear to be an abrupt
transition to the picture of a victory by Yahweh over the
nation's foes, described with a high degree of imaginative
power and, indeed, something of the vigour of the Song
of Deborah.[3]

When the Lord (אֲדֹנָי)[4] doth give the command,
Women in a mighty host spread the good news.
'The kings with their armies flee, they flee!
And she that is home will divide the spoil,
If ye linger there in idleness[5]—
The wings of a dove which is overlaid with silver,
But its pinions with gleaming gold!'
When Shaddai (EVV. 'the Almighty'[6]) scattereth kings,
It is like[7] the falling of snow on Zalmon.[8]

'Sinai' is evidently used with the force of a divine name. Cf. the way in
which 'Carmel' was used not only of the sacred mountain which bore this
name but also of the god who was worshipped there, as shown by O. Eissfeldt, *Der Gott Karmel*, S.B.D.A.W. 1953: 1 (1953), pp. 8 ff., 19, and
K. Galling, 'Der Gott Karmel und die Ächtung der fremden Götter', in
Geschichte und Altes Testament (A. Alt *Festschrift*), B.H.T. 16 (1953),
pp. 105–25; and, for the general principle, see J. Lewy, 'Les Textes paléo-
assyriens et l'Ancien Testament', *R.H.R.* cx (1934), pp. 44 ff. Cf., too, the
defence of the text offered by H. Grimme, *Z.D.M.G.* l (1896), p. 573,
and W. F. Albright, *J.B.L.* liv (1935), p. 204, *B.A.S.O.R.* 62 (Apr. 1936),
p. 30, which is followed, for example, by J. M. Allegro, *V.T.* v (1955), p. 311,
and T. J. Meek, *J.B.L.* lxxix (1960), p. 332. See further in this connexion
Gordon, *Ugaritic Textbook*, pp. 39 f. (§§ 6. 23 f.); but note also H. Birkeland,
'Hebrew *zæ* and Arabic *ḏū*', *S.T.* ii (1950), pp. 201 f.

[1] Cf. G. R. Driver, *Z.A.W.* l (1932), pp. 142 f.
[2] Cf. *The Vitality of the Individual in the Thought of Ancient Israel*, p. 100,
n. 4, 2nd edit., p. 101, n. 6; Albright, *H.U.C.A.* xxiii, p. 21.
[3] vv. 12–15 (EVV. 11–14).
[4] See above, pp. 35 ff., esp. p. 38.
[5] *lit.* 'if ye lie down between the panniers (*or* within the cattle-pens)',
i.e. of behaving in lazy or carefree fashion. Cf. what appears to be the
corresponding idiom in Gen. xlix. 14, Judges v. 16; and see further K.B.,
p. 580, s.v. מִשְׁפְּתַיִם (*or* O. Eissfeldt, *Kleine Schriften*, iii (1966), pp. 61–70).
[6] See, however, W. F. Albright, 'The Names *Shaddai* and *Abram*', *J.B.L.*
liv (1935), pp. 180–93.

(*Notes 7 and 8 on p. 81.*)

The transition in thought, however, is not nearly so abrupt
as may at first appear, for we have already had occasion
to notice that Yahweh's Kingship carries with it, not only
the thought of His power over the cosmic sea and His
consequent control of the rains, but also the prospect of
victory over the nation's foes; and it is obvious that these
foreign kings threaten the life of Israel quite as much as
would the absence of rain. Accordingly we must not be
surprised to find that these two ideas are woven together in
a remarkably impressive way.

At this point attention is focused on the procession itself, as it makes its way into the Temple; and in an opening
apostrophe the imposing mountains of Bashan are deri-
ded for their jealousy of Mount Zion, which Yahweh has
chosen in place of Mount Sinai to be His earthly abode.
Further, we learn that, as in the case of Psalm xxiv, Yahweh's
entry into the Temple is that of a warrior god who is returning in triumph from a victory over His foes; and,
what is more, He is accompanied by those who have opposed His choice of Mount Zion as His earthly home. As
already indicated and as we shall have still further occasion
to realize, these can scarcely be other than the kings of the
nations who have been threatening the existence of the Holy
City.[1]

> O mighty mountain-range of Bashan,[2]
> O lofty mountain-range of Bashan,
> Why do ye look askance, O lofty mountains,
> At the mount that God hath desired for His abode,
> Yea, where Yahweh would settle for ever?

---

[7] The ב of בָּהּ is simply correlative to that of בְּפָרֵשׂ, and the construction
as a whole indicates that the two conceptions are essentially the same.

[8] Probably the modern *Ğebel Ḥaurân*. Cf. Abel, *Géographie de la Palestine*,
i. pp. 377 f.

[1] vv. 16–19 (EVV. 15–18).

[2] *lit.* 'O mountain(-range) of God(s), O mountain(-range) of Bashan'.
The use of the term 'God(s)' is here idiomatic; and, to appreciate the full
force of the original, the reader should consult the careful discussion of this
and related problems by D. W. Thomas, 'A Consideration of some Unusual
Ways of Expressing the Superlative in Hebrew', *V.T.* iii (1953), pp. 209–24.

The chariots of God are thousands upon thousands;[1]
The Lord (אֲדֹנָי) is amid them, He of Sinai[2] is in the sanctuary!
Thou hast ascended on high, leading Thy captives;
Thou hast taken tribute from amongst mankind,
Even those who rebelled at Yah's choice of a home![3]

The jubilation then reaches its peak in the exultant recognition that Israel's God and Saviour, who is extolled elsewhere as the 'Living God',[4] has delivered them from the onslaught of 'Death', and so assured His chosen people that none of their enemies shall escape their vengeance, though they flee to these heights of Bashan or, at the other extreme, seek refuge in the depths of the sea.[5]

Blessed be the Lord (אֲדֹנָי) continually![6]
God beareth for us the burden of our salvation.
God is for us a god who saveth,
And through Yahweh, the Lord (אֲדֹנָי), 'Death' is expelled.[7]
Yea, God doth crush the head of His enemies,[8]
The hairy skull of him who persisteth in his guilt.
The Lord (אֲדֹנָי) said, 'I will bring back from Bashan,[9]
I will bring back from the depths of the sea,
That thou mayest plunge thy foot in blood,
That the tongue of thy dogs may have its share in the foe.'

This passage, with its emphasis upon the fact that 'Death' is

---

[1] G.K., § 97*h*.   [2] See above, p. 79, n. 4.

[3] *lit.* 'at Yah's settling down'. The Hebrew adds 'God', which is obviously a variant of 'Yah'.

[4] See below, p. 103, and *The Vitality of the Individual in the Thought of Ancient Israel*, pp. 105 ff., 2nd edit., pp. 106 ff.

[5] vv. 20–24 (EVV. 19–23).

[6] *lit.* 'every day'.   [7] Or (following the analogy of Ugaritic): And through Yahweh, the Lord, there is deliverance from 'Death'. Cf. Gordon, *Ugaritic Textbook*, pp. 92 f., 98 f. (§§ 10. 1, 11).

[8] See below, p. 132, n. 5.

[9] The writer can find no justification for the proposal to see in the Hebrew בָּשָׁן of this stichos the equivalent of the Ugaritic *btn*, 'serpent', and in the line as a whole a reference to the mythical monster of the Deep. Cf. Gordon, op. cit., 67, i 1 f.; '*nt*, iii 38 (= Herdner, op. cit., 5, i 1 f.; 3, iii 38: cf. Driver, *Canaanite Myths and Legends*, pp. 102 f., 86 f.): and see further, for example, Gaster, *Thespis*, p. 93; Albright, *H.U.C.A.* xxiii, p. 27. This suggestion again fails to do justice to the context (cf. verse 16 (EVV. 15)), and it exaggerates the significance of the parallelism. The ideas actually involved find ready illustration in Amos ix. 3.

the arch-enemy over whom Yahweh has triumphed, is of quite extraordinary importance and needs to be borne in mind, for we shall meet it again.

Meantime, continuing our way through the psalm, we now find that we are given a more detailed account of the procession itself; and the pointed allusion to Yahweh as 'King', coupled with the reference to the instrumentalists and singers, provides what seems to be the necessary context to Psalm xxiv with its theme of Yahweh's Kingship and its obviously processional background centring in the Ark. Further (and this is most important), we learn that Yahweh, the heavenly King, has passed into the Temple in triumphal procession from 'Israel's Spring'; and this can hardly be other than the spring Gihon, which, as early as the time of David, clearly had some special significance in connexion with the ritual of accession to the throne.[1] Finally, it is to be observed that this vindication of Yahweh's universal sovereignty is evidently thought of in close association with the ancient tribal confederation of Israel, for reference is made to figures who are representative, not only of such southern tribes as those of Benjamin and Judah, but also of tribes from the far north such as Zebulun and Naphtali.[2]

What a spectacle[3] was Thy procession, O God,
    The procession of my God, my King (מַלְכִּי),[4] into the sanctuary!
The singers were in front, the minstrels followed behind,
    All flanked by maidens with their timbrels.
In companies they greeted God,
    Even Yahweh, from Israel's Spring.
Benjamin was there, that mettlesome[5] youth,

[1] Cf. 1 Kings i. 33–35, 45 f.; and see above, pp. 32 f.

[2] vv. 25–28 (EVV. 24–27).

[3] *lit.* 'they have seen', i.e. an active form of the Hebrew verb with an indefinite subject, corresponding to a passive construction in English. Cf. LXX and see G.K. § 144 f.   [4] See above, pp. 35 ff., esp. pp. 38 ff..

[5] Cf. the Arabic رَزَّ, which is used of the emission of short, sharp sounds —specifically the 'twanging' of a bow. The reference appears to be to the military prowess of the tribe of Benjamin as exemplified in the use of the bow. Cf. Gen. xlix. 27 (J); Judges xx. 16; 1 Chron. viii. 40, xii. 2: and see further, for example, Lane, op. cit., s.v.

The nobility of honest-spoken[1] Judah,
The nobility of Zebulun and of Naphtali.

Following this dramatic description of Yahweh's royal passage into the Temple, He is summoned to make known His good will and pleasure as regards His subject peoples, who now come to Jerusalem, not to gain spoil for themselves as they had once fondly hoped, but to present to the God of Israel their own tribute of loyalty and obedience.[2]

Issue Thy commands,[3] O my God, as[4] befitteth Thy might,
 The divine might[5] which Thou hast exercised for us!
How potent Thou art[6] on behalf of Jerusalem;
 Kings bring Thee their offerings!
The wild beast of the marshes[7]
 Hath quelled[8] the assembled steers.
Trampling on the bull-like[9] peoples,
 On those whose pleasure was in[10] silver,
He hath scattered the peoples who delighted in war.
They are coming from Egypt with[11] their tribute;[12]
 Cush hath stretched out[13] its hands to God.

---

[1] Dividing the consonantal text of the enigmatic רִגְמָתָם (EVV. '*and* their council') so as to read רֹגֶם תָּם. For √רגם, see above, p. 45, n. 3; and, for Judah's reputation for honest speaking, see Gen. xxxviii. 26 (J), xliv. 18–34 (J).

[2] vv. 29–32 (EVV. 28–31). These verses, as preserved in M.T., are outstandingly difficult; but the difficulties disappear, when one recognizes that the current division and vocalization of the consonantal text are due to the misunderstanding which arose when once the psalm had lost its original *Sitz im Leben*.

[3] Vocalizing the consonantal text so as to read צַוֵּה with LXX, S, and V.

[4] Dividing the consonantal text so as to read אֱלֹהַי כְּעֻזְּךָ.

[5] Dividing the consonantal text so as to read עֹז הָאֱלֹהִים.

[6] Dividing the consonantal text so as to read מַה־יָכָלְךָ. Elsewhere (Num. xiv. 16 (JE); Deut. ix. 28) the *Qal* infin. constr. of יָכֹל occurs as יְכֹלֶת; but, for the coexistence of such masculine and feminine forms, cf. יָבֵשׁ (Isa. xxvii. 11) and יָבְשֶׁת (Gen. viii. 7 (J)). Cf. Albright, op. cit., p. 32, who nevertheless, in the writer's opinion, unnecessarily goes on to seek uniformity of construction by emending the text so as to read יְכֹלְתָּ.

[7] *lit.* 'the reeds'. [8] Vocalizing the consonantal text so as to read גָּעַר.

[9] *lit.* 'bulls of peoples', i.e. an example of the epexegetical genitive or genitive of apposition. Cf. G.K., § 128*f*, and see above, p. 30, n. 1.

[10] Vocalizing the consonantal text so as to read בְּרֹצֵי.

[11] Vocalizing the consonantal text so as to read יַאְתִיוּ. [12] Vide K.B., s.v.

[12] תָּרִיץ should probably be read as תָּרְץ (with no change as regards

The psalm is then brought to a close with a strophe in general praise of Yahweh's universal power, the whole celebrating the fact that He who came riding through the deserts is also the One who rides through the heavens with thundering 'Voice'.[1]

Ye kingdoms of the earth, sing unto God,
  Sing the praises of the Lord (אֲדֹנָי),
Of Him who rideth through the ancient and lofty heavens;
  Lo, He uttereth His Voice, a mighty Voice!
Ascribe might unto God,
  Whose majesty is over Israel,
    And His might in the clouds!
O God, terrible within Thy sanctuary
  Is He who is the God of Israel,
Who giveth might and strength
  To a people divinely blessed![2]

In fact this reference to Yahweh as One who is the 'Rider of the Clouds'[3] links up admirably with the foregoing association of Israel's King with 'Israel's Spring' (i.e. one of the channels connected with the subterranean ocean), for this is wholly appropriate to a festival which associates the coming of the rains with Yahweh's enthronement over the turbulent waters of the great cosmic sea. All in all, it looks as if something dramatic must have happened at 'Israel's Spring'; and we are left with the question as to what this may have been.

IV

We are now in a position to trace back to a still earlier phase the actual course of this ceremony as it came to be celebrated in the capital of the Southern Kingdom; for

the original consonantal text). Cf. the Accadian TARĀṢU ḲĀTA, 'to stretch out the hand'; and see further F. Perles, *Analekten zur Textkritik des Alten Testaments. Neue Folge*, ii (1922), p. 34. This suggestion overcomes the difficulty of construing 'Cush' as both feminine and masculine, i.e. 'She stretcheth forth (*lit.* runneth out) his hands.'

[1] vv. 33–36 (EVV. 32–35).
[2] Vocalizing the consonantal text so as to read לְעַם בְּרוּךְ אֱלֹהִים. Cf. Gen. xxiv. 31, xxvi. 29 (J).   [3] See above, p. 78, n. 6.

Psalm xlviii, another of the familiar enthronement psalms,
indicates the way in which the forementioned victory over
'Death' has been brought about. It opens with a few
general lines of praise in celebration of the fact that Yahweh
reigns as King and, indeed, as the 'great King' in His city
of Zion; and it is to be observed that the sacred mountain
itself is here extolled as being צָפוֹן or, to adopt the form
of transcription made current by the standard English
Versions, 'Zaphon'[1] (EVV. 'the north'), a name which
appears in the Ugaritic texts as that of the mythological
mountain where Baal, the 'Rider of the Clouds', had his
royal throne.[2] The lines in question may be rendered:[3]

> Great is Yahweh and greatly to be praised
>   In the city of our God (*or* in our divine city)!
> His holy mountain is beautiful in elevation,[4]
>   The joy of all the earth,
> Mount Zion, the heights[5] of Zaphon,
>   The city[6] of the mighty King!

The body of the psalm is then taken up with a vivid picture
of the way in which Yahweh, as the stronghold of His
people, has brought discomfiture to the kings of the earth;
and it is to be noted that this has taken place within the
sacred area itself. Thus we read (in further reference to
Mount Zion):[7]

> God in the palaces thereof
>   Hath shown Himself a stronghold.[8]

---

[1] Joshua xiii. 27.

[2] Cf., for example, Gordon, op. cit., 49, i 28–37; 51, iv–v 84 ff.; 'nt, iii–iv
25 ff., 43–48 (= Herdner, op. cit., 6, i 56–65; 4, iv–v 84 ff.; 3, iii–iv 25 ff.,
43–48: cf. Driver, op. cit., pp. 110 f., 96 ff., 86 f.): and see further R. de
Langhe, *Les Textes de Ras Shamra-Ugarit et leurs rapports avec le milieu
biblique de l'Ancien Testament* (1945), ii, pp. 217–44.

[3] vv. 2–3 (EVV. 1–2).

[4] The metrical structure of the poem as a whole makes it clear that the
last two words of verse 2 (EVV. 1) should be construed with verse 3 (EVV. 2).

[5] *lit.* 'recesses'. Cf. O. Eissfeldt, *Baal Zaphon, Zeus Kasios und der Durchzug
der Israeliten durchs Meer* (1932), pp. 15 f.; and see below, p. 94, n. 1.

[6] N.B. קִרְיַת מֶלֶךְ רָב. Cf. p. 42, n. 3.

[7] vv. 4–8 (EVV. 3–7).

[8] Cf. the refrain of Psalm xlvi, as discussed below, pp. 92 ff.

For, lo, the kings assembled,[1]
They came on together.
They saw, so were they startled;
They were dismayed, alarmed.
Trembling laid hold of them there,
Anguish, like a woman in travail,
Like[2] an east wind, when it doth shatter
The fleets of Tarshish.

The fact of this spectacle is then emphasized in the following terms:[3]

As we have heard, so have we seen
In the city of Yahweh of Hosts,
In the city of our God (*or* in our divine city),
Which God maintaineth for ever.

These lines have rightly been interpreted as indicating the use of some form of symbolic ritual of the type familiar to all students of comparative religion;[4] and this theory is supported in principle by the fact that there is no known historical situation which satisfies the conditions laid down by the unmistakable reference to the overthrow of a group of foreign kings within the city itself. What is more, it harmonizes with the obvious vagueness of the picture—so different, for example, from that of the Song of Deborah but so in keeping with a piece of recurrent ritual. Further, it agrees with the statement that what the worshippers have seen has also been described to them; for this points to the fact that they have not only been spectators of some kind of

---

[1] נוֹעֲדוּ. Cf. the use of the cognate term עֵדָה in the simile of the assembled steers, Ps. lxviii. 31 (EVV. 30), as above, p. 84.

[2] *Beth essentiae* (cf. G.K., § 119*i*), i.e. 'a veritable east wind which shattereth etc.'   [3] Verse 9 (EVV. 8).

[4] Cf. Mowinckel, *Psalmenstudien II*, pp. 126 ff., also *Religion og Kultus* (1950), pp. 71 ff. (or, in the German edition, *Religion und Kultus* (1953), pp. 76 f.), *Offersang og sangoffer*, pp. 177 f. = *The Psalms in Israel's Worship*, i, pp. 181 f.: and see in general G. van der Leeuw, *Phänomenologie der Religion* (1933), pp. 349–55 (2nd edit., revised and enlarged (1956), pp. 420–8), E.T. by J. E. Turner, *Religion in Essence and Manifestation: A Study in Phenomenology* (1938), pp. 373–8, or, in the revised French translation by J. Marty, *La Religion dans son essence et ses manifestations: Phénoménologie de la religion* (1948), pp. 364–70.

ritual performance, but have been instructed as to its
meaning by the accompanying mythology. Even stronger
evidence than all this, however, is to be found in the next
line of the psalm; and for the moment we leave one word
untranslated:[1]

> O God, we have . . . Thy devotion (חֶסֶד)
> In the midst of Thy Temple.

The word which we have left untranslated, the *Pi'ēl* of
דמה√, is rendered in the standard English Versions by 'to
think', e.g. in the Revised Version:

> We have thought on thy lovingkindness, O God,
> In the midst of thy temple.

Such a rendering, however, is wholly inadequate. The
verbal form in question, which means literally 'to make
like', is used elsewhere in the Old Testament in one of two
senses: (*a*) that of 'to compare', a rendering which is obviously inappropriate here, and (*b*) that of 'to picture' something in the present which is to happen *in the future*—and
so 'to plan'.[2] The latter is evidently the meaning which is
intended here, and we may render the line thus:

> O God, we have pictured Thy devotion
> In the midst of Thy Temple.

Even so, however, the context shows that this anticipation
of the future is something more than a mere mental 'picture', i.e. something more than that which is seen, as we say,
by the mind's eye. It is a ritual performance or acted
'picture' of a piece with the prophetic symbolism but on the
grand scale—the מָשָׁל *par excellence*.[3]

The next few lines of the psalm then proceed to extol
Yahweh because of this anticipated manifestation of His
righteousness (צֶדֶק) and His corresponding acts of judge-

---

[1] Verse 10 (EVV. 9).

[2] Cf. *The Cultic Prophet in Ancient Israel*, pp. 38 ff., esp. p. 39, n. 1, 2nd
edit., pp. 41 ff., esp. p. 42, n. 2.

[3] Cf. the writer's study of this term in *Wisdom in Israel and in the Ancient
Near East* (H. H. Rowley *Festschrift*), ed. M. Noth and D. W. Thomas,
S.V.T. iii (1955), pp. 162–9.

ment (מִשְׁפָּטִים) in overthrowing the hostile forces which threaten the national life. In other words, we have to note once again that Yahweh's Kingship is thought of as carrying with it the responsibility to act as the heavenly Judge, who from His royal throne can exercise His power in defence of His people.[1]

> Like Thy Name, O God, so doth Thy praise
> Extend to the ends of the earth.
> Thy Right Hand is full of righteousness;[2]
> Let Mount Zion be glad!
> Let the daughters of Judah rejoice
> Because of Thine acts of judgement!

What is even more important, the last few lines of the psalm again deal with a ritual procession; and it will be observed that they close with an emphasis upon the fact that Yahweh is the leader of His people in the struggle against 'Death', i.e. the very same thought which we have already noticed in the case of Psalm lxviii.[3] Accordingly it seems clear that in this psalm we are dealing with the situation immediately preceding the procession which has been engaging our attention in connexion with Psalms xxiv, xlvii, and lxviii. The exhortation to begin this triumphant procession runs as follows:[4]

> March around Zion, go round about her,
> Number her towers,
> Pay heed to her ramparts,
> Pass between her palaces,
> That ye may tell the coming generation
> That such is God!
> Our God, who abideth for ever,
> Is our leader against 'Death'.[5]

---

[1] vv. 11–12 (EVV. 10–11).

[2] It is clear on metrical grounds that the last stichos of verse 11 (EVV. 10) should be taken closely with verse 12 (EVV. 11). Note the resultant example of chiasmus. [3] See above, p. 82.

[4] vv. 13–15 (EVV. 12–14).

[5] Vocalizing the consonantal text so as to read עַל־מָוֶת. These words have long been a *crux interpretum*, and again we can see that the general failure to understand the allusion has been due to the fact that the psalm has been

All in all, therefore, it seems quite clear that the arch-enemy over whom Yahweh has triumphed is 'Death'; and it is tempting to compare the story of Baal's conflict with Mot ('Death') in the mythology of the Ras Shamra tablets and so to find yet another parallel in the field of Canaanite culture as represented by the literature of ancient Ugarit.[1] At the same time it should be borne in mind that there is no indication whatsoever that in this ritual and mythology of the Jerusalem cultus 'Death' is thought of as a god, even though, as we shall see, the Underworld and its forces are represented as threatening the life of the nation as focused in the person of the Messiah. In fact, so far as this ritual performance is concerned, the mass attack of 'Death' is obviously portrayed as an onslaught by the kings (and *ipso facto* the nations) of the earth; and 'Death' is driven out of the city through their discomfiture inasmuch as Yahweh has revealed Himself in some way as the 'stronghold' of His people.[2]

divorced from its original *Sitz im Leben*, so that the obvious rendering seems to make no sense. Indeed this particular example serves the present writer as a stern warning against hasty textual 'emendation'; for, when he began his researches into the Psalter along the lines indicated by 'The Rôle of the King in the Jerusalem Cultus' (as referred to above, p. 7, n. 1), he followed the usual practice of attempting to improve the reading, and only discovered later, as his work developed, that in so doing he was destroying a valuable piece of evidence and an important link in his argument!

[1] Cf. Gordon, op. cit., 49, ii 9–37, vi 9 ff.; 51, vii 42 ff.; 67 (= Herdner, op. cit., 6, ii 9–37, vi 9 ff.; 4, vii 42 ff.; 5: cf. Driver, op. cit., pp. 110 f., 114 f., 100 ff., 102 ff.).

[2] I find it remarkable that, despite the above explicit rejection of any suggestion that 'Death' is here regarded as a god (cf., too, 'The Rôle of the King in the Jerusalem Cultus', pp. 94 f.), I am repeatedly cited in terms which suggest that in my opinion we have here a definite allusion to the god Mot. Cf., for example, H. J. Kraus, B.K.A.T. (1958), 2nd edit. (1961), *in loc.*; S. H. Hooke, *Middle Eastern Mythology* (1963), pp. 84 (cf. p. 94, n. 1), 106 f. (cf. p. 160, n. 4). In the circumstances it seems necessary to point out once again that I was led to pursue the line of study which I have begun in *The Vitality of the Individual in the Thought of Ancient Israel*, because (*a*) I realized that we are here in a very different realm of thought from that which is represented by the Ugaritic texts, and (*b*) it seemed that, to appreciate this, we needed a clear formulation of Israelite ideas concerning 'life' and 'death'. Cf. what I have to say on this matter in *E.T.* lxii (1950–1), p. 41b; also lxviii 1956–7), p. 179b.

Presently we shall see something of the way in which Yahweh's followers enjoy His protection as their 'stronghold'; but we must first examine Psalm cxlix, which apparently introduces the worshippers as themselves sharing in this ritual performance. The psalm opens with a summons to the worshippers, Yahweh's 'votaries' (חֲסִידִים), to offer praise to their God as their Maker and King; and again we meet the thought that Yahweh takes pleasure in His people (or finds them acceptable) and brings them salvation because they are 'humble' or 'submissive' (עָנָו). What is more, we have to note that they are summoned to sing a 'new song'; and this, one need hardly say, is a thought which is particularly appropriate to our festival with its exultant anticipation of a new era of universal dominion and national prosperity.[1]

> Sing unto Yahweh a new song,
> His praise in the assembly of the devout (חֲסִידִים).
> Let Israel be glad because of his Maker,
> Let the children of Zion rejoice in their King.
> Let them praise His Name with dancing,
> Let them sing His praises with timbrel and lyre;
> For Yahweh findeth His people acceptable,[2]
> He adorneth the humble with salvation.

In the latter part of the psalm, however, Yahweh's worshippers or 'votaries' are called upon, not merely to be exultant at the thought of the glory which is coming to them, but to be prepared, sword in hand, to execute the sentence which Yahweh has pronounced or, rather, is about to pronounce upon the nations of the earth; and, significantly enough, this involves their making the kings of these nations their captives.[3]

> Let the devout (חֲסִידִים) exult at the thought of glory;
> Let them break out in applause upon their bedding.

---

[1] vv. 1–4.

[2] Cf., for a valuable discussion of the use of √רצה in a cultic setting, E. Würthwein, 'Kultpolemik oder Kultbescheid?', in *Tradition und Situation* (A. Weiser *Festschrift*), ed. E. Würthwein and O. Kaiser (1963), pp. 115–31.

[3] vv. 5–9.

Let the praises of God be in their throat,
And a two-edged sword in their hand.
To wreak vengeance upon the nations,
    Chastisement upon the peoples,
To bind their kings with chains,
    Their nobility with iron fetters,
To execute upon these the judgement prescribed
    Is an honour which falleth to all His votaries (חֲסִידִים)!

There seems to be only one theory which does justice to this psalm in every detail and without recourse to emendation, i.e. that which sees it as the prelude to a ritual performance of the type to which we have already referred. Accordingly we are brought a stage nearer to the exact timing of the above-mentioned spectacle, for the fact that Yahweh's followers are described as seated or lying upon their bedding indicates that it is at night that they are assembled so expectantly in the Temple.

Fortunately we possess in Psalm xlvi a hymn which may fittingly be said to throw light on this point; and in so doing it also gives some indication of the way in which Yahweh has proved Himself to be the 'stronghold' of His people. It seems to fall into three parts; and of these the first deals with the assurance of Yahweh's help in virtue of His power over the great cosmic sea, which is not merely the source of the rains and the rivers but apparently represents (somewhat like Tiamat, the body of salt water, in the Babylonian Epic of Creation[1]) the primeval forces of darkness.[2]

---

[1] In its current form this myth is probably to be assigned to the period of the First Babylonian Dynasty, i.e. the nineteenth to the sixteenth centuries B.C.; and, as is now well known, it describes the way in which Marduk first subdued the primal chaos by overthrowing the monster Tiamat, the mother of the gods, and her equally monstrous allies under the leadership of her consort, the god Kingu, and then created the visible world by splitting her corpse into two parts and using the one half to form the solid firmament of heaven. In the present connexion it is also worthy of note that the divine assembly, faced with the need to meet the challenge of Tiamat, had previously bestowed upon Marduk 'kingship over the whole of the entire universe'. Tablet iv, line 14. Cf. line 28, 'They gladly did homage, saying "Marduk is King."' Since the publication of the first known fragments of

(*Footnotes 1 and 2 continued on p. 93*.)

We have God as our refuge and strength,[1]
A ready source of help in time of trouble.
Therefore we will not fear, though the earth sway
    And the mountains reel amidst the sea.
Let its waters clamour and break into foam,
    Let the mountains quᵃke at its swelling;
[Yahweh of Hosts is with us,
    The God of Jacob is our stronghold.].[2]

In the second strophe attention is drawn to one of the
currents of the cosmic ocean which, as a good servant but
a bad master, is thought of as ministering to the needs of
the Holy City; and in general the passage recalls, say,
Psalm xxix with its description of Yahweh's enthronement
over the flood and the convulsive effect of His thundering
'Voice'. Indeed we learn that Yahweh's power in the realm
of nature, as shown in His subjection of the turbulent activity of the cosmic sea, has its parallel in what we may
again call the moral realm; but in this case it is revealed in
the overthrow of the kingdoms of the earth, which in their
own way similarly threaten the safety or well-being of the
nation. Accordingly, as in Psalm xlviii, emphasis is laid
upon the fact that Yahweh has proved to be the 'stronghold'
of His people; and in this connexion it is significant (*a*)
that it should be as the 'Most High' that Yahweh preserves
His sacred city, and (*b*) that it is at daybreak that He brings
succour to His people. In short, it is in the person of the
'Most High', worshipped with all the eloquent symbolism

the text by George Smith in *The Chaldean Account of Genesis* (1876) practi-
cally the complete story has been recovered, and a whole series of revised
editions and translations has appeared. A critical edition of the text is available
in A. Deimel, '*Enuma Eliš' sive epos Babylonicum de creatione mundi*, 2nd edit.
rev. (1936), and a convenient transliteration and translation in R. Labat,
Le Poème babylonien de la création (1935). The fullest and most up-to-date
translations into English, however, are those of A. Heidel, *The Babylonian
Genesis*, 2nd edit. rev. (1951), pp. 18–60, and E. A. Speiser in *Ancient Near
Eastern Texts relating to the Old Testament*, ed. J. B. Pritchard, 2nd edit. rev.
(1955), pp. 60–72.   [2] vv. 2–4 (EVV. 1–3).

[1] Or 'protection'? Cf. K.B., p. 693a.
[2] This line is not in the Hebrew text; but it seems likely that in verses 8
and 12 (EVV. 7 and 11) we have a refrain which has fallen out at this particular point.

of the sun, that Yahweh triumphs over the forces of darkness, the gloomy underworld of 'Death', and the kings (or nations) of the earth who threaten the life of His chosen people.[1]

> As for 'The River',[2] its streams make glad the city of God,
>> The most holy abode of the Most High.[3]
> With God in her midst she cannot be shaken;
>> God doth help her as the morning appeareth.
> The nations clamour, the kingdoms reel;
>> At the sound of His Voice the earth is in turmoil.
> Yahweh of Hosts is with us,
>> The God of Jacob is our stronghold.

---

[1] vv. 5–8 (EVV. 4–7). The passages in the canonical prophets, particularly the book of Isaiah, which need to be seen against the background of this festival are so numerous that the writer refrains, for the most part, from drawing attention to them at this stage; but the reader should compare at this point the fragment from the cycle of mythology associated with the 'Most High' which has been preserved for us through its being given an historical application, i.e. Isa. xiv. 12–15, which, as the context shows, celebrates the prospective downfall of some tyrant of the ancient Near East:

> How art thou fallen from heaven,
>> Gleaming One, son of the Dawn!
> Thou, who didst override the nations,
>> Art hewn to earth.
> Yet thou didst say in thine heart,
>> 'I will mount up to heaven;
> Beyond the divine stars
>> Will I raise my throne.
> I will sit on the Mount of Assembly,
>> In the heights (*lit.* recesses) of Zaphon.
> I will climb above the clouds;
>> I will make myself like the Most High!'
> Howbeit to Sheol art thou brought down,
>> To the depths (*lit.* recesses) of the Pit!

The picture is obviously that of a morning star, which strives to reach the height of heaven but only succeeds in being hurled down to the underworld, the more powerful rays of the sun, whose role it is clearly attempting to fill, causing it to fade and disappear. This is not to say, of course, that Yahweh was identified in any way with the sun. On the contrary it was His expressed wish that He should be shrouded in darkness from mortal eyes. Cf., for example, 1 Kings viii. 12 (esp. LXX, i.e. viii. 53a): and see in general the important study by H. Schrade, *Der verborgene Gott: Gottesbild und Gottesvorstellung in Israel und im alten Orient* (1949).

[2] See above, pp. 10 f.

[3] Or, as above, p. 11, n. 3, 'Which the Most High hath sanctified as His abode.'

Finally, the view that we are here dealing with a ritual performance of some kind is confirmed by the vivid phraseology of the third strophe, as it calls upon mankind to gaze on the actual spectacle:[1]

> Come, behold the deeds of Yahweh (   ),[2]
>> As He maketh wars to cease throughout the earth.
> He doth shatter the bow and snap the spear;
>> He doth burn the shields[3] with fire.
> 'Be still and know that I, God,
>> Am high above the nations, high above the earth!'
> Yahweh of Hosts is with us,
>> The God of Jacob is our stronghold.

Indeed, the thought of these last lines is particularly striking; for the ideal which is visualized is one which is pathetically familiar to modern ears, i.e. that of a war which is to end all wars. At the same time it is to be observed that, while Israel is the chosen instrument of God for the achievement of His purpose, which, as we shall see, is one of universal righteousness and justice, the assurance of ultimate victory is found, not in the weapons of His followers, but in His own omnipotence. When all is said and done, the deeds must be Yahweh's deeds, and it is He alone who can really make wars to cease throughout the earth.[4]

We are now in a position to understand Psalm xcvii, which brings us back to the situation indicated by the psalms with which our treatment of this festival began; and in examining it we need to bear in mind that Israel never lived in a vacuum, so that already in early times its

---

[1] vv. 9–12 (EVV. 8–11).

[2] The Hebrew adds, 'Who hath laid waste the earth'; but there is reason to believe on the ground of both syntax and metre that this is a prosaic gloss. Cf., for example, E. Podechard, *Le Psautier: Notes critiques*, i (1949), *in loc.*

[3] M.T. 'wagons'; but it seems likely that the consonantal text should be vocalized so as to read עֲגִלוֹת, a word which is not found elsewhere in the Old Testament but may well have existed as a parallel to the Aramaic עֲגִיל, עֲגִילָא, 'shield'. Cf. LXX and T: and see further, for example, Podechard, op. cit., *in loc.*

[4] Cf. Psalm lxxvi, which has much in common with Psalms xlvi and xlviii, and may well have its original *Sitz im Leben* just here. See above, p. 32, n. 1.

religious thinkers were bound to face the question as to what exactly was Yahweh's relation to the gods of the surrounding nations. The psalm begins with a summons to the world at large to rejoice in the fact that it is Yahweh who is King, and then continues with a description of the way in which He has manifested the basic righteousness and justice of His rule by a dramatic demonstration of His power in the realm of nature. This is pictured in the now familiar terms of earthquake and thunderstorm, the flashes of His lightning not only wiping out His adversaries but illuminating the whole world, so that all peoples have been able to see His 'Glory'. When we come to consider the role of the Davidic King (or the Messiah) in this ritual, we shall be better able to appreciate the meaning of this dramatic intervention on the part of Yahweh. Meantime we may recall that, according to Psalm xxix, the theme on everyone's lips in the Temple was similarly one of 'Glory'.[1]

> It is Yahweh who is King! Let the earth rejoice!
>> Let the many coasts be glad!
> Cloud, deep cloud, is round about Him;
>> Righteousness and justice are the foundation of His throne.
> Fire goeth before Him,
>> Setting His foes ablaze on every side.
> His lightning illumined the world;
>> The earth saw and writhed.
> The mountains melted like wax before Yahweh,
>> Before the Lord of all the earth.
> The heavens have declared His righteousness,
>> And all the peoples have seen His 'Glory'.

In the following lines our attention is directed to the conclusion which is to be drawn from Yahweh's triumph over the nations of the world. It is a proof that these image-worshipping peoples, who are obviously contrasted with the Israelites and their traditional imageless worship of Yahweh,[2] are the wards of inferior gods who in the defeat

---

[1] vv. 1–6.

[2] Cf. H. H. Rowley, 'Moses and the Decalogue', *B.J.R.L.* xxxiv (1951–2), pp. 81–118, esp. pp. 102 ff.; also (in a French edition), *R.H.P.R.* xxxii (1952),

of their own followers have been compelled to acknowledge the supremacy of Yahweh and, what is more, the defeat of their own ambitious schemes to overthrow His righteous rule and produce anarchy in the earth; and again we are reminded of Psalm xxix with its summons to the gods to render to Yahweh the glory due to His Name. In fact, the point of view which occurs here is to be understood in terms of a passage from the so-called 'Song of Moses', as restored on the basis of the Septuagint, i.e.:[1]

> When the Most High gave to the nations their possessions,
> When He divided up mankind,
> Fixing the territories of the peoples
> According to the number of the ⌐gods⌐,[2]
> Yahweh's own share was His own people,
> Jacob was the portion of which He took possession.

Further, it is interesting to observe that Yahweh's supremacy in this way is also expressed in this section of the psalm by means of a double word-play on the appellation 'Most High' (עֶלְיוֹן) like that which we have already observed in the case of Psalm xlvii, i.e. Yahweh is high (עֶלְיוֹן) over the earth, He is highly exalted (*Niph'al* of עָלָה) above all the gods.[3]

> All who serve a graven image are put to shame,
> Those who take pride in worthless idols,
> All the gods having made obeisance to Him.[4]
> Zion hath heard and is glad,
> And the daughters of Judah rejoice,
> Because of Thine acts of judgement, O Yahweh.[5]
> For Thou, Yahweh, art high (עֶלְיוֹן) over all the earth;
> Thou art highly exalted (נַעֲלֵיתָ) above all the gods.

---

pp. 7–40, esp. pp. 25 ff.; and now (with an up-to-date bibliography), in *Men of God: Studies in Old Testament History and Prophecy* (1963), pp. 1–36, esp. pp. 20 ff.   [1] Deut. xxxii. 8–9.

[2] M.T. בְּנֵי יִשְׂרָאֵל. LXX (κατὰ ἀριθμὸν) ἀγγέλων θεοῦ, i.e. reading בְּנֵי אֱלֹהִים. Cf. Job i. 6, ii. 1, xxxviii. 7; and note that the reading of LXX is now confirmed by the fragments of a Hebrew manuscript from Qumran, as described by P. W. Skehan, *B.A.S.O.R.* 136 (Dec. 1954), p. 12, and *J.B.L.* lxxviii (1959), p. 21.   [3] vv. 7–9.

[4] i.e. construing the Hebrew verb as the perfect indicative (cf. R.S.V.) rather than an imperative (cf. EVV.).

[5] Cf. Ps. xlviii. 12 (EVV. 11), as above, p. 89.

In view of this occasion for rejoicing, Yahweh's followers
are then reminded that to love Him carries with it the
responsibility of hating evil; for, when all is said and done,
this is the indispensable condition of success. Yahweh is
there to watch over the lives of His 'votaries' (חֲסִידִים),
those who are devoted to Him or pledged to His service
within the covenant, and it is His responsibility to deliver
them from the power of the 'wicked'. The latter term, as
we have seen,[1] is one which is used categorically of the
nation's enemies, whereas Yahweh's 'votaries' are idealized
as the 'righteous'; and on these, significantly enough, the
glad light is said to have shone. That is to say, it is a
righteous people who have been delivered with the coming
of the dawn from the sorrows of darkness and 'Death'.[2]

> Those who love Yahweh hate[3] evil;
>   He who guardeth the lives[4] of His votaries
>   Doth deliver them from the hand of the wicked.
> Light is sown (*or* risen[5]) for the righteous,[6]
>   And gladness for the upright of heart.
> Be glad in Yahweh, O ye righteous,
>   And give thanks to His holy Name!

We are now in a position to understand Psalm lxxxii,
which has long been regarded as one of the most perplexing
compositions in the whole of the Psalter. It introduces us
at the outset to the heavenly court, and reveals Yahweh as
pronouncing sentence upon the assembled gods of the
nations because of their misrule:[7]

> God (*or* Yahweh)[8] taketh His stand in the divine assembly;
>   Amidst the gods He pronounceth judgement.

The charge against them is that, instead of defending the
rights of the weak and the fatherless, the humble and the
poor, within the territories under their jurisdiction, they

---

[1] Page 78.   [2] vv. 10–12.
[3] Vocalizing the consonantal text so as to read שָׂנְאוּ. Cf. G.K., § 106*g*.
[4] See above, p. 12, n. 1.
[5] i.e. reading זָרַח with one MS., LXX, Jerome, S, and T.
[6] Cf. Ps. cxviii. 27a, as below, p. 127.   [7] Verse 1.
[8] See above, p. 75, n. 3.

have permitted the wicked to dominate the scene and, as
the forces of darkness, to threaten the whole moral basis of
earth's society—a thought which is expressed in the characteristic recognition that the moral realm and the realm of
nature are inextricably related. Thus Yahweh calls them to
task with the words:[1]

> 'How long will ye judge unjustly,
>> And show partiality towards the wicked?
> Secure justice for the weak and the fatherless;
>> Grant the humble and the poor their right.
> Rescue the weak and the poor,
>> Deliver them from the hand of the wicked,
> Who have neither knowledge nor understanding,
>> But live persistently in darkness,
>>> So that all the foundations of the earth are shaken.'

Accordingly, despite their standing as the sons of God,
Yahweh goes on to pronounce what must be the final sentence upon them for failing to live up to this ideal, decree-
ing that as a result they shall die like ordinary human
beings, i.e.:[2]

> 'I admit[3] that ye are gods,
>> And all of you sons of the Most High.
> Nevertheless ye shall die like men,
>> And fall like any ordinary prince.'[4]

This means, of course, that Yahweh will be left to take
charge of their territories and, as the unchallenged, omnipotent, and indeed only God, will be able to enforce the
universal reign of justice; and it is in lively anticipation of
this happy consummation that the psalm draws to a close:[5]

> Arise, O God (*or* Yahweh)! Secure justice for the earth![6]
> For *Thou* wilt take possession of *all* the nations.

The exultation aroused by this thought finds ready illustration in Psalm xcviii,[7] which begins with the now familiar

---

[1] vv. 2–5.   [2] vv. 6–7.   [3] G.K., § 106g.
[4] Cf. Judges xvi. 7 ('like any ordinary man').   [5] Verse 8.
[6] Cf. verse 3.
[7] Cf. Psalm xcvi, which has many points of contact with this and some

summons to the world at large to sing a new song in honour
of Yahweh. As such it is an obvious prelude to the new era
of righteousness and justice which is to dawn for mankind
when Yahweh comes to judge the earth.

> Sing unto Yahweh a new song,
> For He hath performed wondrous things!
> His Right Hand and His holy Arm
> Have wrought salvation for Him.
> Yahweh hath made known His salvation;
> He hath revealed to the nations His righteousness.
> He hath remembered His devotion [to Jacob],[1]
> And His faithfulness to the House of Israel.
> All the ends of the earth have seen
> The salvation of our God.
> Make acclamation unto Yahweh, all the earth;
> Break out in applause, and sing praises!
> Sing praises to Yahweh with the lyre,
> With the lyre and the sound of singing!
> With trumpets and the sound of the horn
> Make acclamation before the King—*Yahweh!*
> Let the sea thunder with all its fullness,
> The world and they that dwell therein;
> Let the rivers clap their hands,
> Let the hills unite in applause,
> Before Yahweh, for He cometh,
> [For He cometh][2] to judge the earth.
> He will judge the world with righteousness,
> And the peoples with equity.

Nevertheless it must be borne in mind that this exultant
anticipation of Yahweh's coming in triumph to judge the
earth is tempered with words of caution; for, as we have
seen, it is only to a righteous nation that Yahweh thus
comes in final demonstration of His universal sovereignty.
That is to say, the festival as a whole serves as a reminder

of the other psalms which are dealt with in the text. At the same time one
must beware of seeing conscious dependence in a case of this kind. It may
well be that we should think, rather, of a common heritage of established
phraseology. Cf. the repetition which so often occurs in the Accadian epics
and annals and in the Ugaritic texts as well as the similar stock phrases in, say,
Homer.   [1] Cf. LXX.   [2] Cf. Ps. xcvi. 13.

to the worshippers that the 'Voice' of Him who rides the
clouds with such catastrophic power is also the 'Voice'
which was heard by their forefathers at Sinai, when Yahweh
first admitted His chosen people to His counsel; and amid
all the disappointment engendered by the passing years it
brings them afresh the challenge to be in very truth the
righteous nation which He then envisaged as the instrument
of His purpose. In short, the key-words for the understanding of this dramatic ritual in its full significance are
to be found in the plea which we met almost at the outset
of our study of these psalms:[1]

> O that *today* ye may hearken to His Voice!

Accordingly, summarizing our discussion thus far, we
may say that the following features can now be recognized
in the festival under consideration. In the first place we
have (*a*) the celebration of Yahweh's original triumph, as
leader of the forces of light, over the forces of darkness as
represented by the monstrous chaos of waters or primeval
ocean; (*b*) His subjection of this cosmic sea and His enthronement as King in the assembly of the gods; and (*c*)
the further demonstration of His might and power in the
creation of the habitable world. Cosmogony, however, gives
place to eschatology; for all this is the prelude to the thought
of His re-creative work, which is expressed in the form of a
ritual drama, and, as such, is wholly in line with what we
are told about prophetic symbolism of the type which appears to have been embraced by the term מָשָׁל. In fact
it is the מָשָׁל *par excellence*, and is designed as an effective demonstration of Yahweh's ultimate will and purpose
for Israel and the world. In this ritual drama the worshippers are given (*a*) an assurance of final victory over 'Death',
i.e. all that obstructs the fullness of life for mankind which
was Yahweh's design in the creation of the habitable world;
(*b*) a summons to a renewal of their faith in Yahweh and His
plans for them and for the world; and (*c*) a challenge to a
renewed endeavour to be faithful to Him and His demands,

---

[1] Ps. xcv. 7c, as above, p. 69.

so that the day may indeed dawn when this vision of a
universal realm of righteousness and peace will be realized,
and His Kingdom will be seen in all its power and glory.
This work of 'salvation' (יְשׁוּעָה), as it is called,[1] is portrayed by means of some kind of mime in which the kings
(i.e. nations) of the earth, representing the forces of darkness
and 'Death' as opposed to light and 'Life' and commonly
designated the 'wicked' (רְשָׁעִים), unite in an attempt to
overthrow Yahweh's covenanted followers, i.e. His 'votaries' (חֲסִידִים) or the 'righteous' (צַדִּיקִים); and victory (or
salvation)[2] is eventually secured through the direct intervention of Yahweh (or the 'Most High') at dawn on this
fateful day. In this way Yahweh reveals His own devotion
(חֶסֶד) and righteousness (צֶדֶק) to His covenant people.
This is not all, however, for Yahweh's earthly victory has
its counterpart in the heavenly places. The rebellion of the
kings of the earth is but a reflection of the rebellious misrule
of the lesser gods in the divine assembly to whom the Most
High had granted jurisdiction over those territories which
were occupied by the other nations of the earth. Accordingly
the overthrow of the kings of the earth corresponds to the
overthrow of these rebellious gods, who, having shown their
unfitness to rule, are condemned to die like any earthly
princes. Thus Yahweh proves to be what has been aptly
called 'the enduring power, not ourselves, which makes for
righteousness';[3] and the helpless, the poor, and the humble,
not merely in Israel but throughout the world, may look
forward to an era of universal righteousness and peace, as
the one omnipotent God comes with judicial power to enforce His beneficent rule upon the earth.

V

Now inasmuch as Yahweh thus enlivens His people with
this dramatic assurance of His will and power to deliver

---

[1] See above, p. 19, n. 2.
[2] Cf., for example, 1 Sam. xiv. 45; and see further Pedersen, *Israel I–II*,
pp. 257 ff., E.T., pp. 330 ff.   [3] See above, p. 13, n. 2.

them from the forces of darkness and 'Death', it is to be expected that the ritual of this festival should have some definite connexion with the earthly king, who, as we have seen, is the focal point of the life of the nation. Accordingly we have now to consider a number of psalms which seem to require interpretation along these lines; and in the nature of the case most of these belong to the class known as royal psalms.[1]

A simple indication of the importance which was undoubtedly attached to the king in this connexion may be found in Psalm lxxxiv, which is best explained as a hymn sung by Yahweh's worshippers in celebration of their pilgrimage from the towns and villages of the land at the time of this autumnal festival. It opens with a vivid description of the emotional response aroused by the thought of the Temple in the hearts of those who have to spend their lives out of sight of the Holy City, and so are unable to enjoy the privileges shared by the chosen few whose duties enable them to make it their permanent home; and it is noteworthy that He in whose honour it stands is addressed or referred to, not merely as Yahweh of Hosts, but also as the 'Living God' (אֵל חַי)[2] and the divine 'King'.[3]

> How lovely is Thy dwelling-place,
>> O Yahweh of Hosts!
> My whole being[4] longeth, yea, pineth
>> For Yahweh's courts;
> My heart and my flesh cry out
>> Unto the Living God!
> Even the sparrow findeth a home
>> And the swallow a nest for itself,
> Laying its young beside Thine altars,
>> O Yahweh of Hosts, my King[5] and my God!
> How happy are they who dwell in Thy house,
>> Who can always be praising Thee!

---

[1] See above, p. 7, n. 1.

[2] Cf. *The Vitality of the Individual in the Thought of Ancient Israel*, pp. 105 ff., 2nd edit., pp. 106 ff.   [3] vv. 2–5 (EVV. 1–4).

[4] For the wide range of meaning associated with the Hebrew term נֶפֶשׁ see op. cit. (n. 2, above), pp. 9 ff., 2nd edit., pp. 3 ff.

[5] Cf. Ps. lxviii. 25 (EVV. 24), as above, p. 83.

In the following lines, however, we learn that even the pilgrim has his own peculiar happiness, for he knows that, following his worship of this 'Living God', the parched and thirsty ground over which he has to travel will soon be transformed, and will be dotted in due course with pools which will be the result of the winter's rains; and this thought spurs him on with increased vigour to meet with God in Zion and to present before Him his special prayer, namely that Yahweh will bless the earthly king in Jerusalem, who is at once the 'shield' of his people and the 'Messiah' of God. Thus the thought of the heavenly King leads on to that of His specially anointed deputy, the reigning member of the House of David; for the Temple, we must be careful to bear in mind, was first and foremost a royal temple and its cultus primarily a royal cultus.[1]

> How happy mankind who make Thee their strength,
> Whose heart is set on pilgrimage![2]
> Passing through the arid[3] valley,
> They convert it into a spring;
> Yea, the early rains clothe it with pools.[4]
> They go from strength to strength,[5]
> Until the God of[6] gods is seen[7] in Zion.
> O Yahweh (   )[8] of Hosts, hear my prayer;
> Hearken, O God of Jacob!

---

[1] vv. 6–10 (EVV. 5–9).   [2] *lit.* 'who have the highways in their heart'.

[3] The point of the comparison is indicated, not only by the context, but also by the Arabic كَلَّ , 'to have little milk' (e.g. of a ewe), 'to have little water' (e.g. of a well), and so generally of that which is unproductive. Cf. Lane, op. cit., s.v.; J. G. Hava, *Arabic–English Dictionary*, rev. edit. (1915), s.v.: and see further König, *Die Psalmen*, p. 304.

[4] Vocalizing the consonantal text so as to read בְּרֵכוֹת. Cf. A.V. and P.B.V. as against R.V. As is clear from the use of this root in both Arabic (بِرْكَة, 'pool') and Hebrew (בְּרֵכָה, id.), rain was regarded as the 'blessing' *par excellence*.

[5] Cf. Jer. ix. 2 (EVV. 3); 2 Cor. iii. 18; and, for the idea, Isa. xl. 31. Alternatively the reference may be to the swelling ranks of the pilgrims.

[6] The consonantal text admits this interpretation, and indeed it was so understood by LXX, Jerome, and S. Cf., too, the Hebrew of Ps. l. 1.

[7] i.e. in all the accompaniment of worship.

[8] The Hebrew adds 'God', but this should be omitted as an intended substitute for 'Yahweh'.

Behold our shield,[1] O God,
And look upon the face of Thy Messiah!

Finally, having reached this focal point at which the worship of the heavenly King and a due regard for the earthly king are linked with the coming of the needed rain, the worshipper reverts to his original theme, and contemplates afresh the incomparable pleasure that awaits the pilgrim in the worship of the Temple:[2]

> For I prefer a day in Thy courts
>   To a thousand elsewhere,[3]
> Hovering on the threshold in the house of my God
>   To dwelling in the tents of wickedness.
> For Yahweh (   )[4] is both sun[5] and shield;
>   He bestoweth grace and glory.

---

[1] The traditional view (following LXX) is that מָגִנֵּנוּ, 'our shield', should be construed as a vocative and therefore as co-ordinate with 'God'; but the parallelism in the Hebrew shows quite clearly that it should be construed as the object of the verb so as to yield an example of chiasmus. Cf., for example, Gunkel, H. K., and Pannier–Renard, S. B., *in loc.* For the same reason one must reject the view, advanced on the basis of Ugaritic, that מָגִנֵּנוּ here means 'our entreaty' = 'we implore'. Cf. Patton, *Canaanite Parallels in the Book of Psalms*, p. 41, where the reader will find other equally untenable examples of this alleged form (including Ps. xlvii. 10 (EVV. 9), as discussed above, p. 76, and Ps. lxxxix. 19 (EVV. 18), as discussed below, p. 109). In fact, here again we see how important it is to examine a form carefully in the light of its context before attempting to interpret it in a novel way in terms of Ugaritic. See above, p. 78, n. 6, and p. 82, n. 9.

[2] vv. 11–13 (EVV. 10–12).

[3] The rendering of this metrical line must be regarded as doubtful. In fact it is almost certain that the consonantal text of the form rendered by 'I prefer' (M.T.: בָּחַרְתִּי) involves some such meaning as 'in my own home', and that this and the following line should be rendered:

> For better is a day in Thy courts
>   Than a thousand in my own . . . (?),
> Better to hover on the threshold in the house of my God
>   Than to dwell in the tents of wickedness.

As yet, however, so far as the present writer is aware, no completely convincing solution of the problem has been offered.

[4] Cf. p. 104, n. 8.

[5] Better 'buckler' or, rather, 'battlement'? Cf. Isa. liv. 12; and see further, for example, Gunkel, op. cit., *in loc.*, Tournay–Schwab, op. cit., *in loc.*, K.B., s.v. Note, however, the words of caution offered by Kraus, op. cit., *in loc.*, with which I am much inclined to agree; for it is also important to

Yahweh[1] doth not withhold what is good
From[2] those who walk in integrity.
O Yahweh of Hosts,
How happy mankind who trust in Thee!

We are now in a position to recognize the real significance of Psalm lxxxix, the theme of which is subject to such sudden change that commentators have been misled into regarding it as a fusion of two and even three originally independent compositions, failing to realize that these transitions are due to its liturgical background;[3] and, as we shall see, there is good reason to believe that the liturgical background in question is that of the festival which we are attempting in some measure to reconstruct.[4] The psalm opens with a hymn in praise of Yahweh; and it is important to note that this combines the thought of Yahweh's devotion and faithfulness to the House of David with the background of thought which we have seen to be proper to this festival. The first two lines run as follows:[5]

I will ever sing of Yahweh's continued devotion;[6]
Through all generations I will make known Thy faithfulness
with my mouth.

bear in mind that, as already observed (pp. 93 f., 101 f.: cf. pp. 134 ff.), the symbolism afforded by the light of the sun is of outstanding importance in the ritual and mythology under review.

[1] On metrical grounds 'Yahweh' should probably be construed with what follows rather than with what precedes.

[2] Cf. Gordon, *Ugaritic Handbook* or *Ugaritic Manual* or *Ugaritic Textbook*, i §§ 10. 1, 11.   [3] See above, p. 25, n. 1.

[4] The writer trusts that the argument of these pages, taken as a whole, provides sufficient answer to the criticism levelled by Mowinckel, *Offersang og sangoffer*, pp. 570 ff., against his use of this psalm (as also Psalms xviii and cxviii) in 'The Rôle of the King in the Jerusalem Cultus'. See above, p. 7, n. 1.

The revised version of Mowinckel's critical comments may now be found in *The Psalms in Israel's Worship*, ii, pp. 253 ff.; and what I have to say in reply may be summed up by expressing surprise at Mowinckel's attitude to the psalms in question in view of his early comment on the psalms which celebrate the Kingship of Yahweh: 'Daß die zeitgeschichtliche Deutung verfehlt ist, geht erstens aus dem völligen Mangel an konkreten geschichtlichen Hindeutungen und Reminiszenzen hervor.' (*Psalmenstudien II*, p. 12.)

[5] vv. 2–3 (EVV. 1–2).

[6] Or 'acts of devotion'.

Yea, I acknowledge[1] that devotion will ever be built up (√בנה);
Along with the heavens themselves Thou wilt maintain (√כון)
Thy faithfulness.

Now such language, with its assurance of Yahweh's devotion
(חֶסֶד) and faithfulness (אֱמוּנָה) is really idiomatic, for it is the
language appropriate to the thought of fulfilling one's part
in a covenant;[2] and this is confirmed by the two following
verses, which introduce a summary quotation of Yahweh's
actual vow under the terms of the Davidic covenant.[3]

'I have made a covenant with My chosen one;
    I have sworn to David My Servant:
"I will maintain (√כון) thy seed for ever;
    Through all generations I will build up (√בנה) thy throne." '

This quotation is introduced with such apparent abrupt-
ness, the 'I' who now speaks being Yahweh, that the text is
commonly supposed to be corrupt, and it has even been
suggested that these lines have been severed from their
supposedly original connexion later in the psalm, where,
as we shall see, we meet with an extended reference to this
Davidic covenant.[4] Such drastic treatment of the text,
however, is completely without justification; for we need
to bear in mind that the introductory lines already quoted
would at once arouse the thought of a covenant in the
minds of the worshippers; and this would be the more
ready in view of the fact that, as we shall see, they are
uttered in the presence of the Davidic king himself. Moreover, there is such a striking parallelism in the language of
the two passages (i.e. in the balanced use of the verbal
forms √בנה and √כון including their general chiastic
arrangement), that their close association must have been

---

[1] Cf. p. 99, n. 3.

[2] The writer hopes to deal with the principle of the בְּרִית and its related
terminology in a subsequent publication. Cf. *The Vitality of the Individual
in the Thought of Ancient Israel*, p. 88, n. 1, 2nd edit., p. 86, n. 7, and p. 103,
n. 4, 2nd edit., p. 105, n. 2.   [3] vv. 4–5 (EVV. 3–4).

[4] Cf., for example, the works of Mowinckel, Gunkel (followed by Kraus,
Die Königsherrschaft Gottes im Alten Testament, pp. 75 ff.; but see now
B.K.A.T., *in loc.*), Buttenwieser, Oesterley, Leslie, and Podechard, as cited
above, p. 25, n. 1.

intended from the first. The sequence of thought is really quite unbroken.[1]

The initial affirmation that Yahweh's faithfulness in respect of this vow is as sure as the heavens themselves is now explained as being due to the fact that He is without peer in the assembly of the gods; for it was He who triumphed over the chaos monster and its allies, and this victory not only ensured His rule over the cosmic sea but also made possible His creation of the ordered world of earth and heaven. It is hardly necessary to add that with this threefold thought we at once enter the realm of ideas which we have already seen to be associated with the conception of Yahweh as the heavenly King and, what is more, with the celebration of the autumnal festival of the Jerusalem cultus in its pre-exilic form.[2]

> The heavens praise Thy wondrous work, O Yahweh,
> Even Thy faithfulness in the assembly of the holy ones.
> For who in the sky can be compared with Yahweh,
> Is like Yahweh among the gods (בְּנֵי אֵלִים)?
> A God who is awesome in the council of the holy ones,
> ⌈He is great⌉[3] and terrible above all who are about Him.
> O Yahweh, God of Hosts, who is like unto Thee,
> Strong, O Yah, and with Thy faithfulness all about Thee?
> It is Thou who dost rule over the swell of the sea;
> When the waves thereof rise, it is Thou who dost still them.
> It was Thou who didst crush Rahab[4] like a corpse,
> Scattering Thine enemies with Thy mighty Arm.

---

[1] Cf. in this connexion the interesting suggestion made by R. B. Y. Scott, 'The Pillars Jachin and Boaz', *J.B.L.* lviii (1939), pp. 143–9.

[2] vv. 6–13 (EVV. 5–12).

[3] Reading רַב הוּא for the extraordinary רַבָּה of M.T. Cf., for example, Gunkel, op. cit., *in loc.*

[4] i.e. the primeval chaos-monster, which makes its appearance in Israel's religious literature as Rahab or Leviathan, the dragon or tortuous serpent with many heads. See in general Job iii. 8, vii. 12, ix. 13, xxvi. 12 f. (cf. xl. 25–xli. 26 (EVV. xli. 1–34)); Pss. lxxiv. 12 ff., civ. 25 f.; Isa. xxvii. 1, xxx. 7, li. 9; Amos ix. 2 f. The conception of Leviathan, the dragon or serpent with many heads, may now be illustrated from the Ugaritic texts, e.g. Gordon, op. cit., 67, i 1 ff.; 'nt, iii 35 ff. (= Herdner, op. cit., 5, i 1 ff.; 3, iii 35 ff.: cf. Driver, *Canaanite Myths and Legends*, pp. 102 f., 86 f.), which not only furnish a close parallel to Isa. xxvii. 1 (cf., too, Job xxvi. 13), but supplement Ps. lxxiv. 13 f. by describing the monster in question as seven-headed. It is

Thine are the heavens, Thine too is the earth;
  It was Thou who didst found the world and all that filleth it.
It was Thou who didst create the north and the south;
  Tabor and Hermon applaud Thy Name!

Further, this assurance of a stability in the realm of nature has its parallel in the assurance of an equal stability in the moral realm. As He is supreme in the assembly of the gods, Yahweh is able to rule the world with the basic principles of righteousness (צֶדֶק) and justice (מִשְׁפָּט); and this means that He never loses sight of the twin factors in His covenant relationship with Israel and the House of David, i.e. devotion and fidelity (חֶסֶד וֶאֱמֶת). Accordingly His followers, who know what it means to share in the 'festal acclamation' (תְּרוּעָה),[1] may live exultantly in the light of His presence. Through Yahweh's righteousness and goodwill they are assured of the nation's supremacy and prosperity; for in the ultimate it is He in His omnipotence who is really Israel's King.[2]

Thine is an Arm with might;
  Thy Hand is strong, and Thy Right Hand on high.
Righteousness and justice are the foundation of Thy throne;
  Devotion and fidelity are present before Thee.
How happy the people who share in[3] the festal acclamation,
  Who walk, O Yahweh, in the light of Thy presence!
In Thy Name they shall rejoice all the day long;
  And through Thy righteousness they shall be exalted.
For Thou in Thy splendour art the source of their strength;
  In Thy goodwill Thou wilt lift up our horn.[4]
For it is Yahweh who is really our shield;
  It is the Holy One of Israel who is really our King.[5]

obvious that we have here (as in the Babylonian Epic of Creation) a motif which, in principle, was the common property of the Near East in the second millennium B.C. and had as its main theme the struggle to create and maintain an ordered world. See further, for example, the careful survey of the material by H. A. Brongers, *De scheppingstradities bij de profeten* (1945), pp. 33–76.   [1] See above, p 75, n. 1.

[2] vv. 14–19 (EVV. 13–18).   [3] *lit.* 'know'.

[4] See above, p. 27, n. 2: and note, accordingly, that K ('Thou wilt lift up our horn') is preferable to Q ('and our horn shall be lifted up').

[5] For the use of לְ as an emphasizing particle, see G. R. Driver, in *Festschrift für Alfred Bertholet* (1950), p. 134; F. Nötscher, *V.T.* iii (1953), p. 379.

Thus the hymn closes, as it began, with the confident ex-
pectation that Yahweh will be loyal to His covenant obligations; and the intervening lines offer the justification for
this assurance. It is because Israel's 'Holy One' is supreme
in the council of the 'holy ones', or (what is the same thing)
it is because the God of Israel is omnipotent in the assembly of the gods; and in His omnipotence as the heavenly
King He not only created the universe but sustains it in
righteousness, for He is faithful and true.

This hymn of praise is then followed by the lengthy
reminder of Yahweh's covenant with the House of David,
which we have already discussed at length;[1] and it must be
repeated here for the sake of continuity, i.e.:[2]

> Of old Thou didst speak by a prophet
>   To Thy votaries, and saidst—
> 'I have bestowed aid upon a manly one,
>   I have exalted a youth from among the people.
> I have found David, My Servant;
>   With My holy oil I have anointed him,
> So that My Hand shall be his constant support,
>   Mine Arm also shall strengthen him.
> No enemy shall oppress him,
>   Nor shall the wrongdoer afflict him;
> But I will beat down his adversaries before him,
>   And I will smite them that hate him.

---

[1] See above, pp. 25 ff.

[2] vv. 20–38 (EVV. 19–37). As indicated above, p. 26, n. 2, the relationship
of these verses to the prophecy of Nathan, as recorded in 2 Sam. vii. 1–17
and 1 Chron. xvii. 1–15, continues to be a matter of dispute. Cf., for example,
the markedly different points of view represented by (a) R. H. Pfeiffer, *Introduction to the Old Testament* (1941), 2nd (English) edit. (1952), pp. 368–73,
who finds the prose narratives to be dependent upon the psalm, which
is itself post-exilic (cf. now Ahlström, *Psalm 89. Eine Liturgie aus dem
Ritual des leidenden Königs*, pp. 182–5, who nevertheless traces the psalm
back to a date at least early in the monarchy); (b) J. L. McKenzie, 'The
Dynastic Oracle: II Samuel 7', *T.S.* viii (1947), pp. 187–218, who finds the
prose narratives on the one hand and the poem on the other to be dependent
upon a common source (cf. now A. Caquot, 'La Prophétie de Nathan et ses
échos lyriques', *S.V.T.* ix (1963), pp. 213–24); and (c) H. van den Bussche,
Le Texte de la prophétie de Nathan sur la dynastie davidique, A.L.B.O. ii. 7
(1948), who accepts the primacy of the prose passages, the text of Chronicles
being superior to that of Samuel.

My faithfulness and My devotion shall be with him,
    And through My Name shall his horn be lifted up.
I will lay his hand also upon the sea,
    And his right hand upon the ocean currents.
He shall cry unto Me, "Thou art my Father,
    My God and the Rock that is my salvation."
I on My part will make him My first-born,
    The highest of earthly kings.
I will always preserve for him My devotion,
    Always keep My covenant true for him.
I will make his seed to endure for ever
    And his throne as the days of heaven.
If his children forsake My law,
    And walk not according to My judgements (*or* rulings),
If they violate My statutes,
    And do not keep My commandments,
I will attend to their rebellion with a rod
    And their iniquity with blows.
But My devotion will I not break off from him,
    Nor will I be untrue to My faithfulness.
I will not violate My covenant,
    Nor alter that which hath passed My Lips.
Once for all have I sworn by My Holiness,
    To David I will not lie;
His seed shall endure for ever,
    And his throne like the sun before Me,
Like the moon, which shall continue for ever,
    A faithful witness in the sky.'

At this point, however, the optimistic note of the earlier verses comes to an end, and there follows a remarkable passage in which bewilderment is expressed at the thought that Yahweh has permitted the defeat and humiliation of His Messiah in a combat which seems likely to prove mortal.[1]

Yet Thou hast spurned and rejected,
    Thou hast been wroth with Thy Messiah.
Thou hast repudiated the covenant with Thy Servant;
    Thou hast brought his crown to pollution in the dust.
Thou hast broken down all his walls;
    Thou hast laid his defences in ruins.

[1] vv. 39–46 (EVV. 38–45).

All the passers-by have despoiled him;
    He has become a mockery to his neighbours.
Thou hast raised on high the right hand of his foes;
    Thou hast made glad all his enemies.
Yea, Thou hast turned back the edge of his sword,[1]
    And hast not upheld him in battle.
Thou hast made an end of his splendour
(*or* Thou hast destroyed ⌐his illustrious sceptre⌐),[2]
    And Thou hast hurled his throne to the ground.
Thou hast shortened the days of his prime;
    Thou hast wrapped him about with shame.

Now we have already seen that at the festival under discussion the celebration of Yahweh's Kingship is the background to a ritual drama in which the kings of the earth
combine to make an attack upon Yahweh's holy city. In the
nature of the case, however, this would also be an attack
upon Yahweh's vicegerent, the Davidic king. Accordingly,
as the celebration of Yahweh's universal Kingship is also
the identical background to the present lament, it seems
reasonable to infer that the defeat or humiliation of the
Davidic king, which is indicated in these lines, is not any
specific historical event, for indeed there is none that can
be made to fit the scene, but is an important element in the
ritual drama. This is confirmed by the language of the last
part of the psalm; for the king himself apparently brings the
liturgy to a close by pleading that he may not be allowed to
die, but may be delivered from the humiliation which he is
suffering at the hands of his foes.[3]

How long, O Yahweh, wilt Thou continue to hide Thyself?
    How long shall Thine anger burn like fire?
Remember, I am ⌐not everlasting;
    As nought⌐[4] hast Thou created all mankind.

[1] Or 'his flashing sword'? Cf. G. R. Driver, in *Studies in Old Testament
Prophecy* (T. H. Robinson *Festschrift*), ed. H. H. Rowley (1950), p. 55.

[2] The text of this somewhat short stichos is commonly, and probably
rightly, suspected of being corrupt; and the alternative rendering given above
is based on the reading מַטֵּה טָהֳרוֹ, which assumes a simple case of
haplography.

[3] vv. 47–52 (EVV. 46–51).

[4] Divide and vocalize the consonantal text so as to read חֶלֶד עֹלָם הַשָּׁוְא.

What man can live and not see death,
Can deliver himself from the hand of Sheol?
Where are Thy former acts of devotion, O Lord,
Which Thou didst swear to David by Thy faithfulness?
Remember, O Lord, the mockery of Thy Servant,[1]
How I bear in my bosom the insults of many peoples,[2]
How Thine enemies make mock, O Yahweh,
How they make mock of Thy Messiah at every step!

Thus we see that at this autumnal festival the Davidic king, for all that he is the specially chosen Servant of the omnipotent, heavenly King, is a suffering Servant. He is the Messiah of Yahweh; but on this occasion, at least, he is a humble Messiah. What we see, however, is a ritual humiliation which in principle is not unlike that suffered by the Babylonian king in the analogous New Year Festival.[3] That is to say, this dramatic deliverance from the kings (or nations) of the earth, this victory over 'Death', is not achieved without an early disaster, which is clearly intended as a lesson in dependence upon Yahweh. Salvation, for king and commoner alike, must come from Israel's God, for all human aids are really worthless to this end.[4]

Now we possess in Psalm ci a composition in the first person which fits remarkably into this context, and in so

The foregoing בַּל‎ corresponds to the Arabic negative لَا (as in 1 Kings xii. 16, Song of Sol. viii. 4), and חָלַד corresponds to the Arabic خَالِد, 'lasting'.

[1] Reading 'Thy Servant' for 'Thy servants' with twenty-four MSS. and S.

[2] Cf. G. R. Driver, 'Once Again Abbreviations', *Textus* iv (1964), p. 81.

[3] Cf., for example, C. J. Gadd, in *Myth and Ritual: Essays on the Myth and Ritual of the Hebrews in relation to the Culture Pattern of the Ancient East*, ed. S. H. Hooke (1933), pp. 53 f.; Labat, *Le Caractère religieux de la royauté assyro-babylonienne*, pp. 167 f.; Frankfort, *Kingship and the Gods*, pp. 319 f. The statement made above in the text corresponds to that which was made by the writer in 'The Rôle of the King in the Jerusalem Cultus', p. 100; and it has been described by L. Černý, *The Day of Yahweh and some Relevant Problems* (1948), p. 69, n. 87, as containing 'a great exaggeration'. This seems to the writer to be without justification and to be based on a failure to pay due regard to the pivotal words 'in principle'; for the principle is surely the same, i.e. that of reminding the king that in the ultimate he holds office by will of his divine overlord, whose responsible servant he is.

[4] Cf. Pss. xx. 7 ff. (EVV. 6 ff.), lx. 13 f. (EVV. 11 f.) = cviii. 13 f. (EVV. 12 f.); Isa. xxxi. 1 ff.; Jer. xvii. 5 ff.; Zech. iv. 6.

doing reveals the Messiah as pleading the justice of his rule and longing for the moment when Yahweh will come to him in his apparent abandonment. Most recent commentators are agreed that the psalm embodies the code of behaviour governing the conduct of an Israelite ruler;[1] and we may safely infer from the reference to 'Yahweh's city' in the last line of the poem that the ruler in question is the Davidic king.[2] Indeed its standpoint is so similar to that of the so-called 'Last Words of David' that it may well mirror the moral code to which the Davidic king (and originally David himself) was pledged under the terms of the Davidic covenant. For our immediate purpose, however, the most remarkable feature of the poem is to be found in the first two lines, for these end with a question which at first sight appears strangely out of keeping with the context:[3]

> Of devotion and justice will I sing;
> Unto Thee, O Yahweh, will I raise a psalm.
> I will make my theme[4] 'A Faultless Way'.
> When wilt Thou come to me?

The question in the last stichos has been found so irrelevant and so incomprehensible that some commentators have felt bound to infer a corruption of the text;[5] but we are now in a position to place it in its full context and so to grasp its purpose. The fact is that the Messiah is pleading

---

[1] e.g. Kirkpatrick, Kittel, Gunkel, König, Schmidt, Herkenne, Calès, Leslie, and Weiser; also Kraus. For a valuable discussion of the form and content of this psalm, see now O. Kaiser, 'Erwägungen zu Psalm 101', *Z.A.W.* lxxiv (1962), pp. 195–205, where stress is rightly laid upon the use of the Qinah rhythm (i.e. the metre which is characteristic of the dirge).

[2] Cf. Ps. xlviii. 2 f., 9 (EVV. 1 f., 8), as above, pp. 85 ff.; Isa. lx. 14.

[3] vv. 1–2a.

[4] The *Hiph'il* of √שכל appears to be used with reference to the composition or use of a Hebrew poem of the type known as a מַשְׂכִּיל (EVV. 'Maschil'). Cf. the use of √זמר in the preceding verse (including the heading to the psalm).

[5] e.g. Duhm, Staerk, Mowinckel (*Kongesalmerne i Det Gamle Testamente*, pp. 50 f.; but see *Offersang og sangoffer*, p. 335, *The Psalms in Israel's Worship*, i, p. 68, and G.T.M.M.M., *in loc.*), Gunkel, Schmidt, Herkenne, Oesterley, Leslie, and Weiser; also Kraus, and E. Dhorme, *B.P.* (*A.T.*), ii (1959).

his loyalty to the Davidic covenant in terms of his devotion (חֶסֶד) and justice (מִשְׁפָּט), and is claiming that his
rule is altogether without fault; he has behaved with
complete integrity.[1] Accordingly he can look confidently for
Yahweh to come to him in his hour of need. He has ful-
filled his own part in the covenant, and it is now for
Yahweh to show a corresponding loyalty or devotion. The
remainder of the psalm then presents us with an elaboration of this defence. That is to say, it offers us not so much
a vow as to the type of rule which he proposes to exercise[2]
but an affirmation of the rule which he is wont to exercise.[3]

> I walk in the integrity of my heart
>> Within my house.
> I set before mine eyes
>> No evil thing.
> I hate him that practiseth[4] deceit;
>> He is no adherent of mine.
> The crooked heart departeth from me;
>> I consort with none who is evil.
> Whoso slandereth his fellow in secret,
>> Him I put to silence.[5]
> As for the lofty of eye and the proud of heart,
>> Him I cannot endure.

[1] The statement which is made above in the text is in line with the usual
understanding of the first metrical line; but Kaiser, op. cit., p. 202 (following
Kraus, B.K.A.T., *in loc.*), thinks that we have here a reference, not (*a*) to the
qualities, subsequently illustrated, which the Davidic king claims to have
shown in fulfilment of his obligations under the covenant, but (*b*) to the
corresponding qualities in Yahweh to which he can appeal in virtue of his
own behaviour in upholding the covenant. This is a tempting suggestion,
for, as Kaiser goes on to make clear, it would serve to strengthen rather
than weaken my argument; but I am not convinced that this interpretation
is required by the parallelism or, again, by the wording of Psalm lxxxix. 2
(EVV. 1) and Isaiah lv. 3.   [2] Cf. P.B.V., A.V., and R.V.

[3] vv. 2b–8. Cf (i) the imperfect forms of the verbs in these verses with
the cohortatives of vv. 1–2a; (ii) the so-called 'negative confession' or
'declaration of innocence' recited by the king in connexion with the ritual of
humiliation at the Babylonian New Year Festival, as described, for example,
by Gadd, loc. cit., and Frankfort, loc. cit. See also Mowinckel, *Psalmenstudien II*, pp. 328 f., *Offersang og sangoffer*, pp. 77, 333 ff. (cf. *The Psalms
in Israel's Worship*, i, pp. 65 ff.); Dürr, *Ursprung und Ausbau der israelitisch-
jüdischen Heilandserwartung*, p. 140, n. 37.

[4] Vocalizing the consonantal text so as to read עֹשֵׂה.   [5] Cf. K.B., s.v.

> Mine eyes are upon the faithful of the land,
> That they may dwell with me.
> Whoso walketh in a faultless way,
> He becometh my servant.
> There doth not dwell within my house
> Any that committeth deception.
> He that telleth lies may not stand
> Before mine eyes.
> Morning by morning I put to silence
> All the wicked in the land,
> Cutting off from Yahweh's city
> All who make trouble.[1]

The language is so simple and direct that comment is unnecessary; but one important conclusion must now be borne in mind, i.e. that the Messiah, in pleading that he has proved worthy of his trust, is affirming not only his own righteousness but also that of his subjects. Whatever their standing in society, Yahweh's חֲסִידִ֫ים or 'votaries' are, one and all, צַדִּיקִים or 'righteous'. In short, the Messiah has purged the nation of its evil and made it a fit instrument for the realization of Yahweh's purposes.

The next work to engage our attention is Psalm xviii,[2] which, as the conclusion shows quite clearly, must have been composed for the use of the Davidic king or Messiah. We have already seen how, in Psalms lxxxix and ci, the Messiah has appealed to Yahweh for deliverance from his distress, and here we have his thanksgiving for answered prayer. It falls clearly into three parts, which celebrate (*a*) his deliverance from 'Death' through the intervention of Yahweh in the person of the 'Most High'; (*b*) his resultant justification or, better perhaps, the consequent vindication

---

[1] The reference is to the role of the king as the supreme judge to whom difficult cases might be referred. Cf. 2 Sam. xv. 1–6; 1 Kings iii. 16–28; Jer. xxi. 12. In the Yemen, for example, it was still the practice only a few years ago for the Imam to sit for an hour every morning under the Tree of Justice in San'a to deal with his subjects' grievances. Cf. A. Rihani, *Arabian Peak and Desert: Travels in Al-Yaman* (1930), pp. 103 f.

[2] Cf. 2 Sam. xxii, which has been followed occasionally in the ensuing translation.

of his righteousness (צֶדֶק); and (c) his triumph over the nations of the earth.

The general situation revealed by the psalm is so clear that little is required in the way of detailed comment. The Messiah begins with a few general lines in praise of Yahweh for His saving power:[1]

> I love Thee, O Yahweh, my strength!
> Yahweh is my crag, my fortress, my deliverer;
> My God is my rock wherein I seek refuge,
> My shield, my saving horn, my tower.
> I call for Yahweh, the subject of my praise,
> And I am delivered from mine enemies.

This is followed by a description of his deliverance which is not only vivid and picturesque but highly instructive. His fight with his powerful foes, who, as we learn from the last part of the psalm, are the nations of the earth, continues to be a struggle with 'Death'. As such, however, it is also a battle with the breakers of the cosmic sea which threatens every moment to engulf him and thus plunge the nation (and indeed, by implication, the whole earth) into chaos.[2]

> Death's breakers[3] engulfed me,
> And the evil torrents o'erwhelmed me.
> Sheol's cords were round about me;
> Death's snares confronted me.
> In my distress I called for Yahweh,
> And unto my God I appealed for help.

As we have already seen, however, this disastrous experience is really designed as a lesson in dependence upon Yahweh; and it is only when the outlook is blackest that the latter

---

[1] vv. 2–4 (EVV. 1–3).

[2] vv. 5–7a (EVV. 4–6a). For the cosmology underlying this scene, see *The Vitality of the Individual in the Thought of Ancient Israel*, pp. 89 ff., and now, especially, 2nd. edit. rev., pp. 88 ff.; also, for valuable comparative data, O. Kaiser, *Die mythische Bedeutung des Meeres in Ägypten, Ugarit und Israel*, B.Z.A.W., 2nd edit. rev. (1962).

[3] Reading 'breakers' with 2 Sam. xxii. 5 rather than 'cords', which occurs again in the following line.

intervenes on behalf of this Messiah who has proved worthy of 'Sonship', and delivers him (and *ipso facto* the nation) from the arch-enemy 'Death'. Moreover, it is significant to find that deliverance comes through the intervention of Yahweh in the person of the 'Most High', for this harmonizes with the fact that the triumphant issue of the ritual combat was found to take place with the intervention of the 'Most High' at daybreak. That is to say, the life of the Messiah is renewed at dawn; and this is a point to be borne in mind, for we shall have occasion to return to it in due course. Moreover, it is wholly in line with what we have already learnt concerning Yahweh's subjection of the cosmic sea, as celebrated at this festival, that He comes to the aid of His Messiah in His role as the 'Rider of the Clouds', and that His theophany is described as taking place in all the terrifying splendour of a thunderstorm.[1]

> In His Palace (*or* Temple) He heard my voice,
>   And my appeal ( )[2] came to His Ears.
> The earth heaved and quaked,
>   While the foundations of the mountains quivered;
>   Yea, they rocked because He was wroth.
> Smoke rose from His Nostril,
>   While fire leapt devouring from His Mouth;
>   Live coals came kindling therefrom.
> He parted[3] the heavens, and descended,
>   With a cloud beneath His Feet.
> He rode upon a cherub[4] and flew;
>   He sped on the wings of the wind.
> He made darkness His covert,
>   His shelter around Him the watery blackness,
>   Masses of cloud which had no brightness.[5]

---

[1] vv. 7b–20 (EVV. 6b–19).

[2] Omitting 'before Him' as a variant of 'to His Ears': cf. 2 Sam. xxii. 7.

[3] Vocalizing the consonantal text so as to read וַיֵּט, 'And He thrust aside' (i.e. like a curtain).

[4] A mythical creature, probably pictured as a winged and human-headed lion. Cf. Gen. iii. 24 (J); Exod. xxv. 18–22 (P); Ps. xcix. 1; Ezek. i. 5–28, x. 1–22, xxviii. 11–19; etc.: and see above, p. 72, n. 1.

[5] Construing the first word of verse 13 (EVV. 12) with verse 12 (EVV. 11). Cf. J. M. P. Smith, in *The Bible: An American Translation* (1935).

Ahead of Him through His clouds there passed
    Hailstones and coals of fire.[1]
Yahweh thundered in the heavens;
    The Most High uttered His Voice ( ).[2]
He sent forth His arrows, scattering them abroad,
    Even lightnings in abundance, making them resound.
Then the bed of the sea[3] could be seen,
    And the foundations of the world were laid bare,
At Thy rebuke, O Yahweh,
    At the tempestuous breathing of Thy Nostril.[4]
He reached from on high, He took me,
    He drew me out of the many waters.[5]
He delivered me from my powerful enemy,
    From my foes, for they were too strong for me.
They confronted me on the day of my calamity;
    But Yahweh became my support.
He set me at liberty;[6]
    He freed me, for He was pleased with me.

It is difficult not to link this dramatic picture with the procession from 'Israel's Spring', which we have already seen to be closely associated with the manifestation of Yahweh's victorious power over the waters of the cosmic sea; and one cannot but conjecture (although this is no more than a conjecture) that something like a baptismal scene within the confines of the spring Gihon may have been the focal point of this dramatic ritual.[7] Be this as it may, it

---

[1] For the significance of the verb עָבַר in this connexion, see Isa. xxxiii. 21; Lam. iii. 44. The rendering in the text is based upon that of Buttenwieser, op. cit., *in loc.*

[2] Omitting 'hailstones and coals of fire' as an obvious duplication from the preceding verse. Cf. LXX and 2 Sam. xxii. 14.

[3] *lit.* 'the watery channels' or (as in 2 Sam. xxii. 16) 'the channels of the sea'; but see also Patton, op. cit., pp. 12 and 34, and F. M. Cross jr. and D. N. Freedman, *J.B.L.* lxxii (1953), p. 26, n. 41.

[4] Or, as in 2 Sam. xxii. 16,

'At the rebuke of Yahweh,
    At the tempestuous breathing of His Nostril.'

[5] See above, p. 63, n. 3.   [6] *lit.* 'He brought me forth into a broad place.'

[7] Cf. J. Steinmann, *David: Roi d'Israël* (1948), pp. 144 f. The reader may also be referred at this point to the interesting comparative data now furnished by C. S. Mann, 'Sacral Kingship—an Ashanti Footnote', *J.S.S.* v (1960), pp. 378–87, esp. 381 f.

will be observed that, following his ascent from the waters of the Underworld, the Messiah knows himself to be the 'Son' in whom his heavenly Father is well-pleased.[1]

It is appropriate, therefore, to find that the Messiah, whom we have already seen in Psalm ci to be pleading his faithfulness to his trust, then goes on to emphasize the fact that by his deliverance from 'Death' he has been vindicated with regard to his 'righteousness' (צֶדֶק); he has been justified or proved 'righteous' (צַדִּיק). Moreover, this is in line with his humility before his God and Father; for it is only a humble people (עַם עָנִי), proved such in the person of their king, whom Yahweh consents to save. It is for man, even when called to the highest office in the service of his Creator, to remember his place in the divine economy. The Davidic king must be taught that he is no more than a vicegerent in the service of the divine King, for only so can he be sure of Yahweh's support in time of need; and in the scene before us the true Messiah, having been vindicated with regard to his righteousness, is assured that his lamp will not be extinguished. In this way we again see that Yahweh's victory is not only the triumph of the 'Living God' over the forces of 'Death' but also the triumph of light over the forces of darkness; and the resultant deliverance of the Messiah from the dark underworld of 'Death' is a dramatic escape from the encircling defences of a prison into the world of light and life which is Yahweh's special creation and care.[2]

> Yahweh doth recompense me according to my righteousness;
>> According to the purity of my hands He maketh me restoration.
> For I have kept Yahweh's ways,
>> And I have not departed wickedly from my God.
> For all His judgements are before me,
>> And I turn not His statutes from me.
> I have been faultless in my relations with Him,
>> And I have abstained from all that would render me guilty.

---

[1] See above, pp. 25 ff., 110 f., and below, pp. 128 ff.
[2] vv. 21–30 (EVV. 20–29).

So Yahweh hath made me restoration according to my
   righteousness,
According to the purity of my hands in His sight.
With the devoted Thou dost prove devoted;
   With him who is faultless Thou dost prove faultless;
With the pure Thou dost prove pure;[1]
   But with the tortuous Thou dost prove ready to wrestle.[2]
For Thou dost save a humble people,
   But lofty eyes Thou dost abase.
For Thou keepest my lamp alight, O Yahweh,
   My God doth illumine my darkness.
For through Thee I break down[3] the fence;
   And through my God I leap the wall.

The Messiah, fresh from Yahweh's triumph in the ritual
combat and his own dramatic escape from the confines of

---

[1] G. R. Driver, *H.T.R.* xxix (1936), pp. 172 f., suggests that the verbal
forms from √ברר in this line should be associated with the Syriac ܟ݁ܒ݂ܪ,
'simple, rude', and the Arabic بَرِيّ, 'wild, savage', so as to secure an example
of synonymous parallelism in contrast to that of the preceding verse, e.g.

   With the boorish Thou dost show Thyself boorish,
     And with the crooked Thou dost show Thyself tortuous.

Once again, however, it seems to the writer that what is an attractive suggestion when considered in comparative isolation becomes untenable when
seen in its full context; for this example scarcely does justice to the use of
√ברר in verses 21 and 25 (EVV. 20 and 24), i.e. כְּבֹר יָדַי, 'according to the
purity of my hands'. Indeed the fact that the second stichos in verse 27 is introduced by the conjunction ו, which is absent from the three preceding
stichoi, serves to point the contrast thus finally introduced. (Professor Driver,
in a private note to the writer, defends his view on the ground that this is
'one of those cases in which a Hebrew author intentionally juxtaposes hom-
onyms with different senses' (cf. *V.T.* iv (1954), pp. 242 f.), and claims that on
his theory verses 26 and 27 (EVV. 25 and 26) offer an example of parallelism, combined with chiasmus, which is decisive; but the writer remains
unconvinced.)   [2] Cf. Gen. xxx. 8 (J).

[3] Vocalizing the consonantal text so as to read אָרֻץ; cf. A.V. mgn. At
the same time there seems to be no justification for taking the further step
of reading גֶּדֶר ('wall') for גְּדוּד. Cf., for example, Duhm, op. cit., *in loc.*
The term גְּדוּד appears to have the primary meaning of 'section' or 'division' (cf. גָּדַד, 'to cut'), whence the traditional rendering of EVV., 'a
troop'. Here, however, it seems to be used of a 'division' with reference to
that which actually divides, i.e. a partition, barrier, or fence. Accordingly it
should be retained, the more so that it is confirmed by the text of 2 Sam.
xxii. 30.

'Death', then goes on to praise Yahweh, the one omnipotent God, in equally picturesque language for this assurance of victory over his enemies and a resultant supremacy amongst the nations of the earth.[1]

> As the God whose way is faultless,
>> Yahweh's speech is without dross;
>>> He is a shield to all who seek refuge in Him.
> For what god is there beside Yahweh,
>> And what rock is there except our God?
> The God who girdeth me with might,
>> And hath rendered my way faultless;
> Who maketh my feet like those of a hind,
>> And setteth me firm on the heights;[2]
> Who traineth my hands for battle,
>> So that mine arms can aim a bow of bronze![3]
> Thou hast given me also Thy saving shield,
>> While Thy Right Hand upholdeth me,
>>> And Thy support[4] maketh me great.
> Thou dost extend my strides beneath me,
>> And mine ankles do not give way.
> I pursue and overtake mine enemies,
>> And I turn not back until making an end of them.
> I smite them so that they cannot rise;
>> They fall beneath my feet.
> Thou hast girded me with might for battle;
>> Thou dost subdue mine opponents beneath me.
> Thou hast made mine enemies turn back before me,
>> And them that hate me I put to silence.
> They appeal for help, but there is none to save them,
>> Even to Yahweh, but He doth not answer them.
> I grind them small like dust before the wind,
>> I crush[5] them like the mire of the streets.

[1] vv. 31–46 (EVV. 30–45).

[2] Reading בָּמֹות for בָּמֹותַי with LXX, Jerome, and S on the ground of dittography.

[3] Cf. G. R. Driver, *W.O.* i (1947–52), p. 410; also *V.T.* i (1951), p. 248, where it is suggested that 'bow' must be used here by synecdoche with reference to a bronze-tipped 'arrow'.

[4] *lit.* 'answer' or 'response', i.e. reading עֲנֹותְךָ in agreement with 2 Sam. xxii. 36. Cf. verse 42 (EVV. 41) with its reference to the vain appeal to Yahweh made by the Messiah's enemies.

[5] See G. R. Driver, *H.T.R.* xxix (1936), pp. 173 f.

Thou dost deliver me from my[1] people's struggles:
Thou dost make me head of the nations;
People serve me that I have not known.
Foreigners cringe before me;
The moment they hear, they obey me.[2]
Foreigners wither away,
Quitting their fastnesses.

The whole psalm is then brought to an end on a note of personal thanksgiving to Him who is obviously the 'Living God':[3]

Yahweh *liveth*![4] Blessed be my rock!
The God who doth save me is supreme,
The God who hath granted me vengeance,
And subdued[5] the peoples beneath me!
As my deliverer from mine angry foes,
Thou dost give me supremacy over mine adversaries,
From violent men Thou dost rescue me.
Therefore I will thank Thee amid the nations, O Yahweh,
I will sing praises to Thy Name,
To Him who doth give great victories[6] to His king
And showeth devotion to His Messiah,
To David and his seed for ever.

In Psalm cxviii we have an obvious companion-piece to the foregoing. It opens with a general summons by or on behalf of the king to offer thanks to Yahweh for His unending devotion (חֶסֶד); and the whole nation, afterwards distinguished as the priesthood and the general body of worshippers, is then bidden to echo this thought of Yahweh's continued regard for His chosen people. It is true that the king is not specifically mentioned, but the language and thought of the psalm as a whole are obviously in harmony with the other psalms in this series which centre in the person of the Messiah; and, of course, if the king is

---

[1] Cf. 2 Sam. xxii. 44.
[2] Reversing the order of the two stichoi as in 2 Sam. xxii. 45.
[3] vv. 47–51 (EVV. 46–50).   [4] Cf. p. 2, n. 2.
[5] It is worthy of note that in the text of our psalm (but not that of 2 Sam. xxii. 48, which reproduces the more familiar √ירד) the Messiah echoes the words of Ps. xlvii. 4 (EVV. 3) with its otherwise unparalleled use of the *Hiph'il* of √דבר, as noticed above, p. 76, n. 1.
[6] EVV. 'deliverance': R.V. mgn. 'Heb. *salvations*'. See above, p. 102, n. 2.

the speaker and it is clear to all the onlookers that he is
filling this particular role, there is no need for him to be
mentioned as such on every occasion.[1] His opening words,
then, may be rendered as follows:[2]

> Give thanks to Yahweh, for He is good;
> For His devotion is everlasting.
> Let Israel say,
> 'For His devotion is everlasting'.
> Let the House of Aaron say,
> 'For His devotion is everlasting'.
> Let those who fear Yahweh[3] say,
> 'For His devotion is everlasting'.

This is followed by words of thanksgiving on the part of
the king, which describe in colourful terms the immediate
ground for the foregoing exhortation to give thanks to
Yahweh for His unceasing devotion; and the reason is that
He has justified His Messiah's trust by delivering him from
the onslaught of the nations.[4]

> Out of my distress I cried unto Yah;
> Yah's answer was to set me at liberty.[5]

[1] de Fraine, *L'Aspect religieux de la royauté israélite*, p. 334, n. 6, takes
the writer to task on the ground that in his earlier work, 'The Rôle of the
King in the Jerusalem Cultus', p. 105, he unblushingly ('sans sourciller')
ascribed verses 5 ff. of this psalm to the king despite the fact that the king is
not specifically mentioned. It is pleasant to find, however, that subsequently
the writer is spared his blushes, for a little later de Fraine himself says of
verse 10, 'il s'agit bien d'un roi qui parle' (op. cit., p. 388, n. 8)!

[2] vv. 1–4.

[3] It is commonly held that in the expression 'those who fear Yahweh'
one should see a reference to proselytes. Cf., for example, Gunkel, op. cit.,
pp. 498 (i.e. on Ps. cxv. 11) and 505 f. (on this passage), and similarly König,
op. cit., pp. 144 and 440. Even if the phrase might be allowed this meaning,
the order in which the groups are mentioned in the case before us should be
enough to make one question the validity of this view; but the fact is that it
reads into a simple description of the devout Israelite a highly specialized
meaning for which there is no real warrant. Cf., for example, K. Lake, in *The
Beginnings of Christianity. Part I: The Acts of the Apostles*, ed. F. J. Foakes
Jackson and Kirsopp Lake, v (1933), Note VIII. 'Proselytes and God-
fearers', pp. 74 ff., who points out that 'eisegesis has often been substituted
for exegesis in treating the phrase in the Old Testament' (p. 82). Cf., too,
Kirkpatrick, op. cit., on Ps. cxv. 11.   [4] vv. 5–14.

[5] *lit.* 'Yah answered me with a broad place.' Note the close parallel in Ps.
xviii. 20 (EVV. 19), as above, p. 119, n. 6.

With Yahweh on my side I do not fear
What man may do to me.
With Yahweh on my side to give me aid,
I gaze in triumph on them that hate me.
It is better to seek refuge in Yahweh
Than to trust in man.
It is better to seek refuge in Yahweh
Than to trust in princes.
All nations surrounded me;
Through the Name of Yahweh I cut them off.[1]
They surrounded me, yea, they surrounded me;
Through the Name of Yahweh I cut them off.
They surrounded me like bees;
They died away[2] like a fire of thistles;
Through the Name of Yahweh I cut them off.
Thou didst press me sore[3] that I might fall,
But Yahweh came to mine aid.
Yah, who is my strength and song,
Hath become my salvation.

In the ensuing lines we are able to discern a little more of
the ritual background of this psalm; for once again, as in
Psalms xxiv and lxviii, we find ourselves in the company of
a procession which is approaching the gates of the Temple
and seeking admission to its precincts. In this case, however,
we find that the focus of interest is not the Ark as the manifestation *par excellence* of the presence of the divine King
amidst His chosen people but His earthly representative,
the Messiah of the House of David; and the whole ceremony,

---

[1] Or 'I warded them off'? Cf. LXX (ἠμυνάμην), and see further G. R.
Driver, *Z.A.W.* lii (1934), p. 54.

[2] Reading the *Qal* for the *Pu'al* of the M.T. The simile is that of a bonfire
of thistles, which blazes up furiously enough at first but quickly dies away.
Cf. the simile of the dying wick in Isa. xliii. 17; and, for the picture, see 2
Sam. xxiii. 6 f. (as above, p. 19).

[3] The placing of this psalm in what appears to be its original setting
throws light on a reading which is commonly emended to נְדַחְיתִי, following LXX, Jerome, and S, so as to yield the meaning 'I was pressed sore';
for it is now possible to explain this reading in terms of an aside addressed
to the leader of the 'kings' of the earth, who, as we have seen, are led captive
to the Temple in this triumphant procession of Yahweh's Messiah. In other
words, the M.T. has happily preserved what is an appropriately dramatic
touch.

as it now appears before our eyes, is one which compels a certain admiration. The Messiah has been made to suffer humiliation; he has been 'chastened sore' and thereby brought close to the gates of the Underworld. Nevertheless through Yahweh's devotion (חֶסֶד) and righteousness (צֶדֶק) his faith has been justified, and he has been delivered from the power of 'Death' and thereby proved righteous (צַדִּיק); but *ipso facto* the people themselves, as forming a psychical whole with its focus in the king and, what is more, as being dependent upon the justice of his rule for the right ordering of society, have also been delivered from 'Death' and proved righteous (צַדִּיק). Thus the well-being of the community is assured; and public testimony is borne to the fact that the key to 'Life' is righteousness (צֶדֶק), the loyal functioning of the corporate whole, based on a resolute faith in Yahweh. Accordingly the procession of the righteous now moves forward through 'the gates of righteousness', through 'the gate whereby the righteous may enter', to continue the ritual in a ceremony with which we have yet to deal.[1]

> Hark to the cries of victory[2]
>   In the tents of the righteous!
> Yahweh's Right Hand acteth mightily,
>   Yahweh's Right Hand is exalted,
>   Yahweh's Right Hand acteth mightily!
> I am not to die but live,
>   And relate the deeds of Yah.
> Yah hath chastened me sore,
>   But He hath not given me over to 'Death'.
> Open for me the gates of righteousness,[3]
>   That I may enter thereby and acknowledge Yah.
> This is that gate of Yahweh,
>   Whereby the righteous may enter.

[1] vv. 15–21.

[2] Or 'salvation', i.e. the same word as in verses 14 and 21. See again p. 102, n. 2.

[3] Cf. the interesting collection of traditional material, Jewish and Christian, assembled by J. Morgenstern, 'The Gates of Righteousness', *H.U.C.A.* vi (1929), pp. 1–37, although the citation of this work must not be construed as an acceptance of the theories developed by Morgenstern in this connexion. Cf. the writer's comment, *E.T.* lxii (1950–1), p. 40; and see above, p. 55, n. 2.

I will acknowledge Thee, for Thou hast answered me,
And hast become my salvation.

These lines are followed by a short hymn of welcome,
which was evidently sung by way of greeting to the incom-
ing procession; and it is wholly in line with our attempted
reconstruction of this festival that the emphasis should be
found to lie upon the fact that this festal day is one on which
Yahweh has acted in a very special way, delivering His
people from darkness and bringing them light as well as life.
Moreover, it is to be observed that this hymn of welcome to
Yahweh's Messiah centres in the cry of הוֹשִׁיעָה נָּא, 'Grant
salvation!', which in the shortened form הוֹשַׁע־נָא has been
made familiar through the Greek of the New Testament as
'Hosanna!'[1]

> The stone which the builders rejected
>   Now doth crown the corner.
> This is Yahweh's doing;
>   It is marvellous in our eyes.
> This is the day on which Yahweh hath acted;
>   Let us rejoice and be glad therein.
> O Yahweh, grant salvation (הוֹשִׁיעָה נָּא)!
>   O Yahweh, grant prosperity!
> Blessed is he that cometh in the Name of Yahweh!
> We greet you from the House of Yahweh;
>   Yahweh is God, and hath given us light![2]

The concluding lines of the psalm then present us with
what appears to be the royal summons to begin the festal
dance as an act of thanksgiving to Yahweh for His lasting
devotion (חֶסֶד); and it is worthy of note that the worshippers appear to have been equipped with festal branches of
some kind. In the circumstances it is reasonable to infer
that these are branches of palm, myrtle, and willow such
as were traditionally associated with the ritual encircle-
ment of the altar in the post-exilic form of the Feast of

---

[1] vv. 22–27a. Cf. Matt. xxi. 9, 15; Mark xi. 9 f.; John xii. 13.
[2] Cf. Ps. xcvii. 11, as above, p. 98, n. 6.

Tabernacles.[1] Finally, it is also worthy of note that this royal summons thus brings us full circle to the summons with which the psalm began.[2]

> Join in the dance with festal boughs
> Up to the horns of the altar!
> Thou art my God, and I will acknowledge Thee;
> My God, I will extol Thee.
> Give thanks to Yahweh, for He is good;
> For His devotion is everlasting.

VI

(a)

We come now to what appears to be the final stage in the dramatic ritual under review, and to appreciate its significance we have to recall that David was promised supremacy over the kings of the earth in virtue of his being the adopted 'Son' of Yahweh; for we now meet with the thought of the eventual fulfilment of this promise in the person of his descendant and ideal successor upon the throne, the true Messiah of the House of David.[3] We have already seen how Yahweh secures the latter's supremacy over the nations by giving him victory in the ritual combat at daybreak on this—'the day on which Yahweh hath acted'. The complementary idea, however, is present at the same time, for this deliverance from 'Death' also marks the renewal of life or rebirth of him who has proved to be the true Messiah; it is the sign of his adoption as the 'Son' of Yahweh, and issues, as one might expect, in his re-enthronement as Yahweh's vicegerent endowed now with universal power. This finds ready illustration in Psalm ii, which shows us the kings of the earth, after their abortive attempt throughout the years to thwart Yahweh's plans to make good His sovereign power through the line of David, being compelled to acknowledge the universal sovereignty of this particular Messiah in virtue of his triumphant enthronement as one

---

[1] Cf., for example, Buttenwieser, op. cit., *in loc.*
[2] vv. 27b–29. [3] See above, pp. 2 f. and 25 ff.

who is justified to be the 'Son' of Yahweh, the divine
King who is enthroned in the heavens. It opens thus:[1]

> Why did the nations become insurgent,
>   And the peoples engage in useless plotting?
> The kings of the earth took up their stand,
>   The rulers conferred together,
>   Against Yahweh and against His Messiah:
> 'Let us snap their bonds asunder,
>   And let us fling their cords off from us.'
> He who is throned in the heavens doth laugh;
>   The Lord maketh mock of them.
> Then He doth speak to them in His anger,
>   And in His wrath He doth dismay them:
> 'But I, as you see,[2] have set up My king
>   Upon Zion, My sacred mountain.'

At this point in the liturgy the Messiah himself is made
to recount an oracle which he has received from Yahweh;
and here we have clear evidence of the complementary
ideas concerning the Messiah's relationship to Yahweh in
terms of 'Sonship' and (in conscious dependence upon his
heavenly Father[3]) his supremacy over the nations of the
earth.[4]

> Let me tell of Yahweh's decree!
>   He hath said to me, 'Thou art My Son;
>   This day have I begotten thee.
> Ask of Me, and I will make
>   The nations thine inheritance,
>   The ends of the earth thy possession.
> Thou shalt crush them with a rod of iron;
>   Thou shalt smash them like a potter's vessel.'

The psalm then draws to a close with an exhortation to
the rebellious kings of the earth to curb their proud spirits
and admit Yahweh's universal sovereignty.[5]

---

[1] vv. 1–6.

[2] These words represent an attempt to reproduce the force of the introductory וַאֲנִי, which serves to underline the contrast between the empty
words of the rebellious kings of the earth and the summary statement of the
heavenly King whose actions speak louder than words.

[3] Note the emphatic 'Ask of Me'.   [4] vv. 7–9.   [5] vv. 10–12.

Now therefore, ye kings, show prudence;
Take warning, ye rulers of earth.

Serve Yahweh with fear;
With trembling kiss ⌐His Feet⌐;[1]
Lest He be angry, and ye vanish away,
For His anger is quickly kindled.
Happy all those who seek refuge in Him![2]

The same association of ideas may be found in Psalm cx, which appears to be an oracle delivered specially for the occasion by one of the cultic prophets whose role in the formal worship of the Temple we have already had occasion to note.[3] The psalm begins with the word נְאֻם which is, of course, the normal term for a prophetic oracle;[4] and the opening lines, which are quite straightforward, may be rendered thus:[5]

Oracle of Yahweh to my lord!

Sit thou at My Right Hand, while I make
Thine enemies a stool for thy feet.
Yahweh doth extend thy powerful sceptre;[6]
Rule from Zion amidst thy foes!

The words which immediately follow have long been a *crux interpretum*, as one may see from a comparison of the

---

[1] The expression נַשְּׁקוּ־בַר at the beginning of verse 12 (A.V. 'Kiss the Son'; R.V. 'Kiss the son') is a well-known *crux interpretum*, as the use of the word בַּר as an Aramaism for 'son' is extremely unlikely in this context. The rendering accepted above involves the assumption that the present text of this stichos has arisen from corruption of an original בְּרְעָדָה נַשְּׁקוּ. (*or* בְרַגְלָיו (לְרַגְלָיו). Cf. A. Bertholet, *Z.A.W.* xxviii (1908), pp. 58 f., 193: and see in general H. H. Rowley, *J.T.S.* xlii (1941), pp. 152 f.

[2] Cf. Ps. cxviii. 8 f., as above, p. 125.   [3] See pp. 22 and 69.

[4] Cf. *The Cultic Prophet in Ancient Israel*, pp. 46 f., 2nd edit., p. 52.

[5] vv. 1–2.

[6] Cf., for the idiom, 1 Sam. xiv. 27: and, for the metaphor, the code of Ḥammurabi (as above, p. 4, n. 4), Epilogue rev. xxvi. 14 f., 'May Shamash lengthen his sceptre', i.e. 'May Shamash extend his rule', which is variously explained (*a*) as the prolonging of one's reign (cf. T. J. Meek, in *Ancient Near Eastern Texts relating to the Old Testament*, p. 178), (*b*) as the enlarging of one's empire (cf. G. R. Driver and J. C. Miles, *The Babylonian Laws*, ii, pp. 100 f., and (*c*) as an extending of one's rule in both time and space (cf. P. Cruveilhier, *Commentaire du code d'Hammourabi* (1938), pp. 268 f. Cf., too, the picturesque idiom which is referred to above, p. 27, n. 2.

Massoretic text with the renderings of the ancient versions. Nevertheless there appears to be little, if anything, wrong with the consonantal text, when it is read in the light of the foregoing discussion. The fact is that it deals in a perfectly straightforward way with the rebirth of the Messiah, which, as we now know, takes place on this eventful day with his deliverance from the Underworld, apparently at the spring Gihon, at dawn or 'as the morning appeareth'; and this carries with it the implication that the Messiah, in all the fresh vigour of his new-won life (which is here symbolized by the morning dew),[1] has been elevated for all time not only to the throne of David but also to the traditional priesthood of Melchizedek.[2]

> Thou hast the homage of[3] thy people on the day of thy birth[4]
> In sacred splendour[5] from the womb of dawn.[6]
> Thou hast the dew wherewith I have begotten thee;[7]
> Yahweh hath sworn beyond recall:
> Thou art priest for ever
> After the order of Melchizedek.

The oracle then comes to an end with a reminder of the way in which Yahweh came to the aid of His hard-pressed Messiah; and in the portrayal of this scene we are given a

---

[1] Cf., for example, Ps. cxxxiii. 3; Isa. xxvi. 19: and see further E. Burrows, 'Psalm 110 (Vulgate 109) Interpreted', in *The Gospel of the Infancy and Other Biblical Essays* (1940), pp. 88 ff.; G. Widengren, *Psalm 110 och det sakrala kungadömet i Israel*, U.U.Å. 1941: 7, 1 (1941), pp. 11 f. As Burrows indicates on the analogy of Ps. cxxxiii. 2 f., there may well be a ritual counterpart to this reference in the fact of anointing from which the title 'Messiah' is derived. See above, p. 14, n. 2.   [2] vv. 3-4.

[3] It is possible that the consonantal text should be vocalized so as to read נָדַבְתָּ, *lit.* 'Thou hast made thy people willing', rather than as M.T., i.e. 'Thy people are all willingness.'

[4] Vocalizing the consonantal text as חִילְךָ, i.e. *Qal* infinitive construct of √חיל with an objective suffix, on the analogy of Isa. xlv. 10.

[5] Many MSS. (in common with Symmachus and Jerome) read 'in the sacred mountains', which seems equally possible in the context.

[6] The anomalous מִשְׁחָר should perhaps be read as שַׁחַר on the ground of dittography.

[7] Or, a little more literally perhaps, 'of My begetting thee', i.e. vocalizing the consonantal text so as to read יְלִדְתִּיךָ with LXX. Cf. Ps. ii. 7 (as above, p. 129); and, for the syntax, see G.K. § 130d.

vivid glimpse of the heavenly King, who is known to all as the omnipotent God who has proved 'mighty in battle',[1] pausing to slake His thirst ere He pursues afresh His work of slaughter and retribution.[2]

> The Lord hath smitten away at thy right hand,
> Judging[3] kings in the day of His anger.
> He hath taken His fill of corpses among the nations;[4]
> He hath crushed heads[5] o'er all the wide earth.
> He would drink from a stream on His way,[6]
> Thus holding His Head on high!

In conclusion we are now in a position to appreciate the original significance of Psalm xxi, for this in turn gains in coherence when studied against the foregoing background of ritual and mythology. It opens with an emphasis upon the fact that the king is able to rejoice in an affirmative response to his plea for 'life' (חַיִּים). Through some great act of 'victory' or 'salvation' (יְשׁוּעָה) on the part of Yahweh, which is not further defined but now stands revealed, this has been vouchsfed to him; and it is described in glowing terms as 'length of days for ever and ever'. What is more, this assurance of answered prayer with its issue in the king's coronation or enthronement is the outcome of a true covenant relationship, whereby the king's trust (√בטח) in Yahweh is matched by a signal act of devotion (חֶסֶד) from Yahweh's side; and it is all of a piece with the liturgical setting which is here proposed for our psalm that Yahweh, who has already figured so prominently as the 'Most High', is again refered to at this point by means of this particular appellation.[7]

> The king is glad, O Yahweh, by reason of Thy might;
> How greatly doth he rejoice because of Thy victory![8]

---

[1] Cf. Ps. xxiv. 8, as above, p. 73.   [2] vv. 5–7.
[3] Construing the first word of verse 6 with verse 5 on the ground of both metre and sense.   [4] Cf. Exod. xv. 9.
[5] Cf. the language of Ps. lxviii. 22 (EVV. 21), as above, p. 82, and that of Hab. iii. 13.
[6] The Hebrew corresponds exactly to the French 'en route'!
[7] vv. 2–8 (EVV. 1–7).   [8] EVV. 'salvation'. Cf. again p. 102, n. 2.

Thou hast granted him the desire of his heart;
　Thou hast not withheld the request of his lips.
For Thou meetest him with goodly blessings;
　Thou settest a crown of gold upon his head.
Life, which he asked of Thee, Thou hast given him,
　Length of days for ever and ever.
His glory is great by reason of Thy victory;[1]
　Honour and majesty Thou dost bestow upon him.
Yea, Thou makest him an everlasting blessing;
　Thou bringest him joy and gladness with Thy presence.
For the king trusteth (בֹּטֵחַ) in Yahweh,
　And in the unshakeable[2] devotion (חֶסֶד) of the Most High.

In the second half of the psalm we meet with the exultant thought that the future may be faced with confidence
by Yahweh's followers, for the dramatic victory which they
have been celebrating is an earnest of that which is to come.
In short, it offers the assurance that in due course Yahweh
will indeed root out those who have been planning mischief against Him and, by implication, His Messiah; and, in
keeping with our earlier study of the triumph of the
heavenly King,[3] He is finally urged to arise that He may
bring to pass this final act of judgement upon those who
have sought to oppose His will.[4]

Thy Hand will reach out to all Thine enemies;
　Thy Right Hand will find out those who hate Thee.
Thou wilt make them like a blazing oven
　In Thine own good time,[5] Yahweh.
In His anger He will swallow them up;
　Fire will devour them.[6]
Thou wilt destroy their fruit from the earth,
　And their seed from amongst mankind.

---

[1] EVV. 'salvation'. Cf. again p. 102, n. 2.
[2] i.e. construing בַּל־יִמּוֹט as a relative clause.
[3] See above, pp. 98 ff. 　　　　　　　[4] vv. 9–14 (EVV. 8–13).
[5] Cf. *The Vitality of the Individual in the Thought of Ancient Israel*, p. 46,
n. 3, 2nd edit., p. 44, n. 3.
[6] It is tempting to omit this line as a gloss on the ground that it is comparatively short and introduces a reference to Yahweh in the 3rd person rather
than a direct address. Cf., for example, Kittel, op. cit., *in loc*. On the other
hand, however, its omission would destroy the balance of the two halves of

Because they intended evil against Thee,
  They planned mischief which they could not effect,
Thou wilt surely make them turn to flight,
  When Thou dost aim at them with Thy bowstrings.
Rise up, O Yahweh, in Thy strength,
  That we may sing the praises of Thy might!

All in all, therefore, enough has been said to prove the
literally vital part played by the Messiah of the House of
David in the ritual and mythology of the Jerusalem cultus
during the period of the Israelite monarchy; and, summarizing our conclusions once again, we may now say that
the following features are to be recognized in the festival
under discussion as celebrated in Solomon's Temple between the tenth and sixth centuries B.C. In the first place we
have (*a*) the celebration of Yahweh's original triumph, as
leader of the forces of light, over the forces of darkness as
represented by the monstrous chaos of waters or primeval
ocean; (*b*) His subjection of this cosmic sea and His enthronement as King in the assembly of the gods; and
(*c*) the further demonstration of His might and power in the
creation of the habitable world. Cosmogony, however, gives
place to eschatology; for all this is the prelude to the
thought of His re-creative work, which is expressed in the
form of a ritual drama, and, as such, is wholly in line with
what we are told about prophetic symbolism of the type
which appears to have been embraced by the term מָשָׁל. In
fact it is the מָשָׁל *par excellence*, and is designed as an effective demonstration of Yahweh's ultimate will and purpose for
Israel and the world. In this ritual drama the worshippers
are given (*a*) an assurance of final victory over 'Death',
i.e. all that obstructs the fullness of life for mankind which
was Yahweh's design in the creation of the habitable world;
(*b*) a summons to a renewal of their faith in Yahweh and His
plans for them and for the world; and (*c*) a challenge to
a renewed endeavour to be faithful to Him and His demands, so that the day may indeed dawn when this vision

the poem, and there is a similar reference to Yahweh rather than a direct
address in verse 8 (EVV. 7).

of a universal realm of righteousness and peace will be realized, and His Kingdom will be seen in all its power and glory. Moreover, the summons and the challenge are directed first and foremost towards the ruling member of the House of David, in whom rest the hopes of Yahweh and His people; for we now know that, humanly speaking, the leading actor in this drama is the Davidic king, in whom the life of the nation as a corporate whole finds its focus. This work of 'salvation' (יְשׁוּעָה), as it is called, is portrayed by means of some kind of mime in which the kings (i.e. nations) of the earth, representing the forces of darkness and 'Death' as opposed to light and 'Life' and commonly designated the 'wicked' (רְשָׁעִים), unite in an attempt to overthrow Yahweh's covenanted followers, i.e. His 'votaries' (חֲסִידִים) or the 'righteous' (צַדִּיקִים), under the leadership of the Messiah. The latter, who is also described as the Servant of Yahweh,[1] suffers an initial humiliation; but this issues in his salvation and that of his people, for it involves the recognition of an ultimate dependence upon Yahweh rather than 'the arm of flesh', and thus sets the seal upon the basic plea of 'fidelity' (אֱמֶת), 'devotion' (חֶסֶד), and 'righteousness' (צֶדֶק) on the part of the Messiah and his subjects.[2] As a result victory (or salvation) is eventually secured through the dramatic intervention of Yahweh Himself in the person of the 'Most High', who makes His presence felt at dawn on this fateful day, and delivers the Messiah and *ipso facto* the nation from the forces of darkness and 'Death'. In this way Yahweh reveals His own 'fidelity' (אֱמֶת),

[1] For the setting of this conception in a wider context, see the valuable study by C. Lindhagen, *The Servant Motif in the Old Testament* (1950).

[2] A consideration of the possibility that the conception of the Suffering Servant in the work of Deutero-Isaiah may have some connexion with that of the Davidic Messiah lies outside the scope of the present study; but the writer hopes to return to the question in another monograph in this series. Meantime the reader may be referred to the careful survey of recent work in this field by H. H. Rowley, 'The Suffering Servant and the Davidic Messiah', O.T.S. viii (1950), pp. 100–36, reprinted in *The Servant of the Lord and other Essays on the Old Testament* (1952), pp. 59–88, and now, with an up-to-date bibliography, ibid., 2nd edit. rev. (1965), pp. 61–93.

'devotion' (חֶסֶד), and 'righteousness' (צֶדֶק) in relation to
His covenant people. Further, this deliverance from 'Death'
marks the renewal of life or the rebirth of the king in question. It is the sign that in virtue of his faithfulness and
basically by reason of his faith this suffering Servant and
humble Messiah has been adopted as 'Son' of Yahweh or,
to express this mediatory office in another way, has become
an everlasting Priest 'after the order of Melchizedek'; and,
as such, he is enthroned on Mount Zion as Yahweh's unmistakable vicegerent upon earth. This is not all, however,
for Yahweh's earthly victory has its counterpart in the
heavenly places. The rebellion of the kings of the earth is
but a reflection of the rebellious misrule of the lesser gods
in the divine assembly, to whom the 'Most High' had granted
the jurisdiction over those territories which were occupied
by the other nations of the earth. Accordingly the overthrow of the kings of the earth corresponds to the overthrow of these rebellious gods, who, having shown their
unfitness to rule, are condemned to die like any earthly
princes. Thus Yahweh proves to be what has been aptly
called 'the enduring power, not ourselves, which makes for
righteousness'; and the helpless, the poor, and the humble,
not merely in Israel but throughout the world, may look
forward to an era of universal righteousness and peace, as
the one omnipotent God comes with judicial power to destroy the wicked, to justify His Messiah and His Messiah's
people in their responsible mission to the world, and to enforce His beneficent rule upon the earth.

(b)

All this, however, is to summarize our conclusions in
close adherence to the terminology of the sacred texts. If
we would adopt more general terms, we must state them
afresh in the following way. In saying 'Amen'[1] to the conditions laid down in the Davidic covenant the king becomes the trustee of Yahweh's chosen people. Henceforth

---

[1] See above, p. 107, n. 1.

it is his responsibility to defend the nation from internal corruption and external attack; and success in the latter connexion is conditioned by his success in the former. In other words, it is the king's function to ensure the 'righteousness' or right relationship within the borders of his territory which will ensure the economic well-being of his people and at the same time will safeguard them from foreign interference. There can be no prosperity and no assurance of continuity for the nation without righteousness; and there can be no righteousness without the fidelity to Yahweh and His laws to which the tribal brotherhood of Israel was pledged under the terms of the Sinaitic covenant. In the ultimate, therefore, the righteousness of the nation is dependent upon the righteousness of the king. Under the changed conditions of the monarchy it is the king's devotion and fidelity to Yahweh under the terms of the Davidic covenant which is the basis of the nation's fidelity and righteousness. Thus the king is in a very real sense the 'shield' of his people; and his first care must be the administration of justice, ensuring obedience to the formal definitions of righteousness which are enshrined in Yahweh's laws and thus maintaining the appropriate balance between the rights and the responsibilities of the individual. It is only in this way that he can ensure the prosperity and the survival of his people, i.e. all that is implied by the Hebrew term for 'life' and so makes it possible and indeed necessary to speak of the continuing and abundant life of the social body or, better, its 'vitality'. Thus, as already indicated, it is the king's duty to remove the obstacles which impede the way of life within and without the borders of the nation (i.e., in other words, to safeguard the liberty of the individual and of the state), so that one and all may follow freely the road which leads to economic prosperity.[1] Accordingly, while the freedom for which the king longs in his dramatic

---

[1] The Hebrew terminology which is normally reproduced as that of 'salvation' (i.e. √ישע and its derivatives) is first and foremost the language of 'freedom' or 'liberty'. See above, p. 19, n. 2.

struggle with the forces of darkness and 'Death' is obviously
freedom to live and, implicitly, to prosper, it is not a freedom
to live altogether in the way of his own choosing or freedom
to prosper at the expense of his fellows. It is a freedom to
be of service, a freedom to live in accordance with the will of
Yahweh and thus to promote, not merely his own personal
welfare, but the well-being of the community as a whole,
i.e. the well-being of the nation for whom he has accepted
responsibility under the terms of the Davidic covenant.

Accordingly, if the argument of these pages is sound, the
ritual of the festival which we have been attempting to
reconstruct was designed to foster the corporate sense of
Israel (i.e. as the tribal brotherhood in covenant relationship with Yahweh) by recalling the traditions of Yahweh's
active intervention on their behalf in the field of history
and the consequent demands which He made upon those
who were so obviously the people of His choice. Under the
changed conditions of the monarchy, however, all this was
set in the wider context furnished by the thought of Yahweh
as the omnipotent, divine King, who is also the Creator and
Sustainer of the universe, which appears to have had its
roots in the earlier worship of Canaan as represented by the
Jebusite cultus in Jerusalem. The implications of Yahweh's
choice of the Hebrews were now unfolded, and the historic epi-
sodes of the Exodus, the Wandering, and the Settlement were
seen in a new light. Yahweh's ultimate purpose was now clear;
it was that of a universal realm of righteousness and peace,
in which not merely the twelve tribes of Israel but all the
nations of the earth should be united in one common life.
This was Israel's mission to the world; and the successful
direction of that mission had been entrusted to the House of
David. The purpose of the Davidic covenant was to ensure
righteousness within Israel and thus make righteousness safe
for the world. The world was in danger of collapsing into
primitive chaos, and it could only be saved from such utter
collapse as Israel succeeded in producing the necessary response to Yahweh's attempt to create an ordered world.

If there is a robust nationalism here, it is a nationalism which is tempered by a sense of responsibility towards Yahweh as the one omnipotent God who is 'the power, not ourselves, which makes for righteousness' and by a lively concern for the establishment of His Kingdom as an actual fact in the international sphere. If it is a nationalism which may give rise to the dream of a sovereign state, it is also one which foresees the breakdown of national barriers and the establishment of a righteousness which the tribal brotherhood of Israel (with its story of a common ancestry and its emphasis upon a community of blood and soil) may ultimately share with all the nations of the earth, as the Creator Himself comes to the aid of His righteous people and so smooths the way for that universal obedience which will ensure the fruits of His beneficent rule for the whole of mankind. Finally (and this is of basic importance), it is also a nationalism which offers no ground for pride, but on the contrary stresses the fact of man's creaturely dependence upon God. There can be no righteousness where there is no humility; and in this respect Israel, like the king himself, is no more than *primus inter pares*. When all is said and done, man everywhere must learn to be humble, if he would inherit the earth.

It should be obvious, of course, that what we have in this dramatic ritual and its attendant mythology is no attempt of a magical or magico-religious kind to present Yahweh with a *fait accompli*, i.e. an *opus operatum* which carries with it the implication that His Hand can be forced, and that He may be manœuvred into giving His worshippers the material blessings which they want. It is, rather, a theory of the universe, a creative vision of an ultimate purpose for them and for the world, which discerns an ideal pattern of behaviour for mankind and must needs be communicated to Yahweh's followers with all the measured symbolism and moving imagery afforded by splendid architecture, exciting drama, rousing music, and stirring verse. It is intended to evoke an awareness of a common life, not only within

Israel but also throughout mankind, and a recognition of the necessity to co-operate for the common good in no narrow nationalistic sense but with a view to the well-being of society at large. It is designed to arouse in the worshippers and especially in the king a lofty sense of the need to unify society in a common admission of dependence upon and responsibility towards the Creator and thus make possible an entry into that fuller life which He has designed for mankind. It is only as His rule is acknowledged in the moral realm, or it is only as His will is done on earth as also in heaven, that the full benefit of His creative activity in the realm of nature can become available for mankind, and that His Kingdom may be seen in the fullness of its glory. In other words, this ritual drama is a summons to convert into actual fact the social ideal which is here depicted in moving symbols culled from all the arts, and its purpose is to give Yahweh's followers the opportunity to renew their willingness and their power to co-operate for the common good, not only of Israel, but also of all mankind. Thus it is the lively hope of a new world which is brought before the king and his subjects with the coming of a new cycle of the year; and who should sympathize with this point of view more readily than we who know that every new year has its own way of inviting new resolutions or the renewal of old resolutions which have worn thin with the passage of time?

Finally in this connexion, it remains to be said that the ritual and mythology under review thus serve to focus the attention of the worshippers, both the king and his subjects, upon what is unquestionably a cardinal dogma of the cultus, i.e. that it is only the righteous, whether this be the individual or the community, who may be expected to 'live' in the full sense which the Hebrew term may imply, and, what is more, that the righteous will 'live' in this way in virtue of his fidelity or faithfulness. Nay more, through this dramatic act of worship the king and his people are given the opportunity year by year, not merely to pledge afresh their devotion and their faithfulness, but also, in renewing their vows, to renew their faith. For, when all is said and done, this ritual drama offers the assurance that, however unequal the struggle may appear, victory is ultimately certain if Israel will only prove steadfast. That is to say, its final implication is one which pervades the Old Testament from beginning to end, i.e. the principle that the righteous will 'live' (with all that this means or may come to mean), not merely in virtue of his faithfulness, but primarily by reason of his faith.[1]

(c)

Looking still more closely at the worship under discussion we see a ritual pattern in which the broadly verifiable data of history are interwoven with an imaginative portrayal of that which made possible the long pageant of human life and that which is to be its ultimate issue (i.e., in more technical language, a cosmogony and an eschatology), both of which clearly belong to the colourful sphere of myth. Accordingly, if there was ever any concentration upon the cycle of the year and the annual revival of the social unit, this has been transcended; and 'salvation' has become a matter of the historical process. The purpose of this ritual and its associated mythology is simply to secure what may be described as a 'frame of mind',[2] the conscious acceptance of a pattern of thought and behaviour which will give direction not only to one's own life but also to the life of society. Its aim is (a) to reaffirm one's belief in the principles underlying the behaviour thus envisaged and one's faith in Yahweh as their author, and (b) to evoke afresh the assent of the will in a renewed pledge of faithfulness to Him and His demands. Accordingly, the memory of Yahweh's earlier dealings with His people is carefully employed as an aid to present faith and faithfulness; and

---

[1] Cf. *The Vitality of the Individual in the Thought of Ancient Israel*, p. 3, *ad init.*, 2nd edit., p. v, *ad init.*

[2] Hebrew: יֵצֶר מַחְשְׁבוֹת הַלֵּב. Cf. ibid., p. 86, 2nd edit., p. 85.

the vision set before the worshippers is the extended one, not merely of a new cycle of the year, but of a new age in which Israel's destiny and indeed the destiny of all mankind will have been realized. Thus, if we have here no formal statement of faith which warrants the word 'creed', there is ample material for the framing of one; and in so far as it is implicit it is quite remarkable for its affirmation concerning the character and purpose of the Godhead as expressed in His sovereignty over space and time and, in particular, its emphasis upon the ultimate welfare of mankind as the guiding motif of His activity in creation and history.

This sovereignty of Yahweh first manifests itself in the creation of the earth as a habitable place for mankind, and it continues to prove itself an actuality in the multifarious processes of nature which form the context of human life; but it still remains to be made effectual in the field of human action, which is continually permitted to oppose His will and thwart His plans for the general good. Nevertheless His determination to ensure His sovereignty even in the realm of man's behaviour is already discernible in the history of His chosen people, who, by their formal acceptance of the covenant obligations imposed at Sinai–Horeb, have consented to be the agents of His purpose in establishing a universal order of society which shall function in perfect harmony with the great cosmic order and so shall form the crown and climax of His activity in creation. With the settlement in Canaan and the founding of the monarchy He is prepared to take the final step for the establishment of His rule in the moral realm; and this is to take place as soon as the House of David fulfils its own covenanted task of raising His chosen people to the required standard of social righteousness and thus forging a community which will be justified in serving as the moral and spiritual leaders of mankind. In other words, Israel is to serve as the great bridge-head in Yahweh's campaign against the forces of evil; and when this has been successfully built up, the time will be ripe (or the vital moment will have arrived)[1] and the great 'Day' will have dawned when He will be justified in intervening decisively in the affairs of men as the sovereign Ruler and Judge of mankind. The latter will then be an organic whole enjoying the fullness of life which has been designed for the human race by the God of Israel, who in His sovereign power is the 'Living God' (אֵל חַי) or the true 'Giver of Life'.[2]

Thus at the point in time represented by any one of these recurrent festal days the worshipper's gaze is directed first, in retrospect, to the beginning of time or the creation of the natural order; in the second place, to Yahweh's control of the natural world and His active concern with the behaviour of mankind on the plane of history; and, in the third place, to the prospect of the consummation of both creation and history in a universal moral order, i.e. the coming of the great 'Day' which will usher in a new era of world-wide righteousness and peace.

Accordingly, in this great act of worship the eschatological hope, which centres in the House of David, finds vivid expression in the contemporary scene, and that which is really yet to be occurs dramatically before one's eyes as a challenge and a means of inspiration for all who are prepared to take it seriously. In particular it brings before each reigning member of the House of David the vision that he may yet be instrumental in preparing the way for the conclusive demonstration of Yahweh's sovereign power and His determination to secure an ordered world, or, in other words, that he himself may have a decisive part to play in the fulfilment of Yahweh's plans for making His Kingship effectual amongst men and ensuring that His will shall be done upon earth as also in heaven. In this way the House of David[3] is reminded that it is the responsibility of the true Messiah to put an end to everything

---

[1] Cf. *The Vitality of the Individual in the Thought of Ancient Israel*, p. 101, n. 2, 2nd edit., p. 102, n. 2.

[2] Vide op. cit., pp. 105 ff., 2nd edit., pp. 106 ff.   [3] Cf. p. 3, n. 3.

which disturbs the right relationship between the various members of society both on the human plane and *vis-à-vis* the Godhead, i.e. to root out from the social body the deadly cancer of sin, which finds expression most forcibly in its avarice and pride, and thus bring his people into that effective unity with one another and with the Creator which will not only ensure their own well-being but will lead to that decisive intervention on the part of Yahweh in the affairs of mankind which will bring about universal righteousness and peace. In short, this great act of worship looks forward to the day when the crisis will have been reached in the persistent struggle between the forces of light and the forces of darkness, i.e. the day when the true Messiah of the House of David, by his own dependence upon the holy Spirit and his own filial devotion to the Godhead, will have justified the decisive intervention of Yahweh, and final victory (i.e. man's full 'salvation' or his enjoyment of perfect freedom) will thus be assured.

INDEX

(a) SUBJECTS

Where relevant page numbers apply to both text and footnotes.

Aaron, 71.
Abdi-Ḥiba, 34 f.
Abiathar, 44 n., 52 n.
Abimelech, 44.
Abishai, 1.
Abram, 35, 47 ff.
Absalom, 53 n., 65 n.
Accadian, 4 n., 65 n.
Achan, 3.
Achish, 44 n.
Addu-nirari, 14 n.
Adonai, 38.
Adonijah, 51 n., 66 n.
Adonis, 38, 58 n.
Adoni-zedek, 35 ff., 47.
Adoption, *see* Messiah.
Ahab, 44.
Ahaz, 3.
Ahimelech, 44.
'Al, 18 n., 50 n.
Almighty, 74 n., 80.
Amariah, 45 n.
Amarna, *see* Tell el-Amarna.
Amen, 136.
Amorite, 35, 63 n.
Angel, 16, 30 n.
Anointed, anointing, 1, 13 ff., 17, 104, 131 n. *See also* Messiah.
Anu, 4 n.
Aramaisms, 18 n.
Araunah, 34.
Ark, 14, 19 ff., 33, 70 ff., 72 ff., 74 ff., 78, 83, 125.
Asaph, 46.
Asher, 43.
Asherah of the Sea, 48 n.
Assembly: of the gods, 63, 66, 92 n., 98 f., 101 f., 108 ff., 134 ff.; divine Mount of, 75 n. *See also* Yahweh.
Atonement, Day of, 57 n.
Autumn festival, 54 ff., 60 ff., 69 f., 103, 108, 113. *See also* Festival.

Ba'al of Tyre, 42 n.
Baal, 62, 67 n., 78 n., 86, 90.
Baalhanan, 51 n.

Babylon, Babylonian, 4 n., 10, 38, 55, 60, 65 n., 92, 108 n., 113, 115 n.
Baptism, 119.
Bashan, 81 f.
Bel, 38.
Benjamin, 83 f.
Bethel, 54 f.
Bethlehem, 21 n.
Blessing, 12, 48, 73, 104 n., 133.
Booths, 58, 69. *See also* Feast of Tabernacles.
Bul, 55.
Byblos, 4 n., 36, 49.

Calendar, 55 ff.
Canaan, Canaanite, 33 ff., 38 ff., 43 ff., 47 ff., 62 n., 68 ff., 74, 77 f., 90, 138.
Carmel, 79 n.
Chaos, 64, 92 n., 101, 108 f., 117, 134, 138.
Cherub, cherubim, 70 ff., 118.
Clouds, Rider of the, 78 n., 85, 100 f., 118.
Combat, *see* Ritual.
Cosmogony, 101, 134, 141.
Cosmology, 10, 59 f., 117 n.
Covenant, 16 ff., 19 ff., 25 ff., 67 f., 98, 102, 106 ff., 109 ff., 113 ff., 132 f., 135 f., 136 ff., 142 f. *See also* Devotion, Faithfulness.
Craftsman of the gods, 79 n.
Creator, creation, 26, 48 n., 59 f., 68 f., 72 ff., 92, 101, 108 ff., 120, 134, 138 ff., 142 ff.
Creatress of the gods, 48 n.
Creed, 142.
Crown, 23, 133.
Cultus, 7 ff., 13 f., 19 ff., 25 ff., 33, 45 n., 49 f., 51 ff., 58, 60 ff., 70 n., 74 f., 90, 96 f., 104, 108, 112 f., 134 ff., 138, 140 f. *See also* Ritual.
Currents, 10 f., 27, 65 ff., 93 f., 111. *See also* Sea.

Dan, 54.

Darkness, 98 f., 101 f., 120 ff., 127, 134 ff., 144.

David: as Messiah, 1, 15, 17 f.; as Son of Yahweh, 27 ff,. 128 ff.; House of, 2 ff., 16 ff., 23 ff., 25 ff., 39, 54, 104, 106, 109 ff., 125 f., 128, 134 f., 138, 143 f.; humility of, 19 ff.; Last Words of, 16 ff., 29, 114; name of, 51; throne of, 19 f., 22 f., 26, 83, 128, 131; and Absalom, 53 n.; and Ahimelech, 44; and Ark, 14, 20, 33; and corporate personality, 27 f.; and covenant, 16 ff., 19 ff., 25 ff., 106 ff.; 110 f., 114 f., 136 ff; and cultus, 33, 51 ff., 83; and dynasty, 1, 13 ff., 19 ff., 25 ff., 51 n.; and extension of personality, 15 f.; and Gihon, 83; and Jebusites, 32 ff., 53; and Jerusalem, 32 ff., 50, 53, 62; and kings of the earth, 25 ff., 110 ff., 128 ff.; and musical guilds, 46; and priests, 46; and Samuel, 15; and Saul, 16, 44; and Solomon, 51 n., 53 n., 66 n.; and divine Spirit, 17 f., 29 f.; and Temple, 14 n., 20; and tribes of Israel, 33; and Yahweh, 15 ff., 19 ff., 25 ff., 33 f., 128.

Dawn, 93 f., 98, 101 f., 118, 128, 130 f., 135.

Dead Sea, 11 n.

Death, 82 f., 85 f., 89 f., 93 f., 98, 101 f., 112 f., 116 ff., 120 ff., 125 ff., 128, 134 ff., 137 f.

Deborah, Song of, 79 f., 87.

Demons, 58 n.

Desert, 78 ff., 85.

Deutero-Isaiah, 60 f., 61 n., 65 n., 135 n.

Devoted, 22 n.

Devotee, 22 n.

Devotion, 22 n., 26 ff., 88, 102, 106 ff., 109 ff., 114 f., 123 ff., 127 f., 132 f., 135 ff., 140 f., 144. *See also* Faithfulness.

Devout, 22 n.

Dew, 131.

Dragon, *see* Monster of the Deep.

Drama, *see* Ritual.

Earth, kings (nations) of the, 10, 25 ff., 74 ff., 80 ff., 86 ff., 91 f.,

93 ff., 95 ff., 98 f., 102, 110 ff., 116 f., 121 ff., 124 f., 128 ff., 135 f., 138 f. *See also* Yahweh.

Ebed-melech, 45 n.

Egypt, Egyptian, 34 f., 62 n., 65 n., 84.

'Ēl, 47 ff.

Elders, council of, 53 n.

Elhanan, 21 n., 51 n.

'Ēlî, 50 n.

Eli, 50 n.

Eliba'al, 9 n.

Elimelech, 43 f.

Elisha, 30 n.

'Elyôn, 49 f. *See also* Most High.

Enlil, 4 n.

Enthronement, 60, 64, 68, 70 ff., 75 n., 85, 93, 101, 126, 128 f., 130 f., 132 f., 134, 136.

Ephrathah, 21.

Esagila, 4 n.

Esarhaddon, 42 n.

Eschatology, 7 f., 58 f., 61 n., 70 f., 101 f., 134 ff., 141 ff.

Ethanim, 55.

Ethiopian, 10 n., 45 n.

Euphrates, 10 f., 27 n., 45 n.

Exile, 65 n.

Exodus, 69 ff., 138.

Faith, 101, 126, 132 f., 134 ff., 141 f.

Faithfulness, 106 ff., 120, 134 ff., 141 f. *See also* Devotion.

Family, 2 f., 80.

Father, heavenly, 29 f., 119 f., 128 f.

Feast: of Ingathering, 55 ff.; of Tabernacles, 55 ff., 69 f., 127 f.

Festival, 54 ff., 60 ff., 69 f., 72, 77, 85, 91, 93 f., 95, 100 ff., 106, 108, 112 f., 115 n., 118, 127, 134 ff., 138. *See also* Autumn festival, Ritual.

Freedom, *see* Salvation.

Gezer, calendar of, 57.

Gideon, 15 f., 44.

Gihon, 32 f., 83, 119, 131.

Giver of Life, 7, 143.

Glory of Yahweh, *see* Yahweh.

God: high, 49 ff., 74; Living, 82, 104, 120, 123, 143; Most High, 47 ff.; omnipotent, 49 f., 68 f., 102, 121 ff., 131 f., 136, 139. *See also* Yahweh.

Godhead, 69, 142, 143 f.
Godly, 22 n.
Gods, rebellious, 102, 136. *See also* Assembly.
Gomorrah, 47.
Guilds, musical, 46.

Ḥammurabi, 4 n., 130 n.
Ḥaremḥab, 4 n.
Heavenly King, *see* Yahweh.
Hebrews, historical traditions of, 61 n., 68 ff., 77 ff.
Hebron, 65 n.
Hermon, 63 n.
High god, 49 ff., 74. *See also* Most High.
Hinnom, 45 n.
History: and ritual, 69 f., 141; and salvation, 141; and Yahweh, 61 n., 138, 141 ff.
Hittite, 35, 44.
Holy, 22 n.; City, 81, 93, 103; One of Israel, 26, 29 f., 110; ones, 108 ff.; Spirit, 29 f., 144.
Horeb, 68, 142. *See also* Sinai.
Hosanna, 127.
Hosts, *see* Yahweh.
Humble, 91, 98 f., 102. *See also* King, Messiah, People, Yahweh.
Humiliation: of king, 25 f.; of Messiah, 111 ff., 115 n., 126, 135. *See also* Ritual.
Humility: of David, 20 f.; of Messiah, 120; and righteousness, 139.
Hymnology, Canaanite, 62 n.

Ichabod, 73 n.
'Il, 37 n.
Ingathering, *see* Feast.
Isaiah, vision of, 64 n.
Israel: divine purpose for, 53, 70, 95, 101, 116, 134 ff., 141 ff.; God of, 7, 37, 66, 82, 113, 143; Holy One of, 26, 29 f., 110; lamp of, 1; Spring of, 83, 85, 119; tribes of, 33, 83 f., 136 ff.

Jacob, 16, 73.
Jair, 21.
Jebusite, 33, 51 n., 52 n., 53, 62, 138.
Jedidiah, 51 n.
Jehoash, 23 f.
Jehoiachin, 45 n.
Jehoshaphat, 4 n.

Jehozadak, 37.
Jeremiah, 38.
Jeroboam I, 54.
Jeroboam II, 44.
Jerusalem: fall of, 1 f.; and Adonizedek, 35 ff., 47; and Ark, 19 ff., 33, 70 ff., 72 ff., 75; and autumn festival, 54 f., 64, 70, 108; and cultus, 19, 25 f., 32 f., 47 ff., 54, 58 f., 62, 74, 90, 108, 134, 138; and David, 32 ff., 50, 53, 62; and Davidic kings, 1; and 'Elyôn, 49 f.; and Hebrew cosmology, 10; and high god, 49 f., 74; and Hinnom, 45 n.; and king, 104; and Melchizedek, 35 ff., 47 ff., 53; and righteousness, 37, 47, 53; and Šālēm, 52 f.; and Ṣedeḳ, 52; and subject peoples, 84; and Tammuz, 51 n.; and Temple, 26 n., 38, 45 n., 54 f. *See also* Jebusite, Ritual.
Jesse, 18, 29.
Jonathan, 43 n.
Jordan, 11 n.
Joseph, 16.
Joshua, 35.
Josiah, 14, 45 n.
Jubilee, 57 n.
Judah, 1, 32, 83 f., 89, 97.
Judge, *see* King, Yahweh.
Judge River, 67 n.
Judges, 43 f.
Justice, 4, 7, 13, 71 f., 95 f., 98 f., 99 ff., 109, 113 ff., 126, 136 ff. *See also* Righteousness.

Kadesh, 63 f.
Karatepe, 45 n., 48 n.
Keret, 4 n., 35.
Kindness, 22 n.
King, earthly: Davidic, 1, 16, 30, 96, 107, 112 ff., 116, 120, 135; as judge, 4 ff., 9, 13, 116 n., 126; as sacrosanct, 16; as shield of his people, 104 f., 137; accession of, 7 f.; anointing of, 13 ff.; humanity of, 29 f.; humiliation of, 25 f.; humility of, 19 ff.; negative confession of, 115 n.; universal sway of, 10 ff.; and covenant, 16 ff., 113 ff., 136 ff.; and cultus, 7 f., 13 f., 96, 112 f., 135; and dynasty, 7 f., 23; and God, 30; and

King (*cont.*)
heavenly King, 105, 112, 120; and humble, 11; and people, 1 ff., 7 f., 11 ff., 30, 104, 126, 136 ff.; and righteousness, 4 ff., 11 ff., 17, 35, 47, 136 ff.; and royal psalms, 7, 17, 102 f.; and Spirit, 14 ff.; and testimony, 23 ff.; and Yahweh, 7 f., 13 ff., 19 f., 29 f., 102, 104 ff., 112, 123 f., 136 ff. *See also* Messiah.

King, heavenly, 33, 38 f, 45 f., 59 f., 64 ff., 68, 70 ff., 74 ff., 77, 83 ff., 86, 88 ff., 95 f., 101, 103 ff., 108 ff., 112 f., 120, 125, 128 f., 132 f., 134 f., 138 ff., 141 ff. *See also* Yahweh.

Kingdom: Northern, 1, 30 n., 39 n., 54; Southern, 1, 30 n., 54, 85.

Kingu, 92 n.

Kiriath-jearim, 21 n.

Laws, 4 ff., 67 n., 136 f.

Lebanon, 12, 63 f.

Leptis Magna, 48 n.

Leviathan, *see* Monster of the Deep.

Life: Giver of, 7, 143; of Messiah, 118, 128 ff., 134 ff.; light and, 101 f., 120, 127, 134 ff. *See also* Society.

Light, *see* Life.

Liturgy, liturgical, 19 f., 25, 29, 38, 51 n., 60 ff., 69 f., 106, 112, 129, 132. *See also* Cultus, Ritual, Worship.

Living God, 82, 104, 120, 123, 143.

Lord, 36 ff.

Lovingkindness, 22 n.

Magic, 34 n., 139 f.

Malchiah, Malchijah, 46.

Malchiel, 43, 47.

Malchiram, 45 n.

Malchi-shua, 43 n., 45.

Malik, 45 n.

Manaḫbiria, 14.

Marcheshvan, 55.

Marduk, 4 n., 38, 92 n.

Mari, 51 n.

Maschil, 114 n.

Massah, 69.

Mediterranean, 11, 27 n.

Melchizedek, 35 ff., 47 ff., 53, 131, 136.

Melqart, 42.

Merciful, 22 n.

Mercy, 22 n.

Meribah, 69.

Messenger of Yahweh, 14 ff.

Messiah: anointed, 1, 14 f., 131 n.; Davidic, 1, 16, 29 f., 96, 113 f., 116, 120, 125 f., 134 ff.; humble, 113, 136; true, 120, 128, 136; as Servant of Yahweh, 28, 113, 135 f.; as Son of Yahweh, 28 f., 117 f., 119 f., 128 ff., 136; as suffering Servant, 113, 135 f.; of God, 104; adoption of, 28, 128 ff., 136; defeat and humiliation of, 111 ff., 125 f, 135; enthronement of, 125 f., 128 f., 132, 136; faithfulness of, 120, 136; humility of, 120, life of, 118, 128 ff., 134 ff.; rebirth of, 128, 136; sonship of, 28, 117 f., 128 ff.; victory of, 113, 121 f., 128, 132 f., 135; and Ark, 125; and covenant, 28, 114, 135 f.; and cultus, 90 104, 113, 134 ff.; and David, 1, 15, 17 f., 131; and deliverance at dawn, 117 f., 128, 130 f., 135; and deliverance from Death, 90, 113, 116 ff., 120 ff., 125 ff., 128, 134 ff.; and divine purpose, 116, 134 ff., 143 f.; and Hosanna, 127; and king, 13 ff., 96, 104, 113 f., 116, 120, 123 f., 132, 135 f.; and kings (nations) of the earth, 90, 113, 117 ff., 121 ff,. 125 n., 128 ff.; and Most High, 18 n., 76 n., 117 f., 135; and people, 1 f., 90, 104, 116, 135 f.; and priesthood of Melchizedek, 130 f., 136; and righteousness, 116, 120, 126, 135 f., 143 f.; and Spirit, 14 ff.; and Yahweh, 1 f., 13 ff., 27 ff., 111 ff., 114 ff., 117 ff., 120 ff., 123 ff., 128 ff., 130 ff., 132 ff., 135 f., 143 f. *See also* Ritual, Yahweh.

Micaiah, 39 n.

Milcom, 43.

Military operations, 56.

Milk, Milku(-i) and compounds, 39 ff.

Milḳart, *see* Melqart.

Mime, 102, 135. *See also* Ritual.

Mind, frame of, 141.

Miriam, Song of, 70 n.

Mission of Israel, *see* Israel, divine purpose for.
Mistress of the gods, 48 n.
Molech, 45 n.
Monarchy, 4 n., 15, 29, 39, 45, 54, 64, 70, 77, 134, 136 ff., 142. *See also* David, King Messiah, Yahweh.
Monster of the Deep, 82 n., 108 n.
Moon, 57.
Moral realm, and Yahweh, 8 f., 13, 74, 93, 98 f., 109, 114, 140, 142. *See also* Nature, realm of.
Moses, 16, 71; Song of, 97.
Most High: as appellation of Yahweh, 74 ff., 93 f., 97, 102, 116 ff., 132, 135 f.; word-play on, 74 ff., 97; Yahweh's intervention as, 93 f., 101 f., 116 ff., 135 f.; and Jerusalem, 11, 47 ff., 93 f.; and Messiah, 18 n., 76 n., 116 ff., 135 f.; and mythology in Isaiah, 94 n.; and Song of Moses, 97; God Most High, 47 ff. *See also* Ritual.
Mot, 90, *see* Death.
Mother of the gods, 92 n.
Muluk, 45 n.
Music of the Temple, 14 n., 22, 46, 83.
Myth, mythology, 49, 53, 58, 61 n., 68, 69 f., 77, 82 n., 86, 88, 90, 92 n., 94 n., 132, 134, 139 ff. *See also* Ritual.

Naaman, 30 n.
Name: royal, 12, 51; divine, 49 ff., 79 n.
Names, theophorous, 38 ff., 53 n.
Naomi, 44.
Naphtali, 83 f.
Nathan, 26 n., 110 n.
Nathan-melech, 45 n.
Nation, 2 ff., 8 f., 13, 17, 75, 79 ff., 90, 93, 98, 100 ff., 109, 117, 123, 135, 136 ff. *See also* People.
Nations, *see* Earth.
Nature, realm of, 8, 13, 64, 74, 93, 96, 98 f., 109, 140, 142 f. *See also* Moral realm.
Navel of the earth, 10 n.
Negative confession, *see* King.
New age, 61 n., 99 ff., 134 ff., 138 ff., 141 ff.

New song, *see* Ritual.
New Year, 57, 70 n., 113, 115 n., 140.
Niqmepa, 4 n.
Nisan, 55.
Nob, 44.
Nuḫashshe, 14 n.

Ocean, 66 f., 85, 93, 101, 134. *See also* Sea.
Oracle, 17 ff., 19 ff., 26 ff., 110 f., 129 ff.

Palestine, 58 n., 59 n.
Pashhur, 46 n.
Peace, 101 f., 134 ff., 138, 143 f. *See also* People, welfare of; Righteousness.
People: chosen, 53, 68 f., 71 f., 75, 79, 82, 93 f., 100 f., 123, 125 f., 136 ff., 142 f.; humble, 79, 91, 120, 136; welfare of, 1 ff., 8 f., 12 f., 64, 79, 91, 93, 136 ff., 139 f., 142, 144; and Ark, 20, 75, 125; and covenant, 67 f., 102, 135 ff., 142 f.; and gift of rain, 67 f., 79, 104; and king, 1 ff., 7 ff., 12 f., 30, 104, 126, 136 ff.; and Messiah, 1 f., 90, 104, 116, 125 f., 135 f.; and righteousness, 4, 13, 53, 71 f., 78 f., 98, 100 ff., 116, 125 ff., 135 f., 136 ff., 140 f., 143 f.; and Yahweh, 8, 20, 53, 64, 68 ff., 71 f., 75, 79 ff., 86, 88 ff., 92 ff., 98, 100 ff., 123 f., 125 f., 134 ff., 136 ff., 141 ff. *See also* Votaries, Worshippers.
Persian Gulf, 11.
Personality: corporate, 2 f., 27 f., 126, 135, 138; extension of the, 15 f., 20, 69.
Philistines, 1, 53 n., 73 n.
Philo of Byblos, 49.
Phinehas, 73 n.
Phoenicia, Phoenician, 4 n., 9 n., 36, 38, 41 ff., 44 n., 45 n., 63 n.
Pilgrimage, 103 ff.
Power, 2, 15; which makes for righteousness, 13, 102, 136, 139; as personal, 13 n.; as supra-personal, 13 n.
Power of Yahweh, *see* Yahweh.
Presence of Yahweh, *see* Yahweh.

Priest, 20 ff., 44, 46 f., 52 n., 71, 123 f.; as messenger of Yahweh, 14.

Priesthood of Melchizedek, 47 ff., 53, 131, 136.

Prince Sea, 67 n. *See also* Judge River.

Procession, 72 ff., 78, 81, 83 f., 89, 119, 125 n., 126 f. *See also* Ritual.

Promises, 24 n., 26, 28 f., 45 n., 67 f., 128. *See also* Covenant.

Prophet, 26, 71 n., 94 n., 110; cultic, 22, 69, 130; as messenger of Yahweh, 14.

Prophetic, 17 ff., 130; symbolism, 88, 101, 134.

Proselytes, 124 n.

Psalms, 18, 20, 28; Canaanite prototypes for, 62 n.; dating of, 60 ff., 71 n.; Ugaritic parallels to, 62 n.; enthronement, 68, 70, 86; liturgical, 60 f.; royal, 7, 17 ff., 25, 26 n., 30 n., 102 ff.; individually discussed: ii, 128 ff.; xviii, 116 ff.; xxi, 132 ff.; xxiv, 72 ff.; xxix, 62 ff.; xlvi, 92 ff.; xlvii, 74 ff.; xlviii, 85 ff.; lxviii, 77 ff.; lxxii, 7 ff.; lxxxii, 98 f.; lxxxiv, 103 ff.; lxxxix, 25 ff., 106 ff.; xciii, 65 ff.; xcv, 68 ff.; xcvii, 95 ff.; xcviii, 99 f.; xcix, 70 ff.; ci, 113 ff.; cx, 130 ff.; cxviii, 123 ff.; cxxxii, 19 ff.; cxlix, 91 f.

Psychical whole, 2 ff.

Punic, 42, 44 n, 45 n., 48 n.

Rahab, 108.

Rain: and cosmic sea, 59 f., 64, 67 f., 81, 85, 92; and Feast of Tabernacles, 57 ff. *See also* People, Ritual, Yahweh.

Ras Shamra, 4 n., 35 f., 40 f., 42 ff., 53 n., 90. *See also* Ugarit, Ugaritic.

Redeemer, 61 n.

Regem-melech, 45 n.

Rider, *see* Clouds.

Righteous, righteousness, 3 ff., 8 f., 12 f., 17, 35 ff., 47, 53, 71 f., 78 f., 88 f., 95 ff., 98, 100 ff., 109, 116 f., 120, 125 ff., 134 ff., 136 ff., 140 f., 142 ff. *See also* King, Messiah, People, Yahweh.

Ritual: accession, 83; anointing, 13 ff., 131; dramatic, 19, 32 n., 87 ff., 92 ff., 96, 101 f., 113, 119, 128, 133, 134 ff., 138 ff.; significance of, 93 f., 101 f., 134 ff., 138 ff., 141 ff.; combat, 111, 118, 121, 128; defeat or humiliation, 111 ff., 115 n., 126, 135; procession, 72 ff., 78, 81, 83 f., 89, 119, 125 n., 125 ff.; and Ark, 19 ff., 72 ff., 74 ff., 83, 125; and autumn festival, 58 f., 60 ff., 77, 91, 93, 95, 101 f., 112 f., 117 f., 127, 134 ff., 138; and cosmic sea, 60, 81, 92 f., 101, 119, 134; and cosmogony, 101, 134, 141; and cultus, 53, 60 f., 90, 134, 138, 140 f.; and dawn, 93 f., 98, 102, 117 f., 128, 131, 135; and Death, 82 f., 85 f., 89 f., 93 f., 98, 101 f., 112 f., 116 ff., 120 ff., 125 ff., 128, 134 ff., 137 f.; and eschatology, 58 f., 61 n., 70, 101, 134, 141; and Feast of Tabernacles, 57 ff., 69 f., 127 f.; and forces of light and darkness, 101 f., 120, 127, 134 ff.; and gift of rain, 58 ff., 81, 85, 92, 104 f.; and Gihon, 32 f., 83, 119, 131; and Jebusites, 33, 53, 62, 138; and Jerusalem, 53, 58 f., 90, 104, 134, 138; and king, 7 ff., 13 ff., 20, 26, 96, 102 ff., 112 f., 115 n., 123 ff., 136 ff.; and kings (nations) of the earth, 80 ff., 86 f., 90 ff., 93 f., 95 ff., 98 f., 101 f., 112 f., 121 ff., 124 f., 128 ff., 135, 138; and Messiah, 14 f., 90, 96, 104, 111 ff., 116 ff., 120 ff., 123 ff., 128 ff., 134 ff.; and Most High, 93 f., 102, 117 ff., 132 f., 135 f.; and mythology, 53, 58, 61 n., 70, 77, 87 f., 90, 92 n., 94 n., 132, 134, 139 f., 141; and new song, 91, 99 f.; and people, 53, 86, 90 ff., 93 f., 98, 102, 120 f., 125 f., 134 ff., 138 f., 140 f.; and rebellious gods, 102, 136; and righteousness, 53, 95 f., 101 f., 120, 125 ff., 135 f., 138 f., 140 f.; and theory of the universe, 139; and victory, 101 f., 113, 121 f., 128, 132 f., 134 ff., 141; and worship, worshippers, 53, 60, 87 f., 91 f., 96, 101 f., 104, 127, 134 f., 138, 139 ff.; and Yahweh, 19 f., 53, 58 f., 60 ff., 70, 77, 83, 86, 90 ff., 95 ff., 101 f.,

104, 108 ff., 111 ff., 116 ff., 121 f.,
125 ff., 128 f., 132 f., 134 ff.,
138 ff.
River, *see* The River.
Ruth, 44.

Sacrifice, 13, 45 n., 58.
Saint, 22 n.
Šālēm, 52 f.
Salem, 32, 35, 48, 53 n.
Salvation, 45, 91, 101 f., 113, 127,
132 f., 135 f., 144; as freedom,
19 n., 137 f., 144; as victory, 101 f.,
113, 127, 132 f., 135 f., 144; and
the historical process, 141.
Samaria, 44, 50 n.
Samuel, 15, 71.
Šapaṭbaʿal, Šipṭibaʿal, 9 n., 41 n.
Saul, 15 f., 44 f.
Sea: of Reeds, 70 n.; Asherah of the,
48 n.; bronze, 60; cosmic, 10 f.,
27 n., 59 f., 64 ff., 81, 85, 92 f.,
101, 108, 117 ff., 134. *See also*
Prince Sea, Rain, Ritual, Yahweh.
Ṣedek, 36 f., 52.
Senir, 63 n.
Serpent, *see* Monster of the Deep.
Servant of Yahweh, *see* Messiah,
Yahweh.
Settlement in Canaan, 38, 43, 53 n.,
70 n., 71, 78 n., 138.
Shaddai, 80.
Shamash, 130 n.
Shechem, 44.
Shema, 24.
Shiloah, 11 n.
Sidonian, 63 n.
Sinai, 68, 79 ff., 101; covenant at, 24,
137, 142. *See also* Yahweh.
Sirion, 63 f.
Society, 13, 61 n., 98 f.; vitality of,
1 ff., 7 ff., 90, 101 f., 127, 134 ff.,
136 ff., 141 ff. *See also* Life,
People, Yahweh.
Sodom, 47.
Solomon, 20, 51 n., 53 n., 54 f., 60,
66 n., 72, 77 n., 134.
Son of Yahweh, *see* David, Messiah,
Yahweh.
Spirit, 14 ff., 29 f., 144; holy 29 f.,
144. *See also* David, Personality
(extension of the), Yahweh.
Spring, and cycle of the year, 56 f.
Suffering Servant, *see* Messiah.

Sun, 93 f., 105.
Šuwardata, 34.
Symbolism, *see* Prophetic.
Synagogues, 60 n.
Syria, 30 n., 35, 50.

Tabernacles, *see* Feast, Rain, Ritual.
Taku, 14 n.
Tammuz, 51 n.
Tell el-Amarna, 14 n., 34, 39, 43 f.,
62 n.
Temple, 92, 125, 130. *See also*
David, Jerusalem, Solomon, Wor-
ship, Worshippers, Yahweh.
Testimony, 23 f., 67. *See also*
Covenant.
Tetragrammaton, 66 n.
The River, 10 f., 93 f. *See also*
Currents, Euphrates, Gihon,
Judge River.
Throne, 8, 19 f., 23, 26, 30 n., 51 n.,
77, 83, 86, 89, 128, 131.
Tiamat, 92.
Tishri, 55, 57.
Tradition, 15, 17, 25 n., 26 n., 35,
43, 49, 52 n., 68, 70 n., 78 n.
Transjordan, 43.
Tree of Justice, 116 n.
Tribes of Israel, *see* Israel.
Tyre, 42.

Ugarit, Ugaritic, 4 n., 35, 37 n.,
40 n., 42 f., 45 n., 48 n., 62, 65 n.,
67 n., 77, 78 n., 82 n., 86, 99 n.,
105 n., 108 n.
Underworld, 42 n., 60 n., 90, 93 f.,
120, 126, 131.
Universal peace, *see* Yahweh.
Universal righteousness, *see* Yahweh.

Victory, *see* Messiah, Ritual, Sal-
vation, Yahweh.
Vitality, *see* Society.
Voice of Yahweh, *see* Yahweh.
Votaries, 22 f., 26, 67 n., 91, 98; as
the righteous, 98, 102, 116, 135.
See also Yahweh.
Vow, 45 n., 107 f., 115.

Wandering, period of the, 69 f., 71,
78 ff., 138.
Welfare, *see* People, Yahweh.
Wicked, 78 f., 98 f., 102, 135 f.
Word-play, 75 f., 97.

Worship, 38 f., 45 n., 47 ff., 59, 62, 67 f., 143 f.; and Temple, 14 n., 22, 38 f., 60, 72 f., 74 f., 96, 104 f., 130. *See also* Ritual, Yahweh.

Worshippers, 49, 68 f., 100 f., 107, 123, 139 f., 143; and Temple, 20, 73, 87 f., 103 f. *See also* Ritual, Yahweh.

Yah, Yahu, 37, 45 n., 82.

Yahweh: of Hosts, 58 f., 74, 103; as Almighty, 74 n.; as Creator, 26, 59 f., 68 ff., 72 ff., 92, 101, 108, 120, 134, 138 ff., 142 ff.; as enduring power which makes for righteousness, 13, 102, 136, 139; as Giver of Life, 7, 143; as God of Israel, 7, 37, 66, 82, 113, 143; as heavenly Father, 29 f., 120, 129; as heavenly King, 33, 38 f., 45 ff., 59 f., 64 ff., 68, 70 ff., 74 ff., 77, 83 ff., 86, 88 ff., 95 f., 101 f., 103 ff., 108 ff., 112 f., 120, 125, 128 f., 131 ff., 134 f., 138 ff., 141 ff.; as Holy One of Israel, 26, 29 f., 110; as Judge, 71 f., 74, 88 f., 91, 95 ff., 133, 143; as Living God, 82, 103, 120, 123, 143; as Most High ('Al, 18 n., 50 n.; 'Elyôn, 49 f.), 11, 53, 74 ff., 93, 97, 102, 116 ff., 132, 136; as Rider of the Clouds, 78 n., 85 f., 101, 118; as (god of) Sinai, 79 ff.; as Stronghold of His people, 86 f., 90 ff.; as supreme God, 26, 59, 66, 69, 71 f., 74 ff., 83, 85, 93 ff., 95 ff., 98 ff., 102, 108 ff., 112 f., 122, 128 f., 131 f., 134 ff., 139, 143 f.; as warrior, 30 n., 73 ff., 81, 131 f.; devotion and faithfulness of, 28 f., 88, 102, 106 ff., 115, 120, 123 ff., 127 f., 132 f., 135 f.; enthronement of, 60, 64 ff., 68, 70, 75 n., 85 f., 93, 101, 134; Glory of, 63 f., 73 f., 95 f.; intervention of, 93 f., 95 f., 101 f., 116 ff., 128 f., 131 f., 135 f., 144; laws of, 3 ff., 67 n., 137; messenger of, 14 ff.; power of, 13, 26, 60, 66 f., 69, 74 f., 78 f., 81, 85, 89, 92 f., 96, 101 f., 116 f., 119, 128, 134 ff., 139; presence of, 20, 72, 75, 78, 109, 125, 135; purpose of, 53, 70, 95, 101, 116,

134 ff., 138 ff., 141 ff., 143 f.; Servant of, 28, 113, 135 f.; Son of, 28 f., 117 f., 119 f., 128 ff., 136; Spirit of, 14 ff., 18, 29 f., 144; throne of, 76, 89; victory of, 77, 80 ff., 85 f., 90, 93, 95 ff., 101 f., 113, 116 f., 120 ff., 128, 131 ff., 134 ff., 144; Voice of, 63 f., 85, 93, 100 f., 119; votaries of, 22 f., 26, 67 n., 91, 98, 102, 116, 135; and Ark, 20, 70 ff., 72 ff., 74 ff., 83, 125; and assembly of the gods, 62 f., 66, 98 f., 101 f., 108 ff., 134 ff.; and cosmic sea, 59 f., 64 ff., 81, 85, 92 f., 101, 108, 117 ff., 134; and cosmogony, 101, 134, 141; and cosmology, 59 f., 117 f.; and covenant, 17 ff., 19 ff., 25 ff., 67 f., 98, 102, 106 ff., 109 ff., 113 f., 132 f., 135 f., 136 ff., 142 f.; and David, 16, 17 f., 20 ff., 25 ff., 33, 128 f.; and Death, 82 f., 85 f., 89 f., 93 f., 98, 101 f., 112 f., 116 ff., 120 ff., 125 ff., 128, 135 f., 137 f.; and eschatology, 58 f., 61 n., 70, 101, 134, 141, 143 f.; and extension of personality, 16, 20, 69; and gift of rain, 59 f., 64, 67 f., 79, 81, 85, 92, 104 f.; and history, 61 n., 138, 141 ff.; and the humble, 20 f., 79, 91, 98 f., 102, 120, 136; and king, 7 f., 13 ff., 20, 30, 102 f., 104 f., 112, 123 f., 136 ff.; and kings (nations) of the earth, 26 ff., 75 ff., 80 ff., 86 ff., 90 ff., 93 ff., 95 ff., 98 f., 102, 110 ff., 116 f., 121 f., 124, 128 ff., 135 f., 138 f.; and Melchizedek, 47 ff., 53, 130 f., 136; and Messiah, 1 f., 13 ff., 27 ff., 111 ff., 113 ff., 116 ff., 120 ff., 123 ff., 128 ff., 130 ff., 132 ff., 134 ff., 144; and new age, 61 n., 99 ff., 134 ff., 138 ff., 141 ff.; and new song, 91, 99 f.; and peace, 101 f., 134 ff., 138, 143 f.; and people, 8, 20, 53, 64, 67 ff., 72, 75, 79 ff., 86, 88 ff., 92 ff., 98, 100 ff., 123 f., 125 f., 134 ff., 136 ff., 142 f.; and righteous, righteousness, 4 ff., 13, 17, 37 n., 53, 71 f., 78 f., 88 f., 95 f., 98, 100 ff., 109 f., 116 f., 120, 125 ff., 134 ff., 138 f., 140 f., 143 f.; and

ritual, 19 f., 53, 58 f., 60 ff., 70, 77, 83, 87, 90 ff., 95 ff., 101 f., 104, 107 ff., 121 f., 125 f., 128 f., 132 f., 134 ff., 138 ff.; and salvation, 82, 91, 101 f., 127, 132 f., 135 f., 141, 144; and universal peace and righteousness, 101 f., 134 ff., 138, 144; and welfare of society, 1 ff., 7 ff., 64, 79, 93 f., 136 ff., 139 ff., 143 f.; and worship, worshippers, 20, 38 f., 49, 53, 59, 62, 68 f., 73, 87 f., 95, 100 ff., 103 ff., 107, 123 f., 139 f., 143 f.; and Zion, 22, 31 ff., 65 n., 70 ff., 72 ff., 75, 81, 85 ff., 136.

Year: cycle of the, 56 f., 61 n., 139 ff.; dying and reviving, 56 f. *See also* New Year.
Yeḥawmilk, 4 n., 9 n., 36.
Yeḥimilk, 4 n., 9 n., 36, 41.
Yemen, 116 n.

Zadok, 52 n.
Zalmon, 80.
Zaphon, 86, 94 n.
Zebulun, 83 f.
Zedek, 37.
Zedekiah, 45 n., 46 n.
Zion, 11, 22, 31 ff., 47 n., 65 n., 70 ff., 72 ff., 75, 81, 85 ff., 136.

INDEX

(b) AUTHORS

Page numbers refer throughout to the footnotes.

Aalen, A., 56, 57.
Abel, F.-M., 47, 59, 81.
Ackroyd, P. R., 32.
Ahlström, G. W., 52, 110.
Aistleitner, J., 48.
Albright, W. F., 5, 27, 37, 41, 42, 43, 44, 46, 47, 50, 60, 62, 77, 78, 79, 80, 82, 84.
Allegro, J. M., 80.
Alt, A., 32, 46, 48, 53, 65.
Anderson, G. W., 7.
Ap-Thomas, D. R., 7.
Arnold, M., 13.
Auerbach, E., 56.

Baethgen, F., 26.
Baly, D., 59.
Barnes, W. E., 24.
Baudissin, W. W. Graf, 6, 37, 38, 40.
Bauer, H., 50.
Begrich, J., 7, 17, 64.
Bentzen, A., 7, 31, 32, 53.
Benzinger, I., 23, 57.
Bergmann, E., 5.
Bernhardt, K. H., 2, 8.
Bertholet, A., 26, 130.
Bewer, J. A., 18.
Birkeland, H., 7, 80.
Black, J. S., 58.
Blanckenhorn, M., 59.
Böhl, F. M. Th., 25, 26, 63.
Bonkamp, B., 26.
Borger, R., 42.
van den Born, A., 24.
Bottéro, J., 52.
Bowden, J. S., 15.
Breasted, J. H., 7.
Briggs, C. A., 32.
Bright, J., 32.
Brongers, H. A., 109.
Buber, M., 39.
Budde, K., 15, 17, 18, 19.
Burney, C. F., 23, 35, 37.
Burrows, E., 10, 131.
van den Bussche, H., 110.

Buttenwieser, M., 25, 26, 107, 119, 128.

Calès, J., 25, 26, 114.
Caquot, A., 110.
Caspari, W., 15.
Causse, A., 17, 24.
Cazelles, H., 4, 46.
Černý, L., 113.
Clemen, C., 42, 49.
Cook, S. A., 3, 37, 51.
Cooke, G., 63.
Cooke, G. A., 11, 35.
Cross, F. M., jr., 50, 62, 119.
Cruveilhier, P., 130.

Dahood, M., 50.
Dalman, G., 59.
Danby, H., 57.
Davies, T. W., 32.
Deimel, A., 5, 93.
Delitzsch, Franz, 21.
Delitzsch, Friedrich, 21.
Dhorme, P. (E.), 15, 17, 24, 37, 72, 114.
Diringer, D., 41, 44, 50, 57.
Dossin, G., 52.
Driver, G. R., 5, 6, 12, 18, 24, 30, 36, 41, 48, 53, 63, 64, 67, 73, 76, 78, 79, 80, 82, 86, 90, 108, 109, 112, 113, 121, 122, 125, 130.
Driver, S. R., 19.
Duhm, B., 25, 26, 114, 121.
Dunand, M., 6, 41, 42.
Dupont-Sommer, A., 6.
Dürr, L., 5, 115.
Dussaud, R., 9, 43.

Eaton, D., 21.
Eissfeldt, O., 3, 7, 21, 23, 37, 40, 42, 45, 48, 49, 65, 72, 74, 80, 86.
Engnell, I., 52.
Eusebius, 42, 49.
Exner, F. M., 59.

Février, J. G., 46.

Finet, A., 52.
Fitzmyer, J. S., 37.
Fohrer, G., 24, 53.
Follet, R., 5.
de Fraine, J., 2, 7, 39, 124.
Frankfort, H., 7, 28, 113, 115.
Frankfort, H. A., 7.
Frazer, J. G., 51.
Freedman, D. N., 50, 119.
Friedrich, J., 42, 46.

Gadd, C. J., 113, 115.
von Gall, A., 33, 37, 39.
Galling, K., 80.
Gaster, T. H., 48, 62, 79, 82.
Gehman, H. S., 24.
Ginsberg, H. L., 6, 36, 37, 62, 78, 79.
Goodenough, E. R., 23.
Goodspeed, E. J., 23.
Gordon, C. H., 6, 36, 37, 40, 41, 48, 50, 53, 63, 67, 78, 79, 80, 82, 86, 90, 106, 108.
Graham, W. C., 72.
Gray, G. B., 41, 43, 56.
Gray, J., 6, 24, 36, 53.
Gressmann, H., 10, 11, 15, 17, 23, 26, 58.
Grimme, H., 80.
de Groot, J., 54.
Gross, H., 10.
Gunkel, H., 7, 11, 17, 21, 25, 26, 31, 52, 71, 105, 107, 108, 114, 124.
Gunneweg, A. H. J., 49.

Hall, H. R., 53.
Harris, Z. S., 42.
Hartwell, H., 25.
Hauer, C. E., jr., 53.
Hava, J. G., 104.
Heidel, A., 93.
Hempel, J., 2, 3, 50, 54.
Herdner, A., 6, 36, 37, 40, 41, 42, 48, 50, 53, 63, 67, 78, 79, 82, 86, 90, 108.
Herkenne, H., 26, 114.
Hertzberg, H. W., 15, 17.
Hilderscheid, H., 59.
Honeyman, A. M., 51.
Hooke, S. H., 8, 32, 62, 90, 113.
Humbert, P., 48, 75.

Irwin, W. A., 7, 48.

Jackson, F. J. F., 124.

Jacobsen, T., 7.
Jaeger, C., 24.
Jean, C. F., 52.
Jeremias, J., 10.
Jirku, A., 63.

Kaiser, O., 91, 114, 115, 117.
Kapelrud, A. S., 4, 65.
Kennedy, A. R. S., 15.
Kenyon, K. M., 33.
Kessler, H., 21.
Kingdon, H. P., 38.
Kirkpatrick, A. F., 15, 20, 21, 26, 27, 44, 78, 114, 124.
Kittel, R., 15, 17, 23, 25, 26, 31, 32, 114, 133.
Klostermann, A., 24.
Knudtzon, J. A., 14, 34, 35, 39, 40.
Koehler, L., 67.
König, E., 25, 104, 114, 124.
Kraus, H. J., 25, 65, 90, 105, 107, 114, 115.
Kutsch, E., 14.

Labat, R., 5, 28, 93, 113.
Lack, R., 51.
Lake, K., 124.
Landersdorfer, S., 23.
Landsberger, B., 52.
Lane, E. W., 12, 83, 104.
Langdon, S., 42.
de Langhe, R., 8, 86.
van der Leeuw, G., 39, 87.
Leslie, E. A., 25, 26, 32, 107, 114.
Levi Della Vida, G., 43, 48, 50.
Lewy, J., 53, 80.
Lidzbarski, M., 42.
Lieberman, S., 5.
Lindhagen, C., 135.
Lipiński, E., 8, 65.
Lods, A., 32.

McHugh, J., 7.
McKenzie, J. L., 110.
Maier, J., 72.
Malamat, A., 4.
Mann, C. S., 119.
Marks, J. H., 49.
Marti, K., 33.
Marty, J., 87.
May, H. G., 24, 48, 63, 72.
Meek, T. J., 5, 51, 80, 130.
Menzies, A., 58.
Mercer, S. A. B., 14, 34, 35, 39, 40.

du Mesnil du Buisson, Comte, 43.
Michel, D., 65.
Miles, J. C., 5, 130.
Möhlenbrink, K., 54.
Montgomery, J. A., 24.
Moore, G. F., 45.
Morgenstern, J., 50, 55, 126.
Moscati, S., 45, 57.
Mowinckel, S., 7, 10, 11, 17, 23, 24, 25, 26, 32, 52, 53, 56, 57, 58, 61, 62, 65, 75, 77, 87, 106, 107, 114, 115.

Neuberg, F. J., 73.
North, C. R., 30.
Noth, M., 7, 13, 18, 32, 33, 40, 41, 43, 45, 50, 51, 59, 88.
Nötscher, F., 25, 26, 109.
Nougayrol, J., 6, 40, 41.
Nowack, W., 15, 17.
Nyberg, H. S., 18, 37, 49, 50, 53.

Obermann, J., 48.
Oesterley, W. O. E., 24, 25, 26, 32, 77, 107, 114.
Östborn, G., 24.

Pannier, E., 44, 105.
Patai, R., 10, 24, 59, 75.
Patton, J. H., 62, 105, 119.
Peake, A. S., 2, 53.
Pedersen, J., 3, 11, 27, 48, 56, 78, 102.
Perles, F., 85.
Pfeiffer, R. H., 110.
Podechard, E., 25, 26, 44, 95, 107.
Pohl, A., 5.
Porteous, N. W., 7, 53.
Porter, J. R., 3, 30.
Posener, G., 34.
Pritchard, J. B., 5, 6, 93.
Procksch, O., 17.

Quell, G., 38.

von Rad, G., 9, 24, 26, 49.
Randon, L., 26.
Renard, H., 44, 105.
Ridderbos, J., 67, 77.
Rihani, A., 116.
Ringgren, H., 37.
Robinson, H. W., 2, 18, 32, 63.
Robinson, T. H., 24, 32, 77.
Ronzevalle, P. S., 50.

Rosenthal, F., 6.
Rost, L., 20.
Rowley, H. H., 8, 49, 51, 53, 61, 62, 96, 112, 130, 135.
Rudolph, W., 44.

Sayce, A. H., 51.
Schmauch, W., 39.
Schmid, H., 50.
Schmidt, H., 25, 26, 32, 77, 114.
Schmidt, W., 39.
Schoff, W. H., 51.
Schrade, H., 94.
Schwab, R., 26, 105.
Scott, R. B. Y., 59, 108.
Sellin, E., 38.
Sethe, K., 34.
Seyrig, H., 43.
Simons, J., 33.
Simpson, D. C., 30.
Skehan, P. W., 97.
Skinner, J., 23, 24, 55.
Smith, G., 93.
Smith, H. P., 15, 17, 32.
Smith, J. M. P., 23, 118.
Smith, R. H., 48.
Smith, W. R., 37.
Snaith, N. H., 24, 54, 56, 57, 58, 61, 70.
Speiser, E. A., 93.
Staerk, W., 25, 26, 114.
Stamm, J. J., 52, 53.
Steinmann, J., 119.
Steve, A.-M., 33, 47, 53.
Sutcliffe, E. F., 60.
Swetnam, J., 36.

Tadmor, H., 52.
Thackeray, H. St. J., 59.
Thomas, D. W., 7, 18, 81, 88.
Thureau-Dangin, F., 37, 40.
Tournay, R., 26, 27, 50, 105.
Trinquet, J., 72.
Turner, J. E., 87.

de Vaux, R., 7, 14, 17, 24, 25, 41, 46, 49, 54, 56, 72.
Vincent, L.-H., 33, 47, 53, 72.
Virolleaud, Ch., 6, 40.
Volz, P., 58.
Vriezen, Th. C., 49.

Wambacq, B. N., 74.
Waterman, L., 23.

Weidner, E. F., 42.
Weiser, A., 25, 26, 27, 114.
Wellhausen, J., 23, 58.
Wensinck, A. J., 10, 58, 59.
Westermarck, E., 48.

Widengren, G., 24, 37, 131.
Wildberger, H., 31, 39.
Wilson, J. A., 7.
Witton-Davies, C., 39.
Würthwein, E., 91.

INDEX

(c) SCRIPTURE REFERENCES

Where relevant page numbers apply to both text and footnotes.
All Old Testament references are to the Hebrew text.

Genesis:

i. 1 ff.	60 n.
iii. 24	118 n.
vi. 2	63 n.
vi. 4	63 n.
vii. 11	60 n.
viii. 2	60 n.
viii. 7	84 n.
xii. 17	4 n.
xiv	49 n.
xiv. 18–20	35 n., 47 ff.
xx. 1–18	44 n.
xx. 3 f.	4 n.
xx. 9	4 n.
xx. 11	18 n.
xx. 17 f.	4 n.
xxi. 22–32	44 n.
xxiv. 31	85 n.
xxvi. 1–33	44 n.
xxvi. 29	85 n.
xxx. 8	121 n.
xxxi. 21	10 n.
xxxvi. 38	51 n.
xxxvii. 15	21 n.
xxxviii. 26	84 n.
xli. 38	16 n.
xliv. 18–34	84 n.
xlvi. 17	43 n.
xlix	16 n.
xlix. 14	80 n.
xlix. 25	60 n.
xlix. 27	83 n.

Exodus:

xv. 1–18	70 n.
xv. 3	30 n.
xv. 9	132 n.
xv. 18	38 n.
xv. 21	70 n.
xix. 6	38 n.
xx. 4	60 n.
xxii. 27	16 n.
xxiii. 16	55 n., 56 n.
xxiii. 31	10 n.

xxv. 18–22	118 n.
xxv. 18 ff.	72 n.
xxxiv. 22	55 n., 56 n.

Leviticus:

xvi. 29	57 n.
xviii. 21	45 n.
xx. 2–5	45 n.
xxiii. 24 f.	57 n.
xxiii. 27	57 n.
xxiii. 34	57 n.
xxiii. 34–36	56 n., 57 n.
xxiii. 39	57 n.
xxiii. 39–44	56 n., 57 n.
xxiii. 42 f.	58 n., 69 n.
xxv. 9	57 n.

Numbers:

x. 35	78 n.
xiv. 16	84 n.
xxii. 5	10 n.
xxiii. 21	38 n.
xxiv. 16	50 n.
xxvi. 45	43 n.
xxix. 1–6	57 n.
xxix. 7	57 n.
xxix. 12	57 n.
xxix. 12–38	56 n., 57 n., 58 n.

Deuteronomy:

iii. 9	63 n.
iv. 18	60 n.
vi. 4 f.	24 n.
ix. 28	84 n.
x. 17	30 n.
xi. 24	27 n.
xvi. 13–15	56 n.
xvi. 16	56 n.
xxxi. 10–13	56 n.
xxxii. 6	48 n.
xxxii. 8	48 n.
xxxii. 8–9	97
xxxii. 13	78 n.
xxxii. 22	60 n.

xxxiii . . . . 16 n.
xxxiii. 5 . . . 38 n.
xxxiii. 12 . . . 50 n.
xxxiii. 13 . . . 60 n.

Joshua:
vii . . . . 3 n.
x. 1–28 . . . 35 n.
xiii. 27 . . . 86 n.
xxiv. 2 . . . 10 n.

Judges:
i. 5–7 . . . 35 n.
iii. 10 . . . 16 n.
iv. 6 . . . 41 n.
iv. 12 . . . 41 n.
v. 1 . . . 41 n.
v. 4–5 . . . 79 n.
v. 5 . . . 79 n.
v. 12 . . . 41 n.
v. 16 . . . 80 n.
vi. 34 ff. . . 15 n., 16 n.
viii. 22 f. . . 16 n.
viii. 23 . . . 38 n.
viii. 31 . . . 44 n.
ix. 1–x. 1 . . . 44 n.
ix. 7–21 . . . 14 n.
xi. 29 ff. . . 15 n., 16 n.
xiii. 25 . . . 15 n., 16 n.
xiv. 6 . . . 15 n., 16 n.
xiv. 19 . . . 15 n., 16 n.
xv. 14 . . . 15 n., 16 n.
xvi. 7 . . . . 99 n.
xvii. 6 . . . 4 n., 5 n.
xx. 16 . . . . 83 n.
xxi. 19 . . . . 55 n.
xxi. 25 . . . 4 n., 5 n.

Ruth:
i. 2 . . . . 44 n.
i. 3 . . . . 44 n.
i. 9 . . . . 22 n.
i. 10 . . . . 18 n.
ii. 3 . . . . 44 n.
iv. 3 . . . . 44 n.
iv. 9 . . . . 44 n.
iv. 11 . . . . 21 n.

1 Samuel:
i–iv . . . . 50 n.
ii. 10 . . . . 50 n.
iv–vii . . . . 20 n.
iv. 1b–vii. 1 . . . 20 n.
iv. 4 . . . . 72 n.

iv. 17 . . . . 21 n.
iv. 19–22 . . . 73 n.
viii. 7 . . . . 38 n.
ix. 11 . . . . 21 n.
x. 1 . . . . 15 n.
x. 6 ff. . . . 15 n.
x. 19 . . . . 18 n.
x. 24 . . . . 12 n.
xi. 6 ff. . . . 15 n, 16 n.
xii. 12 . . . . 38 n.
xiii . . . . 13 n.
xiv. 3 . . . . 50 n.
xiv. 27 . . . 130 n.
xiv. 45 . . . 102 n.
xiv. 49 . . . 45 n.
xiv. 50 . . . 41 n.
xvi. 1–13 . . . 14 n.
xvi. 13 15
xvi. 14 . . . 15 n.
xvii . . . 21 n., 51 n.
xvii. 12 . . . 21 n.
xviii. 14 f. . . 76 n.
xxi. 2–10 . . . 44 n.
xxi. 11–xxii. 2 . . 44 n.
xxii. 6–23 . . . 44 n.
xxiii. 6 . . . 44 n.
xxiv. 7 . . 14 n., 15 n., 16 n.
xxiv. 11 . . 14 n., 15 n., 16 n.
xxv. 43 . . . 41 n.
xxvi. 6 . . . 44 n.
xxvi. 9 . . 14 n., 15 n., 16 n.
xxvi. 11 . . 14 n., 15 n., 16 n.
xxvi. 16 . . 14 n., 15 n.
xxvi. 23 . . 14 n., 15 n., 16 n.
xxvii. 3 . . . 41 n.
xxix. 9 . . . 16 n.
xxx. 7 . . . 44 n.
xxx. 11 . . . 21 n.
xxxi. 2 . . . 45 n.

2 Samuel:
i. 14 . . 14 n., 15 n., 16 n.
i. 16 . . 14 n., 15 n., 16 n.
ii. 1–7 . . . 14 n.
iii. 28 f. . . . 4 n.
v. 1–5 . . . 14 n.
v. 3 . . . . 1 n.
v. 6–8 . . . 53 n.
v. 17 . . . . 1 n.
vi . 13 n., 14 n., 19 n., 20 n.
vi. 2 . . . . 72 n.
vi. 6 f. . . . 20 n.
vii. 1–17 . . 26 n., 110 n.
vii. 14 . . . . 28 n.

2 Samuel (cont.):

viii. 17 . . . 44 n., 52 n.
x. 16 . . . . 10 n.
xi. 1 . . . . 56 n.
xi. 21 . . . . 44 n.
xii. 24 f. . . . 51 n.
xii. 30 . . . . 43 n.
xiv. 1–20 . . . 4 n.
xiv. 9 . . . . 4 n.
xiv. 17 . . . 16 n., 30 n.
xiv. 20 . . . 16 n., 30 n.
xv. 1–6 . . . 4 n., 116 n.
xv. 10 . . . 65 n., 77 n.
xv. 24 ff. . . . 52 n.
xvi. 16 . . . . 12 n.
xvii. 15 . . . . 52 n.
xix. 12 . . . . 52 n.
xix. 22 . . 14 n., 15 n., 16 n.
xix. 28 . . . 16 n., 30 n.
xix. 41–43 . . . 55 n.
xx. 1 . . . . 55 n.
xxi. 1–14 . . . 4 n.
xxi. 17 1
xxi. 19 . . . 21 n., 51 n.
xxii. . . . . 116 n.
xxii. 5 . . . . 117 n.
xxii. 5 f. . . . 60 n.
xxii. 7 . . . . 118 n.
xxii. 8 . . . . 60 n.
xxii. 14 . . . . 119 n.
xxii. 16 . . . . 119 n.
xxii. 16 f. . . . 60 n.
xxii. 30 . . . . 121 n.
xxii. 36 . . . . 122 n.
xxii. 44 . . . . 123 n.
xxii. 45 . . . . 123 n.
xxii. 48 . . . . 123 n.
xxiii. 1 . . . . 50 n.
xxiii. 1–7 . . 16 n., 18 f.
xxiii. 6 f. . . . 125 n.
xxiii. 17 . . . . 12 n.
xxiv . . . . 34 n.
xxiv. 10–25 . . . 4 n.
xxiv. 16 ff. . . . 34 n.
xxiv. 18–25 . . 13 n., 14 n.

1 Kings:

i. 1–ii. 35 . . . 52 n.
i. 11 . . . . 66 n.
i. 18 . . . . 66 n.
i. 25 . . . . 12 n.
i. 28–40 . . . 14 n.
i. 31 . . . . 12 n.
i. 33–35 . . . 83 n.

i. 34 . . . . 12 n.
i. 39 . . . . 12 n.
i. 45 f. . . . . 83 n.
ii. 27 . . . . 50 n.
iii. 4 . . . . 13 n.
iii. 4–28 . . . 5 n.
iii. 15 . . . . 13 n.
iii. 16–28 . . . 116 n.
v. 1 . . . . 10 n.
v. 15–vii. 51 . . . 54 n.
v. 15–viii. 66 . . . 14 n.
vi. 38 . . . . 55 n.
vii. 23–26 . . . 60 n.
viii . . . . 13 n.
viii. 2 . . . 54 n., 55 n.
viii. 12 . . . . 94 n.
viii. 66 . . . . 28 n.
ix. 25 . . . . 13 n.
x. 5 . . . . 13 n.
xi. 5 . . . . 43 n.
xi. 7 . . . . 43 n.
xi. 33 . . . . 43 n.
xi. 36 . . . . 28 n.
xii. 16 . . 28 n., 55 n., 112 n.
xii. 26–32 . . . 14 n.
xii. 26–33 . . . 54 n.
xii. 32 . . . 55 n., 57 n.
xii. 32 f. . . . 55 n.
xii. 32–xiii. 10 . . . 13 n.
xiv. 15 . . . . 10 n.
xv. 12–15 . . . 14 n.
xvii. 1 . . . . 4 n.
xviii. 1 . . . . 4 n.
xviii. 18 . . . 4 n.
xx. 22 . . . . 56 n.
xx. 26 . . . . 56 n.
xxi. 10 . . . . 16 n.
xxi. 13 . . . . 16 n.
xxii. 19 . . . . 39 n.

2 Kings:

iv. 29 . . . . 21 n.
v. 7 . . . . 30 n.
vii. 2 . . . . 60 n.
vii. 19 . . . . 60 n.
viii. 1–6 . . . 4 n.
ix. 1–13 . . . 14 n.
ix. 13 . . . 65 n., 77 n.
x. 15 . . . . 21 n.
x. 18–28 . . 13 n., 14 n.
xi. 4–20 . . . 14 n.
xi. 12 . . . 12 n., 23 n.
xii. 5–17 . . . 14 n.
xvi. 10–18 . . 13 n. 14 n.

xviii. 4 . . . . 14 n.
xix. 14 ff. . . . 13 n.
xix. 15 . . . . 72 n.
xxii. 3–xxiii. 23 . . 14 n.
xxiii. 10 . . . 45 n.
xxiii. 11 . . . 45 n.
xxiii. 13 . . . 43 n.
xxv. 13 . . . 60 n.

1 Chronicles:
i. 49 . . . . 51 n.
ii. 19 . . . . 21 n.
ii. 50 f. . . . 21 n.
iii. 18 . . . . 45 n.
iv. 4 . . . . 21 n.
v. 16 . . . . 63 n.
v. 30–40 . . . 52 n.
vi. 25 . . . . 46 n.
vi. 35–38 . . . 52 n.
vii. 31 . . . . 43 n.
viii. 33 . . . . 45 n.
viii. 35 . . . . 43 n.
viii. 40 . . . . 83 n.
ix. 12 . . . 46 n., 47 n.
ix. 39 . . . . 45 n.
ix. 41 . . . . 43 n.
x. 2 . . . . 45 n.
xi. 46 . . . . 41 n.
xii. 2 . . . . 83 n.
xiii . . 13 n., 14 n., 19 n.
xiii. 6 . . . . 72 n.
xv . . 13 n., 14 n., 19 n.
xv. 16 ff. . . . 14 n.
xvi . . 13 n., 14 n., 19 n.
xvii. 1–15 . 26 n., 110 n.
xviii. 16 . . 44 n., 52 n.
xx. 1 . . . . 56 n.
xx. 2 . . . . 43 n.
xx. 5 . . . 21 n., 51 n.
xxi. 1–xxii. 1 . . 34 n.
xxi. 18–xxii. 1 . 13 n., 14 n.
xxii. 2–19 . . . 14 n.
xxii. 10 . . . . 28 n.
xxiv. 3 . . . . 44 n.
xxiv. 6 . . . . 44 n.
xxiv. 9 . . 46 n., 47 n.
xxiv. 23 . . . 45 n.
xxiv. 31 . . . 44 n.
xxv . . . . 14 n.
xxviii. 6 . . . 28 n.

2 Chronicles:
i. 6 . . . . 13 n.
i. 18–vii. 10 . . . 14 n.

iv. 2 ff. . . . 60 n.
v. 2–vii. 10 . . . 13 n.
v. 3 . . . . 54 n.
vi. 41 f. . . . 20 n.
vii. 8–10 . . . 54 n.
viii. 11 . . . . 21 n.
viii. 12 f. . . . 13 n.
ix. 4 . . . . 13 n.
ix. 26 . . . . 10 n.
xi. 14 f. . . . 14 n.
xiv. 8–14 . . . 13 n.
xv. 1–18 . . . 14 n.
xix. 5–11 . . . 5 n.
xx. 1–30 . . . 13 n.
xxiii. 11 . 12 n., 14 n., 23 n.
xxiv. 4–14 . . . 14 n.
xxvi. 16–20 . . . 13 n.
xxviii. 22–25 . . 13 n., 14 n.
xxix. 3–xxxi. 21 . . 14 n.
xxix. 25 ff. . . . 14 n.
xxxiv. 3–xxxv. 19 . . 14 n.
xxxvi. 10 . . . 56 n.

Ezra:
iii. 4 . . . . 56 n.
x. 25 . . . . 46 n.
x. 31 . . . . 46 n.

Nehemiah:
ii. 3 . . . . 12 n.
iii. 11 . . . . 46 n.
iii. 14 . . . . 46 n.
iii. 31 . . . . 46 n.
viii. 4 . . . . 46 n.
viii. 14–18 . . 56 n., 58 n.
ix. 32 . . . . 30 n.
x. 4 . . . . 46 n.
xi. 12 . . . 46 n., 47 n.
xii. 42 . . . . 46 n.

Job:
i. 6 . . . 63 n., 97 n.
ii. 1 . . . 63 n., 97 n.
iii. 8 . . . . 108 n.
vii. 12 . . . . 108 n.
ix. 13 . . . . 108 n.
xxii. 2 . . . . 76 n.
xxii. 14 . . . . 11 n.
xxvi. 10 . . . . 11 n.
xxvi. 10 ff. . . . 60 n.
xxvi. 12 f. . . . 108 n.
xxvi. 13 . . . . 108 n.
xxxviii. 4 ff. . . . 60 n.
xxxviii. 7 . . 63 n., 97 n.

Job (cont.):

xxxviii. 16 f.	. . .	60 n.
xl. 25–xli. 26	. .	108 n.

Psalms:

ii	. . .	128 ff.
ii. 1–6	. . .	129
ii. 7	. . 24 n.,	131 n.
ii. 7–9	. . .	129
ii. 10–12	. . .	129 f.
vii. 9	. . .	50 n.
xiv. 2	. . .	76 n.
xviii	. . 106 n.,	116 ff.
xviii. 2–4	. . .	117
xviii. 5 f.	. . .	60 n.
xviii. 5–7a	. . .	117
xviii. 7b–20	. . .	118 ff.
xviii. 8 .	. . .	60 n.
xviii. 16 f.	. . .	60 n.
xviii. 20	. . .	124 n.
xviii. 21–30	. . .	120 f.
xviii. 31–46	. . .	122 f.
xviii. 47–51	. . .	123
xviii. 48	. . .	76 n.
xx. 7 ff.	. . .	113 n.
xxi	. . .	132 ff.
xxi. 2–8	. . .	132 f.
xxi. 6	. . .	26 n.
xxi. 8	. . .	133 n.
xxi. 9–14	. . .	133 f.
xxiv	. 72 ff., 75, 81, 83, 89,	125
xxiv. 1 f.	. . .	60 n.
xxiv. 1–2	. . .	72 f.
xxiv. 2	. . 27 n.,	67 n.
xxiv. 3	. . .	75 n.
xxiv. 3–6	. . .	73
xxiv. 7–10	. . .	73 f.
xxiv. 8 .	. . .	132 n.
xxv. 10	. . .	67 n.
xxix	62 ff., 66 f., 73, 77, 93,	96 f.
xxix. 1–2	. . .	63
xxix. 3–9	. . .	63 f.
xxix. 10–11	. . .	64
xxxiii. 6 f.	. . .	60 n.
xxxiv	. . .	44 n.
xli. 2	. . .	76 n.
xlv	. . .	30 n.
xlv. 7	. . .	30 n.
xlvi	. 86 n., 92 ff.,	95 n.
xlvi. 2–4	. . .	92 f.
xlvi. 5 .	. . .	11
xlvi. 5–8	. . .	94
xlvi. 8 .	. . .	93 n.
xlvi. 9–12	. . .	95

xlvi. 12 .	. . .	93 n.
xlvii	. . 74 ff., 89,	97
xlvii. 2–6	. . .	75 f.
xlvii. 4 .	. . .	123 n.
xlvii. 7–10	. . .	76
xlvii. 9 .	. . 65 n.,	77 n.
xlvii. 10	. . .	105 n.
xlviii	. . 85 ff., 93,	95 n.
xlviii. 2 f.	. . .	114 n.
xlviii. 2–3	. . .	86
xlviii. 3	. . .	75 n.
xlviii. 4–8	. . .	86 f.
xlviii. 9	. . 87,	114 n.
xlviii. 10	. . .	88
xlviii. 11–12	. . .	89
xlviii. 12	. . .	97 n.
xlviii. 13–15	. . .	89
l. 1	. . .	104 n.
lii. 2	. . .	44 n.
lx. 13 f.	. . .	113 n.
lxviii	. . 77 ff., 89,	125
lxviii. 2–7	. . .	78 f.
lxviii. 8–11	. . .	79 f.
lxviii. 12–15	. . .	80 f.
lxviii. 16	. . .	82 n.
lxviii. 16–19	. . .	81 f.
lxviii. 18	. . .	79 n.
lxviii. 19	. . .	75 n.
lxviii. 20–24	. . .	82
lxviii. 22	. . .	132 n.
lxviii. 25	. . .	103 n.
lxviii. 25–28	. . .	83 f.
lxviii. 29–32	. . .	84
lxviii. 31	. . .	87 n.
lxviii. 33–36	. . .	85
lxviii. 34	. . .	78 n.
lxix. 16 .	. . .	60 n.
lxxi. 20 .	. . .	60 n.
lxxii	. . . 7 ff.,	17
lxxii. 1–7	. . .	9
lxxii. 8 .	. . 11 n.,	27 n.
lxxii. 8–11	. . .	10
lxxii. 12–14	. . .	11 f.
lxxii. 15–17	. . .	12
lxxiv. 2	. . .	79 n.
lxxiv. 12 ff.	. . .	108 n.
lxxiv. 13 f.	. . .	108 n.
lxxvi	. . .	95 n.
lxxvi. 2 f.	. . .	32
lxxvi. 3	. . .	47 n.
lxxvi. 4	. . .	32 n.
lxxviii. 54	. . .	79 n.
lxxx. 2 .	. . .	72 n.
lxxx. 11	. . .	27 n.

lxxx. 12 . . . 10 n.
lxxxi . . . . 70 n.
lxxxi. 4 . . . 57 n.
lxxxii . . . . 98 f.
lxxxii. 1 . . . 98
lxxxii. 2–5 . . . 99
lxxxii. 3 . . . 99 n.
lxxxii. 6–7 . . . 99
lxxxii. 8 . . . 99
lxxxiv . . . . 103 ff.
lxxxiv. 2–5 . . . 103
lxxxiv. 6–10 . . . 104 f.
lxxxiv. 11–13 . . . 105 f.
lxxxviii. 5–8 . . . 60 n.
lxxxix 17 n., 25 ff., 106 ff., 116
lxxxix. 2 . . . 115 n.
lxxxix. 2–3 . . . 106 f.
lxxxix. 2–19 . . . 26
lxxxix. 4–5 . . . 107
lxxxix. 6–13 . . . 108 f.
lxxxix. 7 . . . 63 n.
lxxxix. 14–19 . . . 109
lxxxix. 19 . . . 105 n.
lxxxix. 20–30 . . . 26 ff.
lxxxix. 20–38 . . 26 n., 110 f.
lxxxix. 20b . . . 29
lxxxix. 21b . . . 28 n.
lxxxix. 31–38 . . . 28 f.
lxxxix. 39 . . . 28 n.
lxxxix. 39–46 . . . 111 f.
lxxxix. 39–52 . . . 29
lxxxix. 47–52 . . . 112 f.
lxxxix. 52 . . . 28 n.
lxxxix. 53 . . . 29 n.
xciii . . . 61 n., 65 ff.
xciii. 3 . . . . 27 n.
xcv . . . 61 n., 68 ff.
xcv. 1–7ab . . . 68
xcv. 2 . . . . 18 n.
xcv. 7c . . . 69, 101
xcv. 8–11 . . . 69
xcvi . . . 61 n., 99 n.
xcvi. 13 . . . 100 n.
xcvii . . . 61 n., 95 ff.
xcvii. 1–6 . . . 96
xcvii. 7–9 . . . 97
xcvii. 10–12 . . . 98
xcvii. 11 . . . 127 n.
xcviii . . . 61 n., 99 f.
xcix . . . . 70 ff.
xcix. 1 . . . . 118 n.
xcix. 1–5 . . . 70 f.
xcix. 3 . . . . 76 n.
xcix. 6–9 . . . 71

c . . . . 70 n.
ci . . 113 ff., 116, 120
ci. 1–2a . . . 114
ci. 2b–8 . . . 115 f.
civ. 25 f. . . . 108 n.
cv. 10 . . . 24 n.
cviii. 13 f. . . . 113 n.
cx . . . 47 n., 130 ff.
cx. 1–2 . . . 130
cx. 3–4 . . . 131
cx. 5–7 . . . 132
cxv. 11 . . . 124 n.
cxvi. 3 . . . . 21 n.
cxviii . . 106 n., 123 ff.
cxviii. 1–4 . . . 124
cxviii. 5–14 . . . 124 f.
cxviii. 7a . . . 71 n.
cxviii. 8 f. . . . 130 n.
cxviii. 15–21 . . . 126 f.
cxviii. 22–27a . . 127
cxviii. 27a . . . 98 n.
cxviii. 27b–29 . . 128
cxxxii . . . 17 n., 19 ff.
cxxxii. 1–10 . . . 20 ff.
cxxxii. 6b . . . 51 n.
cxxxii. 11–18 . . . 22 f.
cxxxii. 12 . . 24 n., 67 n.
cxxxii. 13 . . . 31
cxxxii. 18b . . . 24 n.
cxxxiii. 2f. . . . 131 n.
cxxxiii. 3 . . . 131 n.
cxxxvi. 6 . . . 60 n.
cxxxvii. 1 . . . 27 n.
cxxxix. 13 . . . 48 n.
cxlix . . . . 91 f.
cxlix. 1–4 . . . 91
cxlix. 5–9 . . . 91 f.

Proverbs:
viii. 22 . . . . 48 n.
viii. 24–29 . . . 60 n.
viii. 27 . . . . 11 n.
x. 5 . . . . 76 n.
x. 19 . . . . 76 n.
xiv. 35 . . . . 76 n.
xvi. 20 . . . . 76 n.
xvii. 2 . . . . 76 n.
xxiii. 22 . . . . 79 n.
xxiv. 21 . . . . 16 n.

Song of Solomon:
i. 13 . . . . 51 n.
i. 15 . . . . 30 n.
iv. 1 . . . . 30 n.

Song of Solomon (cont.):

v. 12 . . . . 30 n.
viii. 4 . . . . 112 n.

Isaiah:

vi. 1 ff. . . . 64 n.
vii. 2 . . . . 3 n.
vii. 13 . . . . 3 n.
vii. 17 . . . . 3 n.
vii. 20 . . . . 10 n.
viii. 6 . . . . 11 n.
ix. 5 . . . . 30 n.
x. 21 . . . . 30 n.
xi. 1 ff. . . . 16 n.
xiv. 12–15 . . . 94 n.
xxiv. 18 . . . 60 n.
xxvi. 19 . . . 131 n.
xxvii. 1 . . . . 108 n.
xxvii. 11 . . . 84 n.
xxvii. 12 . . . 10 n.
xxx. 7 . . . . 108 n.
xxx. 33 . . . 45 n.
xxxi. 1 ff. . . . 113 n.
xxxii. 15 . . . 15 n.
xxxiii. 21 . . . 119 n.
xxxvii. 14 ff. . . . 13 n.
xxxvii. 16 . . . 72 n.
xl–lv . . . . 61 n.
xl. 22 . . . . 11 n.
xl. 31 . . . . 104 n.
xli. 14 . . . . 61 n.
xliii. 1 . . . . 61 n.
xliii. 14 . . . 61 n.
xliii. 17 . . . 125 n.
xliv. 3 . . . . 15 n.
xliv. 6 . . . . 61 n.
xliv. 22 . . . . 61 n.
xliv. 23 . . . . 61 n.
xliv. 24 . . . . 61 n.
xliv. 27 . . . . 67 n.
xlv. 10 . . . . 131 n.
xlvi. 1 . . . 38 n.
xlvii. 4 . . . . 61 n.
xlviii. 17 . . . 61 n.
xlviii. 20 . . . 61 n.
xlix. 7 . . . . 61 n.
xlix. 26 . . . . 61 n.
li. 9 . . . . 108 n.
lii. 7 . . . 65 n., 77 n.
lii. 9 . . . . 61 n.
liv. 5 . . . . 61 n.
liv. 8 . . . . 61 n.
liv. 12 . . . . 105 n.
lv. 3 . . . . 115 n.

lx. 14 . . . . 114 n.
lxi. 1 . . . . 16 n.

Jeremiah:

ii. 18 . . . . 10 n.
ix. 2 . . . . 104 n.
xv. 4 . . . . 4 n.
xvii. 5 ff. . . . 113 n.
xxi. 1 . . . 46 n., 47 n.
xxi. 12 . . . . 116 n.
xxiii. 5 . . . . 76 n.
xxx. 9 . . . . 28 n.
xxxii. 18 . . . 30 n.
xxxii. 35 . . . 45 n.
xxxviii. 1 . . 46 n., 47 n.
xxxviii. 6 . . . 46 n.
xxxviii. 7–13 . . . 45 n.
xxxix. 15–18 . . . 45 n.
xlix. 1 . . . . 43 n.
xlix. 3 . . . . 43 n.
l. 2 . . . . 38 n.
li. 44 . . . . 38 n.

Lamentations:

iii. 44 . . . . 119 n.
iv. 20 2

Ezekiel:

i. 5–28 . . . . 118 n.
x. 1–22 . . . . 118 n.
xvi. 3 35
xxvi. 19–21 . . . 60 n.
xxviii. 11–19 . . . 118 n.
xxxiv. 23 f. . . . 28 n.
xxxvii. 24 f. . . . 28 n.
xxxix. 29 . . . 15 n.
xl. 1 . . . . 57 n.
xliii. 7–9 . . . 54 n.
xlvii . . . . 11 n.

Hosea:

iii. 5 . . . . 28 n.

Joel:

iii. 1 f. . . . . 15 n.

Amos:

i. 15 . . . . 43 n.
v. 8 . . . . 60 n.
vii. 10–17 . . . 54 n.
ix. 2 f. . . . . 108 n.
ix. 3 . . . . 82 n.

Jonah:
ii. 4 . . . . 67 n.
ii. 6 f. . . . . 60 n.

Micah:
v. 1 . . . . 21 n.
vii. 12 . . . . 10 n.

Habakkuk:
iii. 13 . . . . 132 n.

Zephaniah:
i. 1 . . . . 45 n.
i. 5 . . . . 43 n.

Haggai:
i. 1 . . . . 37 n.
i. 12 . . . . 37 n.
i. 14 . . . . 37 n.
ii. 2 . . . . 37 n.
ii. 4 . . . . 37 n.

Zechariah:
iv. 6 . . . . 113 n.
vi. 11 . . . . 37 n.
vii. 2 . . . . 45 n.

ix. 9 f. . . . . 11 n.
xii. 10 . . . 15 n.
xiv. 9 . . . . 58 n.
xiv. 16 f. . . 58 f., 78 n.
xiv. 16–19 . . . 56 n.

Malachi:
iii. 10 . . . . 60 n.

Matthew:
xxi. 9 . . . . 127 n.
xxi. 15 . . . . 127 n.

Mark:
xi. 9 f. . . . . 127 n.

John:
vii. 2 . . . . 55 n.
xii. 13 . . . . 127 n.

2 Corinthians:
iii. 18 . . . . 104 n.

Hebrews:
vii. 2 36

INDEX

(d) SELECT HEBREW WORDS AND PHRASES

Where relevant page numbers apply to both text and footnotes.

אָדוֹן 38.

אֲדוֹנָי 38, 80, 82, 85.

אֵל גִּבּוֹר 30 n.

אֱלֹהִים 30 n.

אֵל חַי 103, 143.

אֵל עֶלְיוֹן 49 f.

אֱמוּנָה 107.

אֱמֶת 109, 135 f.

בטח√ 132 f.

בְּנֵי (הָ)אֱלֹהִים 63 n., 97 n.

בְּנֵי אֵלִים 63, 108.

בְּצֵאת הַשָּׁנָה 56.

בְּרִית 17, 107 n.

גָּאַל 61 n.

דמה√ 88.

הוֹשִׁיעָה נָּא 127.

הוֹשַׁע נָא 127.

חיה√ 2 n.

חַיִּים 4, 132.

חֶסֶד 22 n., 88, 102, 107, 109, 114 f., 123, 126 ff., 132 f., 135 f.

חָסִיד 22 n., 91 f., 98, 102, 116, 135.

יְ" מָלַךְ 65 n.

יְחִי הַמֶּלֶךְ 12 n.

יָעִיר 21 n.

יֵצֶר מַחְשְׁבוֹת הַלֵּב 141 n.

יְשׁוּעָה 102, 132, 135.

ישע√ 19 n., 137.

מָוֶת 89 n.

מַלְאָךְ 16.

מֶלֶךְ 12 n., 38 ff., 47, 61 n., 83, 86.

מצא√ 21 n.

מַשְׂכִּיל 114 n.

מָשִׁיחַ 14.

מָשָׁל 88, 101, 134.

מִשְׁפָּט 4, 7 ff., 88 f., 109, 114 f.

נְאֻם 130.

נָהָר 11 n., 27 n., 67 n.

נֶפֶשׁ 12 n., 103 n.

עֵדָה 23 f., 67.

עֵדוּת 23 f.

עַל 18 n.

עלה√ 75 f., 97.

עֶלְיוֹן 11 n., 18 n., 49 f., 75, 97.

עָנָו 91.

עֲנָוָה 20 n.

עָנִי 79, 120.

צַדִּיק 4, 9 n., 36, 78, 102, 116, 120, 126, 135.

צֶדֶק	4 ff., 7 ff., 35 ff., 88 f., 102, 109, 116 f., 120, 126, 135 f.	רָשָׁע	78, 102, 135.
		שָׁלוֹם	4, 9 n., 64.
צְדָקָה	4 ff., 7 ff.	שמע√	21 n.
צָפוֹן	86.	שֹׁפֵט	4.
רוּחַ	15, 63 n.	תְּקוּפַת הַשָּׁנָה	56.
רצה√	91 n.	תְּרוּעָה	109.
		תְּשׁוּבַת הַשָּׁנָה	56.

PRINTED IN GREAT BRITAIN
AT THE UNIVERSITY PRESS, OXFORD
BY VIVIAN RIDLER
PRINTER TO THE UNIVERSITY